*To my mother, father
and sister Jill for
tolerating me
while I grew up.*

SCRAMBLES
in the Canadian Rockies

ALAN KANE

RMB

Copyright © Alan Kane 1992, 2003
Second edition, 2003, reprinted 2006, 2008, 2013

Rocky Mountain Books
www.rmbooks.com

Library and Archives Canada Cataloguing in Publication

Kane, Alan, 1954-
Scrambles in the Canadian Rockies

ISBN 978-0-921102-67-0

1. Hiking—Rocky Mountains, Canadian (B.C. and Alta.)—Guidebooks.*
2. Rocky Mountains, Canadian (B.C. and Alta.)—Guidebooks.*   I. Title.
FC219.K35 1999   917.1104'4   C99-910053-X
F1090.K35 1999

Cover: On Pika Peak with Mount Richardson and the connecting ridge to the left.
Title Page: Mount Hector (left) and a sea of peaks rise
beyond Mount Richardson's summit.
All photos by the author except where noted otherwise.

Printed in Canada

Rocky Mountain Books acknowledges the financial support for its publishing program from the Government of Canada through the Canada Book Fund (CBF) and the Canada Council for the Arts, and from the province of British Columbia through the British Columbia Arts Council and the Book Publishing Tax Credit.

This book was produced using FSC®-certified, acid-free paper, processed chlorine-free and printed with vegetable-based inks.

Disclaimer

The actions described in this book may be considered inherently dangerous activities. Individuals undertake these activities at their own risk. The information put forth in this guide has been collected from a variety of sources and is not guaranteed to be completely accurate or reliable. Many conditions and some information may change owing to weather and numerous other factors beyond the control of the authors and publishers. Individual climbers and/or hikers must determine the risks, use their own judgment, and take full responsibility for their actions. Do not depend on any information found in this book for your own personal safety. Your safety depends on your own good judgment based on your skills, education, and experience.

It is up to the users of this guidebook to acquire the necessary skills for safe experiences and to exercise caution in potentially hazardous areas. The authors and publishers of this guide accept no responsibility for your actions or the results that occur from another's actions, choices, or judgments. If you have any doubt as to your safety or your ability to attempt anything described in this guidebook, do not attempt it.

CONTENTS

Scrambling Areas

A morning view of (L-R) Vice-President, the President and Mount Kerr from the Whaleback.

Approaching the summit of Banded Peak with Mount Cornwall behind.   Photo: Kris Thorsteinsson.

On the brink of a disaster: Debris on Turtle Mountain above Frank Slide.

The final ridge on Mount Engadine, with Mount Assiniboine and Spray Lake behind. Photo: Kris Thorsteinss[

The Lake Louise skyline from Mount Richardson. Left to right: Mounts Hungabee, Lefroy and Victoria.

Photo: Kris Thorsteinsson.   *A party carefully descends steep terrain on Mount Stephen.*

Strenuous scrambling on the crux of Fisher Peak.

Mount Alderson, Alderson Lake (left) and lower Carthew Lake (right) from Mount Carthew.

Observation Peak provides the perfect viewpoint for Bow Lake and Wapta Icefield.

Interesting scrambling on Mount Burstall's east ridge.

Athabasca River valley and Roche Miette from the ridge of Cinquefoil Mountain.

The view northwest toward Cairngorm from Pyramid Mountain.

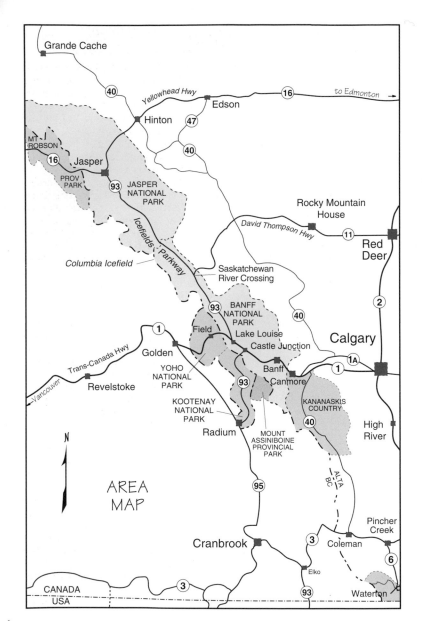

Grande Cache

40

Yellowhead Hwy

16 to Edmonton

Edson

Hinton

47

40

MT ROBSON

16 Jasper

PROV PARK

93 JASPER NATIONAL PARK

Rocky Mountain House

David Thompson Hwy

11 Red Deer

Icefields Parkway

Columbia Icefield

Saskatchewan River Crossing

93 BANFF NATIONAL PARK

40

Field

Lake Louise

Calgary

2

Trans-Canada Hwy

1

Golden

Castle Junction

Vancouver

YOHO NATIONAL PARK

Banff

1A

1

Revelstoke

93

Canmore

KOOTENAY NATIONAL PARK

KANANASKIS COUNTRY

Radium

MOUNT ASSINIBOINE PROVINCIAL PARK

40

High River

N

AREA MAP

95

ALTA BC

Pincher Creek

Cranbrook

3

Coleman

6

CANADA

USA

3

Elko

93

Waterton

14

Preface

When the first edition of *Scrambles in the Canadian Rockies* was published, I had no idea whether there was much of a market for this information. Though I haven't quit my day job, sales have exceeded my expectations. It seems many outdoor enthusiasts want more challenge and a better view, just as I had years earlier. One difference I do notice is that whereas I had taken recognized climbing and mountaineering courses and had significant mountain experience, many users do not. It takes a long time to develop mountain sense and routefinding skills. Although I suggested that readers follow a cautious progression, many folks start out with limited experience, yet see no need for instruction. Often, readers were (and are) totally reliant on a photo with a line and a written description. Casual conversations have revealed that many skipped reading the introduction, the ratings' explanation and the hazard section. I find this a bit worrisome.

Despite naysayer's predictions, there has not been a rash of scrambling deaths. Thousands of boots have tramped up the scree slopes and most folks have avoided trouble. A few accidents are inevitable. It is surprising that we do not see more. Coincidentally, with increased usage many peaks now have a beaten path to the top and little routefinding is necessary. Although many peaks are far more popular than previously, not all routes are crowded and many still offer a respite from the hordes.

Alright, so the peaks are busier, what's new? Well, this book has been completely rewritten, expanded (Now with 50% more scree!), and includes improvements like changes in approach and better ascent routes. Route information comes firsthand: I have personally ascended every described peak in this book and with few exceptions, every variation described too. Readers will find new scrambles in each chapter and traverses or extensions to previously described ascents. Scrambles in two new backcountry areas have been added for those who enjoy multi-peak trips from a central camp. The first is in a wilderness area at Aster Lake in Kananaskis Country. This gem offers a bit of mountaineering, camping, scrambling and requires only a few hours backpacking. The second new backcountry area is Little Yoho Valley in Yoho National Park. Like Aster Lake, all peaks can be ascended from a central camp just a moderate day's backpack in from a road.

A noteworthy change in route description format in this edition is trip time. Previous editions gave ascent time; I have now chosen to give round-trip time (excluding summit breaks). I think this is more useful but I also have ulterior motives. Ascent times created controversy and some folks got peeved when they couldn't meet or beat minimum suggested ascent time.

I would like to say this book is completely error-free, but I must apologize in advance. Despite my best efforts, errors and discrepancies are inevitable and although any information not gained firsthand has been checked as thoroughly as possible, there will be inaccuracies. Guidebook mistakes bug me too, so I try hard to be accurate. Suggestions are welcome and can be forwarded to the publisher to my attention.

To all of you, safe and happy scrambling!

Alan Kane

Acknowledgments

As this bigger, rewritten edition of *Scrambles* goes to press, I have many people to thank. One might think that writing would be easier the second time around, but it is not, and I could not have done it alone. Climbing the peaks is the simple part, and a lot more fun, too, I might add.

Old and new friends and acquaintances provide updates and information, and it is this feedback that makes for a more accurate book. Apart from a clearer trail, perhaps, mountains change little, but access and approach routes do change. In at least two instances, unofficial parking areas that had been in common use for eons were immediately closed by Parks Canada once my book specifically identified them.

Kris Thorsteinsson, with whom I made many ascents over the years, deserves the first thanks. The original idea of this book was his and I will forever be in his debt. Edwin Knox let me in on some scrambles around Waterton Park and shared a personal favourite or two. Thanks to both Steve Tober and Roberto Pavesio who have forwarded insightful comments and suggestions about route descriptions and alternatives. In September 2000, the ever-energetic Mister Pavesio became the first guidebook user to do every scramble in this expanded edition–congratulations Roberto! In 2005 Carol Agar became the first woman to complete all 156 srambles. Congratulations!

I must also thank the following people: Tim Auger, for his invaluable input and help. Harold Brown, Carmie Callanan, Brian Carter, Rick Collier, Gary Fauland, Sim Galloway, Helen Butler, Andy Riggs and Bob Spirko for providing opinions and/or suggestions about new and existing scrambles. Bernard Mueller, who, one sunny day, enthusiastically talked my ear off on The Tower of Babel about many new scrambling possibilities; also Wendy Shanahan, Donna Pletz and Juliette DeChambre of Parks Canada. Thanks also to the following persons whose pictures I have used: David M. Baird, Don Beers, Reg Bonney, Clive Cordery, Gill Daffern, Tony Daffern, Bruno Engler, Leon Kubbernus, Glenn Naylor and Kris Thorsteinsson. Lastly, thanks to Brad White for the great aerial shots, courtesy of Parks Canada.

Place name explanations were mainly taken from *Place Names of the Canadian Alps* by Boles, Laurilla and Putnam, *Over 2000 Place Names of Alberta* by Holmgren and Holmgren, or *Place Names of Glacier/Waterton National Parks* by Jack Holterman. I would never have had the time to research these myself.

Tidbits and trivia about geology and natural history were gathered from Ben Gadd's excellent volume, *Handbook of the Canadian Rockies*.

Two guidebooks have proven invaluable throughout my ascents. They are *The Rocky Mountains of Canada North* by Boles, Krushzyna and Putnam, and *The Rocky Mountains of Canada South* by Krushzyna and Putnam. The scope of these two books is enormous, and my little offering pales in comparison. Similarly, had it not been for Patton and Robinson's *The Canadian Rockies Trail Guide* appearing about 25 years ago, I might have simply become a couch potato. Thanks, guys. Lastly, Dr. Gordon Boake, Dr. James Sie and Carey Jones, physiotherapist, have all been instrumental in helping my bad back over the years. Without their assistance, this edition may never have been completed.

Introduction

More guidebooks continue to appear for our mountain playgrounds, but this book is the only volume specifically focusing on nontechnical ascents of selected mountains in the Canadian Rockies. These nontechnical ascents, or scrambles, continue to appeal to people with a wide range of abilities. Strong hikers and backpackers who want more challenge and a better view will find this book opens many exciting opportunities. Climbers who simply want a hassle-free way of getting out, getting in shape or salvaging a day should also find this information useful. As one alpinist noted, these scramble routes make really good descent routes. Lastly, if you're like me, and find that big climbs with heavy packs are hard on the body, you'll probably appreciate these easier routes. "No pain, no gain" need not apply when speaking of elevation.

I have endeavoured to give concise, detailed information about level of difficulty, starting point, approaches, identity, height, elevation gain and round-trip time. Appropriate maps and any special equipment needed have also been noted. Critics have said that with all this preparation done, the adventure is gone. All you need to do now is buy, read and go conquer. In reality, despite the best information, mountains may still provide unexpected adventure with loose rock, unbridged streams and rapidly changing weather. Furthermore, a slight misinterpretation of the description can also inject new life into a normally straightforward route, as evidenced by periodic epics. Anyone stalwartly opposed to a detailed description can simply pioneer along without it anyway. My foremost aim is to give enough information so you can plan an outing on short notice, avoid nasty surprises and get to the top. I make no apologies to scramblers who experience problems owing to low cloud, fog, snow and ascents by moonlight. The premise is that you can at least see where you are going, even though it may not always be totally necessary. A modicum of ability helps too!

The Canadian Rockies encompass a huge area. This book includes a variety of mountains over a wide cross section of this area. Some are famous postcard peaks close to tourist havens, while others are fairly obscure. Not surprisingly, most peaks are quite close to population centres. Difficulties range from little more than a strenuous hike up a very big hill, to more complex ascents involving scrambling up cliff bands, traversing narrow ridges, ascending steep gullies and moving up moderately steep snow slopes. On some routes you may need to know how to use specialized equipment such as an ice axe, crampons and very occasionally, a length of climbing rope. Often the described route is not the only way up, but is a route that has proven itself. Many of these routes have been in common use for decades, although more esthetic (technical) lines often exist if you're a purist.

Most scrambles in this book are day trips and so do not require a backpack full of camping gear. Many begin at roadside or have very good approach trails, so opportunities to experience quintessential Rockies bushwhacking, sadly, are few. Adequate detail about trailheads and approaches is included but for more detail, *The Canadian Rockies Trail Guide* by Brian Patton and Bart Robinson covers the national parks areas while Gillean Daffern's *Kananaskis Country Trail Guides* cover Kananaskis Country.

Preserving What is Left

Despite developer's and industry's best efforts, much of the Rockies is still a pristine and special place, but every time you wander off an established trail to shortcut a switchback or tramp across a delicate alpine meadow, damage occurs. If enough people do this, a dirt path develops; then rain creates a muddy track. Successive parties detour around it, widening the mudhole, and so it goes. Think before you boldly charge off the trail to blaze your own way. Just because you don't see a single soul on the route does not mean nobody else ever goes there, so don't discard your snotty tissue or drink can along the way. Logical, I know, but the evidence shows that it does escape some people. Mountain usage is rising steadily so we must all do what we can to keep these places as unspoiled as possible. If seeing a teahouse being built on a mountain riles you, take a stand against it. Our elected officials have shown they are only too happy to approve development, despite strong public opinion against it. Blame it on M-O-N-E-Y. If Banff and Canmore are indicators, then clearly much of the business sector sees the Rockies as their own quick ticket to riches, even if it is a national park. Preservation be damned.

We recreationalists cannot afford to sit back and idly watch our special places disappear, but bit by bit, that is precisely what is happening. If we hikers, climbers, bikers and scramblers cannot treat the mountains with care and respect, then we cannot fault developers and politicians, even if they desecrate on a vastly larger scale.

Avoiding Death by Scrambling

Scrambling cannot only be hazardous to your life, but it can end it completely. Scrambling kills. For one reason or another, people have already died on routes described in this book. Over the last few years, a typical scrambling accident has involved a young male from Eastern Canada working a summer job in either Banff or Lake Louise. This person is full of energy and surrounded by impressive looking mountains, but has no experience.

By distributing pamphlets to employers and displaying posters, Parks Canada has tried to inform this group in an effort to reduce future accidents. Unfortunately, the trend will probably continue, despite an abundance of information available. Still, information alone won't always keep you out of trouble. All the reading in the world is no substitute for experience, and it is not the intention of the author to suggest otherwise.

Undertaking any of the trips mentioned in this volume is a potentially **HAZARDOUS ACTIVITY** and **COULD KILL YOU**. Particular phrases used in route descriptions may lead the reader to believe that little danger or difficulty is involved. This is NOT TRUE. Mountains are inherently dangerous and scrambling can be doubly dangerous. Participants are advised to go with caution and select a route within their level of ability and experience. If you're not sure what your abilities are, maybe you don't have any ability. Those without proper skills and experience should enroll in an appropriate course given by a recognized mountain school or Union Internatíonale des Associations d'Alpinisme (UIAA) approved mountain guide. I fully advocate appropriate training, however, you should keep one fact in mind: Many courses teach you the basic moves for moderate rock climbs, but unfortunately few, if any, teach you how to **avoid** technical rock climbing. Avoiding technical rock defines scrambling. Knowing the basics is important, but routefinding is a more important element to safe scrambling. In reality routefinding cannot be taught, but is a skill that develops (hopefully!) over time.

Once you have proper training under your pack belt, the next step is to go with experienced people. Clubs such as the Alpine Club of Canada bring climbers together and offer courses, group outings and a chance to meet potential trip partners.

The biggest killer in the mountains might well be blind enthusiasm. Do not allow it to overshadow good judgement; keep your goal in perspective. Realize that no matter how hard you push or how fast you go, somebody will always be faster than you. Instead, you may as well settle for having fun and doing it safely. If conditions don't seem right or you do not feel comfortable on the route, be smart and **TURN BACK**. It could save your life.

Anyone climbing mountains should strive to develop and refine their mountain skills and to rely less on the skill and judgement of others. As you do, your level of confidence and margin of safety will rise accordingly. That way, you will be less dependent on written route information and can make sound decisions on your own. **Do not put unbridled faith in the information contained in this or any other guidebook.** Develop and use your own judgement too. Persons following any advice or suggestions within these pages do so entirely at their own risk. The risk in scrambling is **DYING**. Be careful.

Climbing Schools

Here are a few of the longer-established schools. Check locally for others.

Yamnuska Inc.
1316 Railway Avenue
Canmore, AB T1W 1P6
Ph (403) 678-4164

Peter Amann Guiding
P.O. Box 1495
Jasper, AB T0E 1E0
Ph (780) 852-3237

Jasper Climbing School
P.O. Box 452
Jasper, AB T0E 1M0
Ph (780) 852-3964

Rescue Dynamics
5109 - 17A Avenue N.W.
Edmonton, AB T6L 1K5
Ph (780) 461-5040
resqdyn@compusmart.ab.ca

Useful Guidebooks

The Canadian Rockies Trail Guide by Brian Patton and Bart Robinson
Kananaskis Country Trail Guide volumes 1 and 2 by Gillean Daffern
Hiking Lake Louise by Mike Potter
The Wonder of Yoho by Don Beers
The World of Lake Louise by Don Beers
Backcountry Banff by Mike Potter
Banff-Assiniboine: A Beautiful World by Don Beers
Jasper-Robson: A Taste of Heaven by Don Beers
Backcountry Biking in the Canadian Rockies by Doug Eastcott

SCRAMBLING IN THE CANADIAN ROCKIES

The Canadian Rockies are truly one of the great mountain ranges of the world and are unique in many ways. Although they do not attain the lofty 14,000 ft. elevations of their counterparts in the United States, the Canadian Rockies are undeniably craggier and more impressive. Similarly, while particular peaks in the Cascade Range of the Pacific Northwest may be somewhat more rugged, many barely rise above tree line. The volcanoes, obviously, are an exception. Yet upon reaching the summit of a Cascade volcano, one sees perhaps only two or three other volcanoes rising skyward with few summits of note in between.

Europe's Alps may outshine Canada's Rockies for sheer magnificence of form, but sadly from every summit one sees a proliferation of mountain railways, gondola lifts, roads and hotels. The climber pampers himself in warm huts offering hot meals, wine and bedding. Routefinding involves following paint splotches and hordes of other people, and not surprisingly, any feeling of wilderness has long since disappeared.

Great ranges like the Himalayas and the Andes do surpass the Rockies in many respects, but access can be both dangerous and difficult. To many, simply staying healthy throughout the visit presents a considerable challenge, never mind trying to reach a summit.

By comparison, Canada's Rockies boast the grandeur of innumerable craggy, glaciated peaks, difficult and remote, yet also offer a myriad of easier ascents close to roads. Glacially-scoured basins contain pristine alpine lakes and flower-strewn meadows. Elk, bear and moose roam free and from every mountaintop one witnesses an endless sea of summits—entertainment for a lifetime. Welcome to the Canadian Rockies!

Climate and Season

Summer in the Canadian Rockies is short. Sometimes it doesn't even show up. The climbing season is highly affected by weather patterns and conditions in any given area vary from year to year and range to range. An old timer once remarked that a year in the Rockies is 10 months of winter and two months of poor sleddin'. He probably hadn't visited the Columbia Icefields: 12 months of good sleddin'!

The early scrambling season is confined to the eastern part of the Rockies in the Front Ranges. These areas are generally a little warmer and experience less precipitation, whether snow or rain. Typical examples of these areas lie east of Canmore, east of Jasper and in parts of the Crowsnest Pass. Here, south and west-facing slopes come into condition as early as May and June. East-facing slopes require a few weeks more. North-facing slopes take longer yet, and in a cold wet year, snow patches persist all year.

Travelling farther west in the Rockies, temperatures are slightly cooler and precipitation is greater, especially along the Continental Divide and the Main Ranges. Lake Louise is wetter than Banff, which is wetter than Kananaskis Valley. Some of the most inclement weather occurs at the Columbia Icefields between Lake Louise and Jasper. The mean yearly temperature is a brisk -2.1° Celsius, making Banff's +2.5° balmy by comparison. Farther south, Denver, Colorado tops in at a sizzling +10°! Tropical, you might say.

Not only are the Main Ranges cooler, but they also include the highest peaks. It is often mid-July or later before snowfree climbing conditions occur here. Ideal conditions may be as brief as a couple of weeks or may not even occur in a cool, wet year. Conversely, an extended autumn or Indian Summer can stretch the scrambling season past September, up to October and even into November. In 1997, a powerful El Niño year, folks were still bagging peaks in early December. Autumn often rewards the optimist with crisp mornings, periods of stable weather and no crowds or insects. The drawback is the shorter daylight.

Mountain Bikes

Mountain bikes are of limited use for scrambles in this book. Bike use is severely restricted in the national parks and is allowed only on fire roads such as Redearth Creek. Kananaskis Country has fewer biking restrictions, although few scrambles actually require or benefit from a mountain bike. One notable exception is Little Elbow Recreation Area, where most approaches use old roads.

Registration

Voluntary registration is available in national and provincial parks at warden and ranger offices and at information centres in Kananaskis Country. Registration gives park staff justification for purchasing rescue equipment and maintaining trained personnel, so it is a worthwhile step based on that alone. Remember, if you do register, you are legally required to sign in upon returning. If you fail to sign in, an unnecessary and costly search could be initi-

ated, and YOU can be billed for the entire amount. Be aware that rescues are NEVER initiated until the following day, so you should always carry warm clothing, extra food and be prepared to survive a night out. It is worthwhile informing others of your plans or, if you do not register, leave an itinerary somewhere in your vehicle. Eventually authorities will scour it for clues and will know where to pick up your body to keep the mountain pristine. At the time of writing, the cost of rescues is still borne by the Canadian taxpayer, but with government budget cutbacks this may well change in the future. Although the rescue budget in one park in a recent year amounted to much less than 0.5% of their total budget, outdoor adventurers in the mountains are perceived by government as generating little direct revenue, and by some taxpayers as being a drain on finances. This misinformation makes us an easy target. Accordingly, future rescue budgets may be reduced with the shortfall being covered through some form of a surcharge. This is in spite of hefty price increases in park passes coupled with the imposition of backcountry overnight fees.

Permits

All visitors stopping in a national park require a valid national park pass, available at park entrance gates and information centres. In addition, overnight stays in the national park backcountry campsites require a backcountry permit and cost about $6 per night. Reservations may also be required in certain heavily used areas such as Skoki near Lake Louise. At time of writing, there are no additional permits required for picnicking, sightseeing, photographing or shopping—yet.

Time, Directions and Grid References

In this book suggested round-trip time covers a range and is based both on personal experience and that of acquaintances. This time assumes the participant is fit, able and doesn't dawdle. Persons who hike, bike and jog regularly should fall into this category. Anyone who occasionally strolls the interpretive paths for exercise will be out of their league on these scrambles. A general guideline for a comfortable ascent pace is 300 m (1000 ft.) per hour, and fit parties will have few problems maintaining this pace.

Directions given are referenced relative to the direction of travel and where any doubt might arise, a compass bearing is included too.

Maps listed are the 1:50,000 scale National Topographic System series. These are available at many information centres and outdoor stores. To pinpoint a precise location, six digit references to grid coordinates are frequently mentioned in this book, and an explanation of this locating method may be found on the border of each map. Note that these locations are estimated only from the map and not by global positioning systems (GPS). Maps shown in this book are intended only to show the positions of mountains relative to highways.

Gradings

First of all, ratings apply only when conditions are DRY. Simple descriptions of easy, moderate and difficult have been adopted and where appropriate, additional information such as the exposure (potential fall distance) may be included. This grading system does not equate directly to existing systems of grading climbs. Easy and moderate scrambles are in the UIAA class I to class II range. Scrambles rated as difficult would normally be about YDS class 3 to 4, UIAA class -III. In some instances there could be a move or two approaching fifth class. For example, Mount Smuts may have a section of about 5.2 or 5.3, but routes do not generally involve any climbing near that level. A better explanation of these ratings might be:

Easy—mostly hiking, much hands in pockets stuff, little exposure, no maintained trail. Not surprisingly, easy scrambles are not really scrambling at all but are mostly off-trail hiking. Mount Bourgeau and the south peak of Mount Indefatigable are prime examples. UIAA Class I; almost idiot-proof.

Moderate—frequent use of handholds required, possible exposure but not usually enough to be a "death fall." Some routefinding involved. e.g. Big Sister, Cascade Mountain and Mount Kidd. Class II.

Difficult—much use of handholds required, sections may be steep, loose and exposed, or rock could be smooth and downsloping. Fall distance may be significant enough to be fatal. Routefinding skills are generally necessary to determine the most practical and feasible way for specific sections. Less experienced parties might prefer the security of a climbing rope for short sections, and being off-route may well require technical climbing. Anyone with vertigo or a fear of heights should avoid scrambles rated as difficult. Sounds logical, but you'd be surprised. Examples are Mount Lady Macdonald, Mount Whyte and Mount Carnarvon. YDS 3rd or 4th class, rarely YDS class 5 or UIAA III.

As compared to other forms of rock such as quartzite, limestone is a high-friction medium. Nonetheless, when wet, snowy or icy, scramble routes become much harder. Many scrambles are then climbs and mountaineering ascents that require technical climbing gear and use of anchors and belay techniques. **THESE SCRAMBLE RATINGS ARE APPLICABLE ONLY IN OPTIMAL CONDITIONS: DRY AND FREE OF SNOW.** Some years dry conditions may not even occur on some routes.

Unroped scrambling is one of the most potentially dangerous mountain activities, especially where exposure (fall distance) is significant. This fact is well supported by accident statistics. Slipping on snow, slipping on loose rock and handhold pullout are leading causes. Just because another party has made the ascent or descent safely does not mean it will be safe for you too. Consider that the other party might just be top-notch alpinists and are simply out having an easy day.

Be aware that climbing back down is more difficult than climbing up. If the ascent makes you uncomfortable, it is certain to be tougher on descent. Think of this before committing yourself: Could you climb back down? If you are unsure, consider an alternate objective. An easier route on a different mountain may be much more enjoyable. Scrambling should not be thought of as a high-risk "extreme" wild and crazy adventure sport. It is not. It is a rewarding recreation that should be done as safely as possible.

Equipment

The best footwear for scrambling is a pair of sturdy leather boots with a cleated Vibram sole and a half or three-quarter shank for rigidity. Running shoes and ultra-light hiking boots are unsuitable, giving too little ankle support and protection on talus slopes. They also wear out quickly. At the other extreme are plastic mountaineering boots with an insulated liner. These are hot, sweaty and clumsy. Save those dainty dancing slippers for ice routes and glaciers.

Ski poles are steadily gaining favour in North America and the Rockies and are a great asset on scree slopes. They especially save wear and tear on the knees on descent and are invaluable for stream crossings. The three-section collapsible models are easily stowed in a pack and weigh little. Careful—they can collapse unexpectedly! Recommended.

Certain routes may warrant carrying an ice axe and perhaps crampons, depending on snow remaining. Many parties carry an ice axe as a matter of course. You must also know how to use this equipment: See the list of instructional schools for appropriate courses. Steeper routes where you must ascend rock bands are likely places to wear a helmet, especially if other parties are on the route ahead of you.

Clothing

Versatility is the key word in dressing for success in the mountains. Functional synthetics that can be layered to cover a wide variety of mountain weather and temperatures are what the fashionable scramblers are wearing this season. This wardrobe should include a raincoat (such as GoreTex), windpants, toque, wool gloves, cap, pile or fleece jacket, a wool or synthetic shirt and a synthetic undershirt. A pair of calf-height gaiters keeps debris out of boots. Although cotton shirts depicting loons and bears may be fine for Main Street Banff, they provide little warmth when wet and are downright miserable on a chilly mountain top. Damp clothing can result in a drop in body core temperature, a condition known as hypothermia. Further deterioration can result in death. This condition includes cold hands and feet, fatigue, irritability, excessive shivering, dullness, inability to use the hands, lack of coordination, slurred speech, apathy, and irrational actions. And all because of a loon shirt! But seriously, should any of these symptoms be present, get the victim into the warmest, driest clothing available. Have him eat and drink (not alcohol) and get him moving toward tree line and home. If he cannot continue, build a fire to warm him up. When you do get him back to safety, buy him a warmer shirt: Hypothermia is easier to prevent than to treat.

Necessary Extras

Good sunblock cream (spf 15 or more), glacier glasses or good sunglasses that eliminate UV rays, lip sunscreen, compass, 1-litre waterbottle, a large handkerchief and toilet paper identify the "old hand" versus the newcomer on the mountain. Consider carrying a small first aid kit, either homemade or commercially packed. No trip is complete without pictures, and what better excuse for a breather than to take a photo or two? Lastly, with the arrival of small cellular phones, more people are carrying these in the mountains. Personally, I find them intrusive. Phones are no substitute for brains or ability, yet incompetent parties who get in trouble are using them to call Parks rescue staff. This, if anything, is real justification for user-borne rescue costs. If you do take a phone, save that call for a real emergency.

HAZARDS

Mountains are inherently dangerous places. Scrambling is a dangerous undertaking in an inherently dangerous place. Increased demand for adventure is revealing a disturbing trend in the populace. It is an attitude problem, and it is people's penchant for passing the blame when they get in trouble. Sure, this adventure stuff makes great conversation, but when an accident happens, blame yourself and no one else. If you cannot take responsibility for your actions, do the rest of us a favour and stay home. Unlike the United States, where individuals have successfully won large sums of money in ridiculous negligence lawsuits, precedent setting cases in Canada have taken a much more sensible approach. The onus of responsibility has been placed squarely on the participant—right where it belongs. How refreshing! Forewarned is forearmed though, so here are some hazards that can occur in the mountains.

Rockfall

It should come as no surprise that the Canadian Rockies harbour more than their share of loose rock. Witness the huge slopes of rubble that provide easy routes to the top. The Canadian Rockies are composed primarily of limestone, with lesser amounts of quartzite in areas near the Continental Divide. The overall quality of limestone is often poor and handholds may pull out unexpectedly. A good thump with your hand will often give a hint of how solid the hold is. "Good rock" is a relative term and it may lie under much loose rubble, especially on ledges. Anyone with an aversion to loose rock and rubble will find few scrambles in the Canadian Rockies to their liking. Besides the danger of loose handholds, another, perhaps greater threat is party-induced rockfall.

Rockfall can kill. Apparently, some parties are seemingly oblivious to the dangers of flying rock. Often, with a bit of thought and care, one can ascend even steep, loose terrain and knock down virtually nothing. Unthinking or bumbling individuals, on the other hand, may unleash virtual torrents of stones. These become deadly missiles to anyone below, even when wearing a helmet. Have you ever had the terrifying experience of hearing a rock suddenly whiz by close to your head, or having it bound down the slope in your direction? If so, then you should have a good idea of the consequences of being hit: Major facial injuries, a broken arm, a concussion or death. Though it is not recommended you climb below others, if you are the upper party, taking this as license to be careless is both ignorant and dangerous. Remember that a helmet protects only the head. While many scramble routes are not steep enough for this hazard to be of concern, steeper routes, particularly gullies, should be suspect. Gullies act as funnels for dislodged debris and in these you should be particularly careful.

Another source of rockfall is as a result of direct sun melting snow or ice that secures otherwise loose rock in place. This has caused at least one death in the recent past and probably more.

Weather

Fickle is probably the best description for mountain weather. Rain, snow and thunderstorms can and do occur with almost no warning throughout much of the season. All may occur during a single afternoon. You might even get sunshine, too. Temperatures can dip below freezing in the Rockies even in the middle of summer, while temperatures on a hot scree slope may cause heatstroke. Weather forecasters sound downright convincing when they predict those warm sunny weekends, but be forewarned: Conditions can change rapidly. Mountain weather forecasting in the Canadian Rockies is far from an exact science, and even when forecasters are repeatedly wrong, they will still keep their job. Many a climbing group has been caught off guard on a big peak when severe weather arrived unexpectedly. Epics and deaths have occurred as a result. Keep your eyes open for changes. Of interest are new digital watches with altimeters and a built-in barometric trend indicator. If you've invested in one of these, a decline in air pressure overnight may warn of deteriorating weather over the next 24 hours.

Avalanches

On most open south- and west-facing ridge routes, snowslides occur early in the season and do not pose a serious avalanche threat to scramblers except in spring. Gullies and big faces can be another matter. These should be carefully assessed for avalanche potential before venturing onto them. Is there evidence of sluffing or sliding nearby? Are there tracks or runnels where snow has partially slid? Firm snow on a rubble slope

alleviates the toil of an ascent and provides a glissade on descent, but too much snow may potentially avalanche once softened by the sun. This dictates an early start to avoid the possibility. Better yet, wait until the snow has melted. Wet snow avalanches occur largely during spring and early summer, and although they move slowly as compared to powder snow and slab avalanches, they rapidly set up like concrete.

Elk and Bears

Few animals present a threat in the Rockies. The exceptions are moose or elk with calves, and bears, particularly if the bear has cubs. Keep your distance from any elk with a calf. Tourists in Banff can't seem to grasp this idea and almost yearly somebody gets charged or kicked by a protective mother. Research has shown the human voice (e.g., singing, yelling) to be a better bear deterrent than bells or other noisemakers. Stay alert and holler before coming over a rise or around a corner. An unexpected intrusion annoys most folks and bears generally have a very low tolerance for surprises. They are also a whole lot bigger! Making noise warns them of your presence and gives them a chance to steer out of your path.

When camping, hang anything smelling even remotely edible at least 4 m up a tree, or better yet, between two trees. Keep your camp clean and do not leave wash water or food bits around to entice bears. The cliche "a fed bear is a dead bear" says it all. Once they develop a taste for human food, they become a dangerous nuisance and are usually killed.

Watch for bear tracks and droppings along the trail. It doesn't take an expert to distinguish between types of bear scat: If it contains a bell, suspect a grizzly. Just kidding. Grizzlies do not stalk people as a source of food, but will bluff charge or attack to eliminate a perceived threat, especially if they have cubs. This is when you may have to play dead. Curl up in a ball and cover your head and neck if possible. Black bears, though smaller, can be very dangerous and have been known to stalk humans in a predatory manner. In a situation like this you should be very aggressive. Yell, throw objects and do whatever it takes to convince the beast that you are defending your territory and will not go without a good fight. Do **NOT** play dead in these circumstances, otherwise, it could happen. Know how to identify each type. Grizzlies have a broader, dished face and a shoulder hump. Blacks are smaller, have a forehead "bump" and the shoulder is not humped. An excellent reference book is *Bear Attacks: Their Causes and Avoidance* by Dr. Stephen Herrero.

More people venturing into the backcountry are arming themselves with an aerosol container of pepper-based spray in case of a bear attack. These cans fit in a holster that can be attached to your belt or pack strap. If a bear appears threatening, you calmly check wind direction so that neither you nor others will receive any of the debilitating spray, then carefully aim at the animal's face and shoot once it is within range. Easy, eh? The spray burns the eyes, rendering the victim near-helpless—temporarily. However, a panic-stricken human may not be thinking clearly enough to operate it correctly. From personal experience, it seems the busiest trails near most-heavily populated areas (least likely to harbour bears) will record the greatest crowds armed with bear spray. Although I do not at this time carry it, it does have its merits. Grizzlies often attack the head

and facial areas and leave the victim badly scarred both physically and emotionally. Extensive plastic surgery is often required to try to correct the damage.

Insects

These little pests are not hazards but are a definite nuisance. In the early season, wood ticks and mosquitos are the main complaint. Later, horseflies and small black flies take a turn. Bug repellents with an active ingredient called DEET are generally most effective, and some repellents now combine a sunscreen with an insect repellent. They do not include a perfume though. Good bug lotions are smelly, sting your eyes, burn your lips and can ruin plastics or synthetics if you're not careful.

In Canada, everyone has the right to bare arms. Biting insects are very happy when we exercise this freedom. Long-sleeved shirts, pants, gaiters and a hat are effective deterrent against insects though, especially ticks. Wood ticks prefer hairy parts of the body. Finding and removing them by yourself can be a real trick. They have been known to carry Rocky Mountain Spotted Fever, but fortunately, this is extremely rare. Of more concern is the potential for them to carry Lyme disease, a progressive and debilitating condition affecting the nervous system. Ticks can be removed by gently tugging on them with a pair of tweezers. If bitten, consider saving the tick for analysis by medical people. This will be of considerable value if you experience any unusual symptoms like fever, a rash or ring around the bite, a headache or flu-like symptoms. Though not widespread right now, Lyme disease has been identified in at least two instances in western Canada so far.

Water

Ah, that beautiful, fresh mountain water. Well, not always, according to health officials. While I believe most water in the Canadian Rockies (or at least in the parks) is pure enough to drink right from the stream, the potential does exist for you to contact Giardia, also known as Beaver Fever. At this time, researchers in Calgary have developed a vaccine against this malady and are now seeking government approval for it. Until then, here's what it's all about.

Giardia is a protozoan parasite that can contaminate surface water and will make life very miserable if you are unlucky enough to ingest it. Symptoms can take up to 15 days to appear and include persistent diarrhea, cramps, weakness and loss of appetite. It does not seem to run rampant despite what health officials suggest, but naturally, the closer you are to heavily-used areas, the more likely you are to encounter it. Most backcountry folks I know drink from streams and have since the last ice age (well, almost). I know of nobody ever contacting the bug. Specific areas of the Rockies (Elk Valley, British Columbia, I believe) have reported cases, but generally, the higher up in the mountains you go, the smaller the risk. Furthermore, if everyone kept his dog out of the backcountry, the risk would remain small. Dogs and beavers are key carriers of the parasite, but everyone visiting the backcountry should also dispose of human waste properly. Humans may carry the bug but may not always realize it.

Here's how to dispose of human waste. Bury feces at least 15 cm deep and 60 m (200 ft.) away from any water source. Above tree line and where soil is lacking, current thinking suggests using a flat rock and the smear technique to spread feces on other rocks. The sun's ultraviolet rays will then cause natural bio-degradation, although toilet paper must be burned. If you use this smear technique, please do it well off the route and nowhere near the summit. UV is most intense (and effective) on the southwest aspect.

If you have any suspicions about the potability of your drinking water, there are a few choices for treating it. Most expensive is to purify it using a commercially available filter and pump, available at better outdoor stores. Boiling for 10 minutes will also do the trick. The simplest method is to use a purifying agent like iodine. Crystals are available, or use four-eight drops of tincture of iodine (at pharmacies) per litre of water, shake well and wait 10 minutes. Adding a few drink crystals helps mask the resultant taste. Note that iodine will permanently taint the linings of some collapsible water bags, whereupon neither cheap wine, tomato juice nor baking soda will remove the odour. Whew! Now that you've survived reading all this, onward!

WATERTON LAKES

Mount Galwey	2348 m	difficult	
Mount Crandell	2378 m	moderate	p. 34
Bertha Peak	2440 m	easy	p. 37
Mount Carthew	2630 m	easy	p. 38
Buchanan Peak	2409 m	difficult	p. 39
Mount Alderson	2692 m	easy	p. 40
Mount Blakiston	2910 m	moderate	p. 41
Hawkins Horseshoe	2683 m	moderate	p. 43
Mount Lineham	2730 m	easy	p. 44
Akamina Ridge	2600 m	moderate	p. 46

Alderson Lake below Mount Alderson as seen from Mount Carthew.

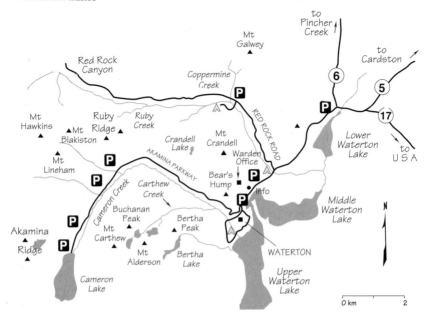

Waterton Lakes National Park, the most southerly area covered in this book, is the Canadian section of International Peace Park. Glacier Park in the United States forms the American portion. Though small, this 518 sq. km preserve in the southwest corner of Alberta is a popular getaway for southern Albertans, boasting a fine network of hiking and backpacking trails. So far, Waterton has avoided the crass commercialism and overdevelopment that bedevils Banff and Jasper. Visitors familiar with those towns will welcome the quieter pace found here.

Serious mountaineering or climbing opportunities are largely absent in Waterton owing to the poor quality of rock and absence of glaciation. Some of the oldest sedimentary rock in the Rockies is found here but it has not improved with age.

The enthusiast will still find a few good scrambles but many ascents, though scenic, are simple scree walk-ups. Compared to Lake Louise, Waterton offers a kinder, gentler landscape. Mountain peaks are smaller and ascents typically demand correspondingly less effort.

Waterton Park is notorious for wind. Gales seem to blow regularly here, to the joy of board-sailors but to the chagrin of campers in the town campground. For many, setting up camp here is a defining moment that reveals that not all tents are created equal. In both winter and spring, Waterton is real chinook country. Chinooks are warm, westerly or southwesterly winds that arrive sporadically during the coldest months and promote rapid snow melting. This helps guarantee a little longer scrambling season than what can be expected farther north. If snow persists in Kananaskis and Bow Valley, try heading to Waterton for a spring weekend.

Although lying next to the prairie, past glaciation has altered Waterton's craggy landscape. Mountain walls have been sculpted into craggy sentinels. Many peaks display high, castellated towers of horizontally-bedded layers. One might expect such striking attractions to guarantee sound rock, but unfortunately it is generally poor and untrustworthy. Colourful red and green outcrops of argillites are also prevalent in the mountains. These are a type of mudstone, but not surprisingly, this, too, is generally flakey and unsound. Park policy does not encourage technical climbing because of unreliable rock and anyone considering steeper routes on these peaks should check his life insurance policy.

Access to Waterton Park is via Highway 6 from Pincher Creek, some 48 km north and by Highway 5 connecting to Cardston, 45 km east. Famous Chief Mountain Highway provides access from the United States but is open in summer only. Located within Waterton Park is 16 km-long Akamina Parkway beginning right in the townsite and terminating at Cameron Lake. Red Rock Canyon Road, 15 km in length, starts a few kilometres to the northeast.

Facilities in Waterton are just what you would expect in a tourist-oriented town. From about mid-May to late September, you can probably find most anything needed in the way of groceries, service stations, restaurants, camping and hiking supplies, souvenirs and ice cream. Everything is within convenient walking distance downtown. Visitors require a national park permit and this can be purchased at the entrance gate. When you tire of tramping around the mountains, scenic boat rides on the lake are popular and horse rides are available, too. Mountain bikes and pedal carts are available in town for the mildly adventurous.

Accommodation Several campsites are found nearby, both in and outside the park. Within the park, showers are available at the townsite campground only. When the thrill of camping wears off, local hotels, motels, chalets and motor inns will be happy to take your money.

The **Parks Information** building is found just before the town centre across from the majestic Prince of Wales Hotel, a historic Waterton landmark on the open shores of the lake.

Wardens are happy to provide advice on current mountain conditions, weather forecasts and tips to keep you out of trouble in your pursuits. Just ask. The Warden Office and Maintenance Compound are west of the golf course on the right-hand side as you drive into town.

MOUNT GALWEY 2348 m

Difficulty Difficult scrambling for a short distance via southwest aspect
Round trip time 3.5-7 hours
Height gain 960 m
Map 82 H/4 Waterton Lakes

As you drive north toward Redrock Canyon, it is hard to miss Mount Galwey. Rolling, verdant hills beginning at road's edge lead to stark, dry slopes crowned by a blunt arrowhead summit. The very shape begs investigation. Judging by register entries, many do just that—repeatedly. It is easier than the view suggests. Try from late May on.

Follow Redrock Canyon Road in Waterton National Park 7.8 km and park at Coppermine Creek picnic area.

Beginning at Coppermine Creek picnic area, follow what begins as a promising trail up undulating hills on the right-hand side of the stream. Stay well above the drainage to avoid a narrow, canyon-like section and tramp along the rounded crest of the open ridge that leads directly toward Mount Galwey. En route you pass a sizeable outcrop of rich red rock—red argillite of the Appekunny Formation. Where the ridge meets the peak, angle left crossing above the headwaters of the right-hand (south) fork of Coppermine Creek. Continue working diagonally up and left circling the peak in a clockwise direction. Now you are above a scree basin feeding the north fork of Coppermine Creek. Galwey's defences are weaker on this side.

Prairie view through window near the summit.

Mount Galwey from Coppermine Creek picnic area.

Although the strata are downsloping and rubbly as you plod around, this unstable terrain improves as you reach the steeper sections. A key landmark to watch for, unless it topples one day, is a rock pinnacle capped by a much larger rock poised against the skyline. It resembles a mushroom: a very big mushroom. Some distance below it, a gully breaks the first steep rock band steering you toward vertical blocks stained yellow with lichen. Ascend this gully. This chute narrows as you climb, and the black band—possibly quartzite—is fabulously solid. Too bad there is so little.

As you emerge on a level platform, possibilities look few. Now you are higher than the point where a north-trending ridge abuts the summit mass of the peak. Although it looks exposed, the correct way lies southward past a rock "wing" projecting airily over the abyss. There really isn't a sheer drop, but merely a sloping scree bay a few metres below. Traverse into it on small but solid ledges—the crux. Now you are onto a more southerly aspect and almost up. Just off to the right, a rectangular window through a solid wall of rock frames a view of prairies lying east. Follow the path of least resistance and scramble easily up to the flat summit. Although the north end is higher, this south end is Mount Galwey and is shown as the summit on all maps.

Mount Galwey is named for Lieutenant Galwey, an astronomer with the BBC—not a radio station, but the British Boundary Commission.

MOUNT CRANDELL 2378 m

Difficulty Difficult scrambling via Bear's hump; moderate via Tick Ridge
Round trip time 4-7 hours
Height gain 1040 m
Map 82 H/4 Waterton Lakes

Mount Crandell offers an opportunity to scramble up a small summit on the very doorstep of Waterton townsite. Three different routes, discussed in decreasing order of difficulty, can be readily combined to effect a traverse. In spite of a radio repeater on top, the ascent is worth doing. Try from May on.

Depending on your choice of route, access is either from Bear's Hump behind Waterton Park Tourist Information Booth or from Waterton Park Warden's Office, 5 km east of the townsite.

Mount Crandell and townsite as seen from Crypt Lake trail. Approximate ascent line from Bear's Hump is shown. B Bear's Hump, T Tick Ridge, D descent.

Bear's Hump Approach

Most demanding of the three described routes is an ascent from Bear's Hump. Starting from the Tourist Information Booth, follow the signed path that fizzles to scratchings of an animal trail shortly beyond Bear's Hump. Continue directly up to the first steep wall. Here the route

Photo: David M. Baird.

suddenly takes on a serious nature. For the next couple of hundred vertical metres, you must work your way left on ledges—many of which are treed to some extent—and search for weaknesses that allow you to ascend successive cliff bands. The rock is solid but often smooth. It is impossible to even attempt to describe an exact line as possibilities are many and the best line depends largely on your skill at routefinding. In critical spots you'll see paths made by streetwise bighorn sheep who eventually tire of panhandling around town and come here to get away from it all. When these paths do appear, it is often worth following them. Sheep are no fools: Despite superb climbing skills, they often choose the easiest available line.

After surmounting several rock bands, you emerge onto easier terrain within a huge bowl that acts as a collecting basin for waterfalls cascading toward Akamina Parkway. The skyline ridge on your right is a narrow and challenging continuation of the ascent. Coincidentally, Tick Ridge, beginning near the Warden's Office, intersects at this point.

You can either scramble on the crest of this airy cockscomb or, easier, wander and scramble along the foot of it on the left (west) side to avoid the most tenuous bits. At some point, though, you will find the crest preferable to traversing alongside. By then difficulties on the ridge will be much less daunting. Challenges diminish as you approach the summit, and the last stretch is just a walk. Owing to the degree of routefinding required, this particular ascent line would present significant challenges as a means of descent. I cannot recommend it for that purpose. Similarly, until you top out there is no quick way off. Gullies end in cliffs. The usual descent route is described lastly.

A foreshortened view of Bear's Hump route from the townsite.

Tick Ridge

The most popular ascent line starts close to the Park Warden's Office/Maintenance Compound. It is obvious and readily studied from the highway.

Walk uphill through the grassy meadow just north of the Warden's parking lot, aiming for the bottom of the big southeast-facing drainage gully where a stream flows. The ridge rising diagonally to the left offers a no-nonsense line of ascent and requires only minor detours into trees to overcome a couple of steeper steps. It then joins the cockscomb described above under the Bear's Hump approach.

Southeast Slopes

The easiest route, used most frequently for a quick **descent**, uses open slopes on the right (north) side of this same southeast-facing drainage gully emerging slightly north of the Warden's Office.

From the summit, drop down through larch forest, angling left as you lose elevation. Keep left of the main drainage system that becomes better defined as you descend. Do not follow the creek down into narrow confines. Instead, stay well above it on open slopes to the left, going overtop a jutting promontory, easily seen from the road. Scramble down the path of least resistance aiming roughly for the stream's exit point at the meadow below. Heavy rains in 1995 widened the streambed so you may be able to avoid the bush more easily now. Total descent time may well be less than one hour.

Mount Crandell is named for a Calgary businessman, Edward Henry Crandell, who had been drawn to the short-lived oil seep "Discovery Well," on Cameron Creek, identified today by a roadside monument.

Tick Ridge route on Mount Crandell.

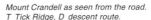

Mount Crandell as seen from the road.
T Tick Ridge, D descent route.

BERTHA PEAK 2440 m

Difficulty Easy to moderate scramble
Round trip time 4-7 hours
Height gain 1150 m
Map 82 H/4 Waterton Lakes

Bertha Peak is an easy ascent from nearby Bertha Lake. The lake is a popular day hike from Waterton townsite, but the mountain will be far less crowded. Less ambitious partners can loll at the lake while you gaze over steep cliffs to the masses far below, or glimpse big peaks in Glacier National Park. An ice axe could be needed for early season trips; try from mid-June on.

Drive into Waterton townsite past the Information Centre and along Evergreen Avenue across from the campground. Continue past Cameron Falls where a gravel side road leads to the signed trailhead for Bertha Lake in a small parking area on the right among cottages.

From the parking area, follow the signed Bertha Lake trail reaching the lake in about 1.5 hours (don't miss the cut-off at 1.5 km). You can see your objective from the lakeshore and it does not look particularly challenging. The route consists of broken slopes of shale with short rock

Bertha Peak as seen from near the lake. S summit.

steps and starts behind the campground on the west shore. As you cross the bridge over Bertha Brook, note the waterfalls that originate in a hidden basin above the campground. (They may dry up in late season.) Easy angled terrain to the right of these cascades works well on ascent, but there are any number of potential routes up. Avoid steep spots as much of the rock is loose shale. Small waterworn gullies are often solid, but of course, no scramble is complete without tedious loose scree somewhere. Just so you know where you are going, the true summit lies at the right-hand end of the skyline ridge. This finale is merely a gentle hands-in-pockets walk up a broad slope of lichen-covered rock plates.

The summit grants a clear view straight down the front cliffs to Bertha Lake and the myriad switchbacks leading to it. Vimy Peak and ridge beckon across Upper Waterton Lake, while impressively larger mountains in Glacier National Park punctuate the horizon to the south. Mount Alderson, lying southwest, is the dominant adjacent peak and is ascended from Cameron Lake on Akamina Parkway. Once you have had enough Waterton wind, **return** the same way.

Who was Bertha? Bertha was a counterfeiter who found that Waterton folks didn't like her type around, and to prove it, they locked her up. Nobody minded her name, though, so they let it stay.

MOUNT CARTHEW 2630 m

Difficulty Easy
Round trip time 4-6 hours
Height gain 1000 m
Map 82 G/1 Sage Creek

Though more of a plod than a scramble, Mount Carthew is sometimes ascended by day-trippers hiking Carthew-Alderson trail or as a destination in itself. The ascent is a minor but worthwhile diversion from the trail. From the top you can wistfully study more impressive summits in nearby Glacier Park and a choice of two routes up offer variety. Try from late June on.

From Waterton townsite, follow Akamina Parkway about 16 km to Cameron Lake. Carthew trail begins on a boardwalk to the left close to the canoe concession.

Follow the wide trail as it rises in a series of switchbacks through deep forest, easing off to reach the shore of pristine Summit Lake in about an hour. Most parties continue past this pond to the high point of the Carthew-Alderson traverse, a saddle between those peaks. Although called Carthew summit, it would be better described as Carthew-Alderson Pass or col. Regardless, a simple hike up scree on the left leads to the ridge and summit 380 m above.

Waterton Park Warden Edwin Knox showed me a more enjoyable off-trail variation that I will share, but please don't trample the vegetation. Gain Mount Carthew's southwest ridge at a point about 10 minutes past Summit Lake. Angle left up the hillside through open forest. Once you gain the wide ridge, expect no particular difficulties en

route to the top. Part way up, you will ascend a small boulderfield, above which are two precarious rock "stacks" on the skyline. After a short 10 m descent to the ridge, the view continues to improve. Cameron Lake, Mounts Chapman and Custer to the south vie for attention. Just before the summit, the normal route from Carthew trail merges. As a descent route, it is quick and dirty—especially if you fall down.

The summit is a prime example of a locally widespread rock called red argillite. This is pretty much the same stuff as at Red Rock Canyon, except you can drive there. Without the presence of oxygen eons ago, this once iron-rich rock wouldn't have rusted, and red argillite would instead be green argillite. Neat, eh?

Below the summit are three Carthew Lakes occupying successively lower bowls. Such lakes are called "pater noster" lakes. Looking southeast, the summit of Mount Alderson's west ridge is obviously straightforward from the hiking trail, and obsessive folks may decide to head up there next.

The best scenery undoubtedly lies to the south and west in Glacier Park where Mounts Chapman and Custer provide the backdrop for Nooney and Wurdeman lakes. Immediately west of Cameron Lake lies broad, undulating Akamina Ridge, a worthwhile ridge walk described in this section.

Returning to the hiking trail, you can either go back to Cameron Lake (shorter) or extend your day by continuing the hike past Alderson Lake and eventually reach Waterton townsite. Allow at least three hours from top to town. **Note:** A hiker's shuttle travels to Cameron Lake each morning. Check at the Information Centre near Prince of Wales Hotel.

Opposite: View of the hiking trail, SW southwest ridge and S summit.

BUCHANAN PEAK 2409 m

Difficulty Difficult scrambling
Time 1-1.5 hours from Mount Carthew, several hours to continue to townsite

You can continue north from Mount Carthew to Buchanan Peak, but it is harder and less pleasant than ascending Mount Carthew. Though initially easy, the descent to the col gets more serious at two successively steeper bands of rock. Waterton offers little rock solid enough to form cliffs, and where it does, cliffs are usually rubble-strewn and loose. Here is no exception. Know your ability and use great care with all handholds. Work down to the left to less steep cliffs and find a feasible spot to downclimb to scree. Unlike Mount Carthew, Buchanan is not simply a hike but with care, experienced scramblers can reach the intervening col and the next high point (1 hour). A lesser point on the SSE ridge is the actual summit as shown on maps.

On **descent**, you can follow the ridge extending southeast toward Alderson Lake. Keeping some distance below the crest is preferable and where possible, use bighorn sheep trails: they know the way. Depending on your route, about one-third of the way down you may encounter short awkward descents on downsloping rock. The remainder is easier and continues right down to the farthest end of the ridge to meet the hiking trail below. Although illogical, you could also ascend this ridge.

Doing both peaks will occupy a full day, and from here it would make little sense to hike back up past Carthew Lakes to reach Cameron Lake. You might as well hike downhill to town. Just remember, if your car is at Cameron Lake, it is about 18 km away from where you'll finish in town. That shuttle service makes a lot more sense now, doesn't it?

MOUNT ALDERSON 2692 m

Difficulty Easy; minimal scrambling
Round trip time 6-9 hours
Height gain 1100 m
Map 82 H/4 Waterton Lakes

Mount Alderson is the other popular peak-bagger's objective on the Carthew-Alderson trail, Mount Carthew being the first. Although it is little more than a hike, it ranks as a fine viewpoint and probably sees less traffic than does its counterpart. Try from late June on.

Begin from Cameron Lake as for Mount Carthew and hike past Summit Lake to the high point on Carthew's south shoulder (two hours). Lose about 50 m as you descend to the saddle near upper Carthew Lake. Then simply ascend the reddish slope to the ridge undulating eastward and reach the summit of Mount Alderson. Allow one-two hours from the low point.

The view to the bigger summits in Glacier National Park is an inspiring companion to your trek. Most Waterton Park area peaks are small in stature and the scene Mother Nature has painted here is pastoral. Gentle hues of red and green argillite above tree line, deep blue lakes and sky (if you're lucky) and golden prairies to the east impart a feeling of

serenity. Often, though, the wind conspires to keep you on your toes (or blow you off them!) rather than let you dreamily wander in an elevated, euphoric daze.

Although most of the ascent is merely hiking, two steps in the ridge require short descents. The first step on good rock is easily descended on the left side; the second step is better turned by scrambling down a succession of downsloping shaley ledges on the right. No further problems are encountered. The **return** is via the same way.

According to *Over 2000 Place Names of Alberta* by Holmgren and Holmgren, Lieutenant General E. A. Alderson commanded the Canadian Expeditionary Force in France, 1915-16.

MOUNT BLAKISTON 2910 m

Difficulty Moderate scrambling
Round trip time 6-10 hours
Height gain 1410 m
Map 82 G/1 Sage Creek

Ease of both approach and ascent has established Waterton's highest point as a most popular scramble. A well-graded approach trail leads to steep but direct rubble slopes guaranteed to have the fittest people puffing to the top. Energetic parties can undertake an enjoyable traverse to include Mounts Hawkins and Lineham. Carry an ice axe for any remaining snow patches. Try from mid June on.

From Waterton townsite, follow Akamina Parkway 9.4 km to Lineham Falls trailhead on the north side of the road. **Note:** Upper part of the ascent route is visible from Rowe Lakes trailhead, 1.3 km farther down the highway.

Follow the wide, well-graded Lineham Falls trail as it switchbacks onto luxuriant grassy slopes, then seeks the depths of sombre forest. In one hour, you suddenly escape shady coniferous forest and are greeted with the first view of Lineham Creek cascading dramatically over a vertical headwall. More importantly, though, this clearing you have entered is an avalanche run-out zone from Mount Blakiston, and is the usual line of ascent. Look for bits of a trail along the right side of the drainage.

A search for difficulties reveals only brief rock steps, and the angle of the terrain seems modest. Left of the highest point, the guard band of dark, castellated cliffs has eroded to allow easy passage to the ridge. Most rock steps between seem surmountable in perhaps as little as a single bound. By comparison, when seen from nearby Mount Lineham, this route appears discouragingly long and incredibly steep. The truth, however, lies somewhere between those two perceptions.

Opposite: Carthew Lakes and the gentle ascent ridge of Mount Alderson as seen from Carthew.

Follow the faint trail along the right side of the gully. Stunted evergreens, defying yearly avalanches, huddle precariously in the lee of the first bluffs you approach. In June, it may be feasible to go up consolidated remnants of climax avalanches, however, for this you will definitely need an ice axe. Eventually the angle steepens and if snowy, you will probably prefer ascending nearby talus instead.

Although Mount Lineham obstructs much scenery initially, step by tedious step peaks in nearby Glacier Park and British Columbia emerge on the horizon. As you draw closer to the final cliffs, notice a couloir directly under the summit. It starts at the first weakness left of the nasty east face drop-off and offers a more interesting finish than the wide gully. Grovel up exasperatingly loose scree to a band of locally-widespread red argillite supporting these black summit cliffs. If you climb the couloir, steep but wonderfully firm rock flaunting fluorescent yellow lichen quickly eases and directs you to the top. It is a great bit of scrambling, but ends all too soon.

Little distance separates prairie from peak in Waterton, allowing the eye to roam freely between eroded summits and rolling grasslands to the east. Cameron Lake is visible to the south and beyond, mightier peaks in

Glacier National Park reach skyward. Barely visible is the broad Flathead Basin farther west.

To **descend**, avoid the summit cliffs by walking a short way down the ridge, turn left and return the same way. Lower down, there can be good glissading early in the season, although some stretches are too steep while others end abruptly on rock. Carry an ice axe and know how to properly self-arrest. Park wardens have not forgotten a past incident on this mountain where a glissade into rocks resulted in a broken bone.

One other hazard for persons ascending snow slopes is the possibility of breaking through snow weakened by water flowing over underlying rock steps. If snow depth is significant, there may be no evidence such rock steps even exist—until you fall in. This has been responsible for at least one fatality elsewhere in the Rockies.

Mount Blakiston is named for Lieutenant Thomas Blakiston, explorer, ornithologist and member of the Palliser Expedition. After a falling out with Palliser he was sent packing, which he did, visiting China, Australia, New Zealand and England before finally settling in the United States.

Mount Blakiston's ascent route looks deceptively steep when viewed from Mount Lineham.

Blakiston

Mount Blakiston, Lineham Lakes and part of the Hawkins Horseshoe from Mount Lineham.

HAWKINS HORSESHOE 2683 m

Difficulty Moderate scrambling
Round trip time 9-12 hours
Height gain approximately 1850 m

From Mount Blakiston, ambitious parties can make a delightful, albeit long, traverse in a grand horseshoe circling Lineham Lakes basin to bag Mounts Hawkins and Lineham, then exit via Rowe Lakes trail. There is much to view, problems are few, and you'll need just one vehicle, not two.

From Mount Blakiston, follow the summit ridge west as it descends gently, jogs southwest, rises to a high point, then heads west over to the bump called Mount Hawkins. Underfoot, in spite of notorious Waterton winds, small grassy patches and pincushion-like clumps of purple moss campion cling to the shale in the hollows.

From Mount Hawkins, the broad ridge continues, curving south to meet the popular Tamarack trail, identified by short metal poles driven into the shale. Again the ridge undulates as it heads east for the summit of Mount Lineham. While this traverse does have a propensity for needlessly losing and regaining elevation, no difficulties are encountered in completing the entire horseshoe. Much of it is wonderful, wide-open hiking, with five Lineham Lakes competing for camera time against a skyline of summits all around. **Note**: You cannot shortcut through Lineham Basin to Lineham Falls trail. Lineham Falls headwall is a tricky technical climb and is not recommended for scramblers.

From Mount Lineham, **descend** south-facing slopes to Rowe Lakes trail. Turn left and reach the road in about 40 minutes. Lineham Falls trailhead is 1.3 km from Rowe Lakes trailhead.

MOUNT LINEHAM 2730 m

Difficulty An easy ascent
Round trip time 4-7 hours
Height gain 1100 m
Map 82 G/1 Sage Creek

Mount Lineham's south aspect presents little more than a steep walk, although many hikers trudge to the top by the more circuitous Tamarack trail/west ridge approach. The summit gives a fine view of Mount Blakiston and the Hawkins Horseshoe traverse that finishes here. In early season, snow-covered south slopes are the perfect angle for practising self-arrest, and glissading conditions can be tremendous then, too. Try from about June on.

From Waterton townsite, follow Akamina Highway 10.4 km to Rowe Lakes/Tamarack trailhead on the north side of the road. Park here.

Hike Rowe Lakes trail for about an hour to the first avalanche slope, then turn right. Apart from thrashing through avalanche greenery for the initial distance, the route is easy. Keep in mind that although this patch of vegetation is small, avalanche areas like this provide much fodder of a grizzly bear's diet, including glacier lilies and false hellebore.

If you don't have a bell or a noisy partner, this might be the ideal place to sing as loudly as you like. Once through the avalanche vegetation, the route is a walkup, but you'll grovel on hands and knees in places.

Cone-shaped Chief Mountain rises above many scree slopes to the southeast and is of special interest to geologists. It was the leading edge of a once-massive 6.5 km-thick wall of rock extending hundreds of kilometres north to Mount Kidd

Snow on these gentle south slopes covers the rubble and allows a glissade.

Photo: Gillean Daffern.   *The scenic west ridge of Mount Lineham presents no difficulties.*

in Kananaskis. Pushed northeast as a largely continuous sheet, it travelled a horizontal distance of some 70 km or so. Geologists, always anxious to find faults, did not let this event slip by unnoticed. They called this the Lewis Thrust, and although similar incidents have occurred elsewhere in the world, few can rival this big push in sheer size. In normal mountain-building circumstances the oldest rock would lie at the bottom of the heap, but when such faulting occurs, older rock rides up onto younger rock, thereby reversing the usual sequence. Because of this occurrence 80 million years ago, part of what would have been British Columbia instead rests in Alberta.

An alternative and scenic but longer **descent** uses part of the Tamarack trail. This loop gives you a view of Lineham Lakes basin that you don't see from the south slopes. From the top, wander down the often-windy west ridge and join the Tamarack trail that descends left into the valley. Pass the Rowe Lakes cutoff and continue back to your vehicle. It is 8.5 km from Lineham Ridge/Tamarack junction to the parking lot. This option is straightforward, but does make for a more complete and longer day whether you choose it for ascent or descent.

Mount Lineham commemorates John Lineham, a transplanted Englishman and a notable Alberta pioneer, largely credited with establishing the town of Okotoks. His ventures and adventures included freighting, oil, a lumber mill or two, and politics. Excepting oil exploration in Waterton, he tended to be successful in all his undertakings.

AKAMINA RIDGE 2600 m

Difficulty Easy with one moderate step
Round trip time 6+ hours to traverse
Height gain 1300 m
Map 82 G/1 Sage Creek

A bit of bush, a little scrambling and oodles of pleasant ridge walking above tree line sum up this loop. The trip starts and ends in Alberta, but the finest portion crosses briefly into British Columbia. Impressive peaks in nearby Glacier Park, Montana, are your companions. Try this trip from late June on.

From Waterton townsite drive 15 km along Akamina Parkway to Akamina Pass trailhead, located about 1 km before Cameron Lake.

Hike up the trail reaching Akamina Pass in about half an hour. This pass marks the Alberta/British Columbia boundary and you will notice a definite cutline identifying it. Follow this cutline south (left). The amount of bushwhacking on this cutline depends entirely on when it was last cleared—recently, you hope! Much of the cutline has an obvious trail and once you reach stands of alpine larch, travel is easy and scenic.

Head straight up the ridge. Note that this ridge is also easily reached (and may be preferable) via open rubble slopes at the back left corner of Forum Lake. Then hike up the ridge to rockbands and traverse right 50-100 m. Look for a break in the cliff that will allow you to scramble easily up ledges. As you ascend, tiny Forum Lake nestles below on your right while larger Cameron Lake sparkles on your left. You'll probably top out near an impressively large cairn, two-three hours from the trailhead. Looking southwest, upper Kintla Lake is visible while to the south, Mount Custer invites attention. Admittedly, the showiest

Pleasant wandering toward the high point of Akamina Ridge.

peaks rise south of the border. Here, anyway! As a matter of interest, nearby Forum Peak is the geographic apex of Alberta, British Columbia and Montana. Rebellious Canadians can surreptitiously touch American soil (and rock) here without stopping at Customs or answering questions!

Continue traversing west (right) along the breezy ridge toward Wall Lake. For survival, vegetation clings to the scant soil in long rows that parallel prevailing winds. Expect no problems as you ascend scree to the high point of the traverse at 117323, a likely place to lunch and absorb the panorama. Near the far (north) end of Akamina Ridge, watch for a good trail leading down to

*Opposite: Forum Peak (left) and
Akamina Ridge route as seen from the road.
P Akamina Pass, C crux.*

the right through open forest and hillsides cloaked in Indian paintbrush. This route roughly follows a small drainage down to Wall Lake where it is signed "Bennet Pass/North Kintla Creek." Wall Lake attracts campers and fishermen alike, and upon arriving you will feel one large step closer to civilization. The trail continues along the left (west) shore of the lake, then out to the main valley trail where you turn right to return to Akamina Pass. Allow an easy hour and a half.

According to *Place Names of Glacier/ Waterton National Parks* by Jack Holterman, in the Kootenai Indian dialect, "Akamina" means "benchland." Akamina-Kishenina Provincial Park is a very recent addition to British Columbia's list of provincial parks, with this 100 sq. km tract gaining its designation in 1995.

CROWSNEST PASS

Turtle Mountain	2204 m	easy	p. 50
Mount Tecumseh	2547 m	moderate	p. 52
Sentry Mountain	2410 m	moderate	p. 54
Crowsnest Mountain	2785 m	moderate	p. 57
Mount Ward	2530 m	easy	p. 59
Window Mountain	2576 m	easy	p. 60
Allison Peak	2645 m	difficult	p. 61

From the final slopes of Crowsnest Mountain, Seven Sisters extends north like a great wing.

The Crowsnest Pass area of southern Alberta does not lie within any national or provincial park and so is not a busy tourist destination like nearby Waterton. Although lacking a well-developed trail system like a national park, this is no obstacle for scramblers. What the area lacks in established trails, it makes up for with both current and disused logging and mining access roads, and is therefore also popular with mountain bikers. Underbrush is virtually nonexistent owing to the dry climate.

Geographically, Crowsnest Pass is situated north of Waterton Park near the eastern edge of the mountains and close to the provincial border. The only major road is Highway 3. As one travels west from Pincher Creek, this picturesque route passes through a succession of small towns including Bellevue, Blairmore and Coleman, then continues to Sparwood in British Columbia and farther. The Pass region is well known for disasters that have occurred in the past. Most noteworthy is the Frank Slide of 1903, when 74 million tonnes of rock avalanched down from Turtle Mountain onto the coal mining town of Frank lying at its base. The town was buried and some 70 persons were killed. Today, an

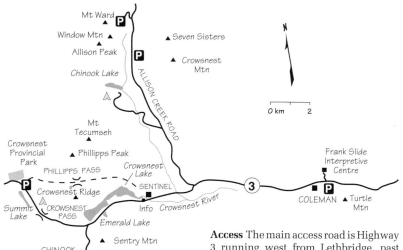

interpretive centre nearby commemorates the disaster. Scramblers can ascend Turtle Mountain for a unique bird's-eye view of the destruction.

Chinooks define the climate here, which results in a longer, drier season for exploring and climbing. Limestone rock found in the Pass is perhaps a little better quality than adjacent Waterton Park, but like that area, peaks are comparatively small. Many caves have been discovered here, and spelunking has perhaps been as popular as scrambling in the past. So, too, are both fly fishing and mountain biking, and one also finds a disproportionate number of four-wheelers and all-terrain-vehicle lovers. Whatever your pursuit, remember that as this is not a park, rescue service is not available. In the event of an accident, volunteers and RCMP would have to respond, not park rescue personnel. No system of registration is available here either.

Access The main access road is Highway 3 running west from Lethbridge, past Pincher Creek and continuing to Fernie in British Columbia. Forestry Trunk Road 940, a gravel road travelling through the southern part of Kananaskis Country, exits (or starts) at Coleman, but is of limited use for access.

Facilities and Accommodation Despite what local merchants would prefer, Crowsnest Pass is not a tourist destination like neighbouring Waterton, which in turn is not a tourist destination like Banff. Life goes on much the same throughout the year and the pace tends to be mellow. A few campgrounds service the area, notably at Chinook Lake on Allison Creek Road, while motels, service stations, stores and restaurants are found in the towns. Limited camping and hiking supplies are available in local sporting goods or hardware stores if needed.

Information The Tourist Information Booth is across from the hamlet of Sentinel, 6.6 km east of the B.C./Alberta border, closed during winter.

TURTLE MOUNTAIN 2204 m

Difficulty An easy scramble
Round trip time 4-8 hours
Height gain 900 m
Maps 82 G/9 Blairmore,
82 G/8 Beaver Mines

Turtle Mountain is best known as the site of the tragic Frank Slide of 1903. Without warning, 74 million tonnes of the mountain crashed down, burying the coal mining town of Frank directly below. At least 70 people were killed. This straightforward trek takes you up to and across the ridge between the two summits where the massive rockslide began, and is far more interesting than the limited view from the nearby visitor centre. Furthermore, the ascent lets you gaze straight down the scarred face on the widespread devastation below. As this area is in the chinook belt, the ascent has a comparatively long season and is usually feasible from early May on.

Drive into the east entrance to Blairmore in Crowsnest Pass, cross the railway tracks and follow streets and avenues toward Turtle Mountain at the east edge of the town. Near 134th Street and 15th Avenue, turn onto a gravel road where there is parking space under telephone lines. The ascent route begins close by.

The trail begins along the base of slabs at the northwest end of the mountain, which faces Blairmore. This well-beaten trail is used regularly by the locals. It makes a couple of short switchbacks and climbs up near the upper rock cut (clearly visible) to gain the main ridge of the peak. As you continue, the path rises through stretches of coniferous

summit

Turtle Mountain from the visitor centre. Ascent route follows skyline ridge from right to left.

forest interspersed with occasional short bits of slab. Much of the way follows the open ridge crest, giving a fine view of Crowsnest Mountain and summits farther west in British Columbia. Trees along here are fully exposed to notoriously strong chinook winds, which explains why so few have branches on the windward side.

The endeavour gets more interesting upon reaching the first summit. Here you can look across the still-scarred face where the slide ripped loose and cascaded onto the town of Frank. Impressive, yes, but the best is yet to come. To reach the second summit, lose a slight amount of elevation to a saddle and pass a hodgepodge of rock debris that stands on your left. This section between the summits reveals great stress fractures in the surface. Even today, huge boulders are still perched precariously near the escarpment, so you should stay well back. Unstable rock still overhangs the face in many places. Finish the ascent by tramping up rubble to the top, which is about half an hour from the first summit.

The second summit gives a more comprehensive perspective of the area and in particular, the incredible horizontal distance that the slide debris travelled. Until recently it was believed that a cushion of air trapped under the moving rock allowed it to travel this great distance, but recent discoveries have now led to a different conclusion. Currently popular is the explanation that smaller particles settle to the bottom and act as ball bearings for larger particles, allowing the big stuff to travel greater horizontal distances. It is generally conceded that the mountain's structure and shape made it prone to sliding, and that the coal mining within was not the culprit. Turtle Mountain's geological structure is an anticline or an upside-down "U," a shape that creates tension forces on the outer layers

Heading toward the main peak.

of the curve where the strata bend downward. This, along with water seeping between layers, probably helped to loosen and lubricate the strata, eventually releasing the horrific avalanche of rock debris that you see today.

Ongoing measurements of the mountain through various methods over the years have not detected further movement and monitoring may stop in future. If so, expect some sort of movement the next day! Until the slide, the mountain was rounded like a turtle's back and the name made perfect sense.

It is possible, apparently, to traverse the peak by continuing farther to the south, descending steep slopes through trees to the east, then heading cross-country toward a farm. Finish by walking into the hamlet of Hillcrest, 4.5 km east of Blairmore. Needless to say, you would require an additional car or a bike. Snow prevented my continuation. For more detailed information, consult *Hiking the Historic Crowsnest Pass* by Tracy and Ross. Most folks return the same way.

MOUNT TECUMSEH 2547 m

Difficulty Moderate scrambling on scree and slabs via south slopes
Round trip time 5-9 hours; 3-6 hours from Phillipps Pass
Height gain 1175 m in total; 975 m from Phillipps Pass
Map 82 G/10 Crowsnest

Mount Tecumseh offers little in the way of difficulty or exposure and is a pleasant outing in the Crowsnest Pass area. Expect minimal exposure but a lot of scree on this small peak. A bike or four-wheel drive is invaluable for the approach. Try from June on.

The ascent begins from Phillipps Pass situated 2 km north of and running parallel to Crowsnest Pass, which separates Mount Tecumseh from Crowsnest Ridge. Crowsnest Ridge is crowned by a highly-visible microwave tower. The gravel access road through Phillipps Pass can be reached from either the east or west end as follows:

From the west, drive to Crowsnest Provincial Park, 2 km west of the B.C./Alberta boundary on Highway 3. Just west of the park a gravel road leads from the highway to the hydro line right-of-way, it can also be reached from the provincial park paved parking lot if the seasonal barricade has been removed. Once on the right-of-way, make a brief detour left into trees and then reach the open flats of Phillipps Pass. Park 4.2 km from Crowsnest Provincial Park, or 0.7 km east of a fenced-in, metal-clad building. This is at the mouth of the drainage emerging at 698017 near a steel hydro-line support tower. This rough access road is suitable for four-wheel-drive vehicles and bikes only.

From the east, drive into the hamlet of Sentinel on the north side of Highway 3 across from the Tourist Information Booth, 6.6 km east of the B.C./Alberta boundary, and follow 26th Street 0.5 km across railway tracks. Although cabled off, a gravel road connecting to Phillipps Pass begins on the north side of the tracks in front of a house on the hill. Hike or bike 3.3 km to the ascent drainage described above.

Walk upstream along the often dry streambed draining the south side of Mount Tecumseh. There isn't really a trail but travel is easy. The abrasive action of water over time has carved solid limestone into a delightful series of "sinks" joined by twisting, smooth-walled channels that are fun to try and ascend directly. You can also trudge along either side if you are not this easily amused.

Within an hour the streambed disappears and you reach a landscape of immense boulders, apparently debris from steep slabs up to the right. Shortly beyond these crumbling rocks turn sharply left past a stand of evergreens and into a scree basin between steep walls of Phillipps Peak and Mount Tecumseh. Although you may have been tempted to continue directly ahead for the top rather than turn left into this basin, cliff bands of downsloping rock complicate more direct lines to the summit. The suggested route allows you to sneak up from the southwest on scree and talus.

From the basin, either tramp straight up or angle slightly to the right as you go. The objective is to gain the ridge above, which leads easily to the summit just east. Contrary to expectations, the crest of the ridge is mostly a plod with no exposure. A metal survey pole crowns the top.

Mount Tecumseh and Phillipps Peak. Route starts from Phillipps Pass. P Phillipps Peak, T Tecumseh.

From the top, the most notable features of the landscape are lonely Crowsnest Mountain and Seven Sisters sitting well apart from the Highrock Range. At one time they were one section of a massive and continuous thick sheet of limestone, pushed in hundreds of kilometres from the west that rode up over existing younger rocks beneath. Geologists identify this north-south demarcation line as the Lewis Thrust. Owing to the erosion of Allison Creek, Crowsnest Mountain, a visible reminder of this cataclysmic upheaval, has become a klippe—an outlier isolated from the main range.

You may wonder why the high point two pinnacles to the west deserves a separate title. Phillipps Peak and Tecumseh were both in use until Tecumseh was officially adopted. The runner-up title was bestowed upon a lower point to the west. You can ascend Phillipps Peak starting farther west along Phillipps Pass and circle left to gain the west ridge. Expect a short section of difficult scrambling on the ridge before the highest point.

There are various explanations for the name of this peak and pass. Michel Phillipps of Elko, B.C. was the first white person to make use of the pass, apparently while scouting out trapping territory in 1873. Bison had used it for centuries but Indians had for some reason avoided it. The mining ghost town of Michel lies just a few kilometres west. Tecumseh, a Shawnee Indian war chief, rallied other Indian tribes into an allied force to combat an American territorial expansion. His forces joined with those of the British and Canadian in 1812, a crucial time during the conflict. In a tragic twist of fate, he died fighting his own people.

SENTRY MOUNTAIN 2410 m

Difficulty Moderate scrambling via west ridge; minimal exposure
Round trip tlme 4-7 hours
Height gain 1025 m
Map 82 G/10 Crowsnest

Diminutive Sentry Mountain guards over the windy gap of Crowsnest Pass, where blustery west winds whip the waters of Crowsnest Lake into a maelstrom of whitecaps. This ascent is largely a nontechnical ridge walk that becomes more interesting near the top. Good views throughout.

You can approach the west ridge of this peak directly from almost anywhere along the first couple of kilometres of Chinook Coal Road. Since the initial and perhaps only real challenge is crossing the creek, you should take the time to scout out the best crossing point along this stretch. Late summer flows are typically only calf-deep but rocks are slimy.

Drive to Chinook Coal Road located 3.7 km east of the B.C./Alberta boundary and 4.8 km west of the Tourist Information Booth on Highway 3 in Crowsnest Pass. Follow the road south for about 1.7 km and park alongside an open pit mine at the foot of Sentry Mountain's west ridge.

Cross the stream and tramp to the top of the limestone quarry. The terrain above this point is easy going through open forest as you hike steadily upwards; occasionally a game trail materializes to coax you along, only to disappear at the first open clearing. The ridge is broad for the first few hundred metres of elevation gain, but becomes more clearly defined higher up. Scattered whitebark pine is interspersed with bleached, twisted trunks stretching dry limbs skyward—a stark reminder of the enduring effects of a past forest fire. Underfoot, the stony landscape is graced by patches of Kinnikinnick or Bearberry. Kinnikinnick is an Indian word that roughly translates to "smokable," and rough it is, too. No wonder gifts of tobacco were popular.

Enjoy the fine view to the south and west as you draw nearer to a "bumpy" portion of the ridge. This part gets a little more interesting, and there are about 275 vertical metres left to go now. Each hump seems to rise a little more steeply, suggesting a drop-off on the other side. Erosion has been thorough, though, and you can continue along quite nicely. One brief notch requires a minor detour to the left on scree and ledges, but not until close to the top does a more serious-looking obstacle rear up. The entire ridge appears protected by a slabby, triangular rock face, seemingly straddling the route. Tackling it directly is a challenge many won't bother with, despite good solid rock. Alternatively, either side will suffice to dodge around it. A detour to the right necessitates a short scramble down to scree, followed by a plod back up and around this stony outcrop. The left side detour may be a better choice. It involves no elevation loss and, with a bit of imagination, you may even see a path.

With this 20 or 30 m behind you, the actual summit is close. The ridge crest narrows dramatically in a couple of places, but except for one point where you must descend a 2 m step, you can avoid most airy bits entirely on scree along the right (south) side. If exposure doesn't bother you, the most sporting route follows right on the crest.

The summit is spacious enough for relaxing without fear of rolling off in your sleep. You'll notice that you could probably wander south along the ridge for quite a distance before encountering any problems, although this would first necessitate about 200 m elevation loss. Conversely, it is easier to sit on your gluteus maximus, stare at big peaks in the west and debate which one is 3359 m Mount Harrison. This was the last Rockies' peak over 3353 m (11,000 ft.) to be climbed. About 1963, cartographers researching new data "found" it, although nobody else knew it had gone missing.

The photo suggests many promising routes up Sentry Mountain and this is by no means the one and only. Other routes may involve more loose rubble than does this particular option. Some years the roadside quarry does not operate and then you could approach the west ridge by driving into the quarry and hike to the west ridge from there. This would eliminate the creek crossing, but the heaps of rock debris are not a particularly esthetic start to the trip.

The west ridge of Sentry Mountain as seen from Crowsnest Ridge. Many route possibilities exist.

CROWSNEST MOUNTAIN 2785 m

Difficulty Moderate scrambling via the north side
Round trip time 4-7 hours
Height gain 1100 m
Map 82 G/15 Crowsnest

"Like the sacred Fuji Yama of Japan, Crow's Nest mountain rises abruptly out of the earth, with no other mountains within miles," wrote P. D. McTavish. He was recounting the second recorded ascent of the peak in 1905. His relatively inexperienced party took a circuitous route and it seems they encountered serious climbing. By comparison, the "tourist route" used today is much easier and, incidentally, was first ascended in 1915 as a solo trip. It is an eye-catching little peak and worth the time if you're in the area. Try from June on.

Drive to Allison Creek Road in Crowsnest Pass, 9.6 km east of the Alberta/B.C. boundary and 14 km west of Frank Slide Interpretive Centre on Highway 3. Follow this road for 9.7 km to a hiking trail sign. Park 0.3 km beyond on the cutline right-of-way.

From the parking area under the cutline walk south 150 m to a marked path. It is well used and easy to follow as it heads to tree line. Pine forest gives way to scree slopes at the north end of the peak where multi-pinnacled Seven Sisters Mountain joins Crowsnest Mountain. There may be flagging, but if it isn't visible, ascend scree to the right of the black waterfall marks at the first band of cliffs. Climb through the lower rock steps, then traverse left on a scree ledge below the black, wet walls of the second cliff. More than one trail can be found below the traverse ledge but they should all rejoin at that spot.

To overcome the second cliff band you must scramble up a long gully to the left.

Toward the top of this gully move left and avoid the damper, dirtier right branch. A ring piton is in place on the right side should anyone be carrying a rope and feel the need to use it, but if the rock is dry it is unnecessary. Annoying dogs, children or spouses could be tethered here too. Above this gully the way is evident, and you should have no problems as you zigzag up gentle scree to the top.

Gould Dome and more prominent Tornado Mountain dominate the view to the north; Mount Ptolemy is the highest point in the cluster of summits lying nearby to the south.

Two theories confuse the origins of the Crowsnest name. One concerns a slaughter of Crow Indians by Blackfoot Indians near the town of Frank, where they were corralled, or in a "nest." According to Reverend John McDougall, though, "on this trail through the mountains there was a nest which was occupied annually by crows" and this explanation is more in favour.

Descend by the same route.

Crowsnest Mountain showing route of ascent.
L lower rock steps, T traverse, G gully.
Photo: Tony Daffern.

Photos: Gillean Daffern.

Crowsnest Mountain: Above scree and the first rock band, the route traverses left below second rock band. It then enters gully on left to reach scree slopes above.

Entering the gully in the second rock band. Note black water and lichen marks on wall.

MOUNT WARD 2530 m

Difficulty Easy scramble
Round trip time 2.5-5 hours
Height gain 625 m
Maps 82 G/15 Tornado Mountain
82 G/10 Crowsnest

Despite the simplicity of the ascent and its proximity to locally-popular Window Mountain Lake, Mount Ward has largely been overlooked in favour of locally famous Crowsnest Mountain nearby. Still, the view from the top is worthwhile and allows a close look at the scramble route up to the huge window in nearby Window Mountain, another Crowsnest area landmark. This is a comparatively short trip that can be extended to a full day to include more difficult scrambling along connecting ridges south to Allison Peak. Try from June on.

From Highway 3, turn north onto Allison Creek Road, 9.6 km east of the Alberta/B.C. boundary and 14 km west of Frank Slide Interpretive Centre. Follow the road for 16.8 km and turn left onto Window Mountain Lake Road (not signed). Drive through a logged area (rough) and park at about 1.3 km. A small parking spot (three vehicles maximum) is reached 2.7 km from Allison Creek Road.

From the parking area the trail soon narrows and heads into the trees, intent on surmounting as quickly as possible the treed hump between vehicle and lake. After angling up over this hump, it descends slightly and you pass along the right side of a small marsh, reaching Window Mountain Lake in about 20 minutes. The lake is a pretty place sheltered by Mount Ward to the south and a high, open ridge to the west. This ridge is

W the Window, S Window Mountain summit, A Allison Peak from Mount Ward.

59

not Mount Ward, however, if desired, its north end can be reached by angling north up open slopes.

Scramblers bound for Mount Ward should hike around the right-hand shore to the far end where an obvious slope leads up into a small valley and easy west slopes of the peak. Occasionally, animal trails are encountered in the moss and scree higher up but are not needed. Glancing back, you will notice that the open ridge just west of the lake would make a possible variation for the return.

From Mount Ward several other easy ascents nearby are apparent including an unnamed peak immediately north of Racehorse Pass and an 8100 ft. (2470 m) point 1.5 km northwest of the lake.

(**Note**: The road to Racehorse Pass begins 1.6 km north of Window Mountain Lake turn-off and requires a bike because of a barricade.)

After you have studied Crowsnest Mountain, patchwork clearcuts to the north and the distant peaks to the west, either return the same way or continue south to 2645 m Allison Peak.

WINDOW MOUNTAIN 2576 m

The intriguing window on nearby Window Mountain (702130 on 82 G/10) lying immediately south is apparent. The route to the window is the rubbly chute directly beneath it, readily reached from clearcuts to the east via logging skid trails about 2.5

km south of Window Mountain Lake turn-off. Furthermore, from the low point in Mount Ward's southwest ridge, it MAY be possible to angle diagonally down to the rocky valley to reach the bottom of the scree gully leading to the Window. If so, rather than return the same way, descend east to logged areas and circle back around the east side of Mount Ward to your vehicle.

The safest way to the top of Window Mountain is via scree slopes and westward-sloping ledges starting above the two large snow patches visible in the picture on p. 59.

According to *Over 2000 Place Names of Alberta* by Holmgren and Holmgren, Captain A. E. Ward was Secretary of the British Boundary Commission, Lake of the Woods to the Rockies in 1917.

Route up to Window Mountain's window. Inset: Crowsnest Mountain seen through the window.

Window Mtn

Window Mountain from the road. Mount Ward would be to the right; Mount Allison is far to the left.

ALLISON PEAK 2645 m

Difficulty Difficult, exposed and loose
Round trip time 3-5 hours from Mount Ward
Height gain about 250 m
Height loss about 250 m

Climbers and experienced, capable scramblers can continue south along the connecting ridge to reach Allison Peak. The traverse involves occasional detours to either side of the ridge as necessary. Some parties find the bit from Mount Ward to the intersection of Window Mountain more challenging than the section of ridge that continues south to Allison Peak. Avoid this traverse unless it

is free of snow. A few minutes before reaching the top of Allison Peak you might find the 1 m x 2 m window through this ridge, close to the crest. **Return** all the long way back to Mount Ward and Window Mountain Lake.

Although attempting the summit of Window Mountain via the connecting ridge may look feasible, descending to the low point is dangerous owing to large, loose blocks of rock and steep rubble-covered slabs. The terrain is very exposed and cannot be recommended.

Douglas Allison, a one-time member of the Royal North West Mounted Police, lived near the creek now bearing his name.

CANMORE AND BOW VALLEY

Heart Mountain	2135 m	moderate	p. 66
Mount Yamnuska	2240 m	easy	p. 68
Mount Fable	2702 m	moderate	p. 70
Traverse to Gap Peak	2440 m	moderate	p. 71
East End of Rundle	2590 m	easy	p. 73
Grotto Mountain	2706 m	easy	p. 74
Middle Sister	2769 m	easy	p. 76
Mount Lady Macdonald	2605 m	difficult	p. 78
Squaw's Tit	2500 m	moderate	p. 80
Ha Ling Peak	2408 m	easy	p. 81
Big Sister	2936 m	moderate	p. 83
Mount Lawrence Grassi	2685 m	moderate	p. 84
Rimwall Summit	2680 m	moderate	p. 85
Mount Baldy	2192 m	moderate	p. 87

This chapter covers scrambles that lie within or close to the Canmore Corridor as well as the extreme north ends of Kananaskis Valley and Spray Lake. Because of their close proximity to urban centres of Canmore and Calgary, these outings are well-travelled and attract many enthusiasts for much of the year.

Geographically, this area is a part of the Rocky Mountain Front Ranges and because of its easterly position in the range, is comparatively dry. Higher peaks to the west collect more precipitation while these peaks around Canmore often experience a rain shadow effect. As a result, the season for scrambling is noticeably longer here. A further phenomenon affecting the scrambling season here is the warm, strong chinook wind that in winter periodically blasts

peaks like Heart and Grotto Mountain devoid of snow. On occasion, Christmas or New Year's ascents can be undertaken owing to minimal snowcover.

The Front Range topography in this area is defined by long limestone ridges generally aligned northwest to southeast. Strata display a pronounced dip to the southwest and, as in much of the Rockies, it is this aspect that usually grants an easy way to the top. An exception to this phenomenon is Mount Yamnuska, which flaunts a near vertical south face. This is because of a locally significant geologic event called the McConnell Thrust.

Like Kananaskis Valley, the Canmore Corridor is a good area to frequent when unsettled weather hits the Rockies. By heading up almost any peak in this

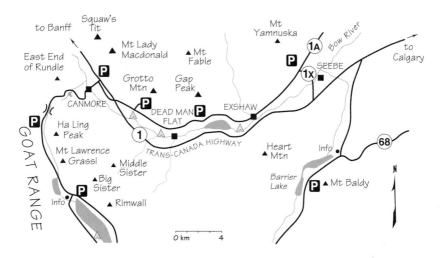

chapter, you are far more likely to salvage a day of poor weather than if you headed farther west. Unfortunately, unbridled development threatens to ruin the charm of Canmore. Since the original edition of this book, the rate of development has been unprecedented. Comparing the view from Lady Macdonald in 1990 to that of today, one now sees a patchwork landscape of hotels, condos and golf courses—none of which existed previously. Not even the summit of Mount Lady Macdonald has been spared. For years now, a partially-constructed teahouse has defiled the upper slopes. However, it is difficult to say which would be worse, the possibility of having it completed and then suffer noisy helicopter traffic, or having it left as a half-finished eyesore. Either way, the idea was ill-conceived and should never have been granted government permission to proceed.

Apart from development, this little corner of the Rockies is a pretty place and scramblers can pass many pleasant hours ascending nearby peaks. To reduce impact on slopes of certain peaks, a local volunteer group, Canmore Trailminders, has constructed trails to the top of a few of the more popular summits. Because south aspects of these mountains come into shape early in the season, particular spots attract a sizeable population of bighorn sheep. Sheep are hosts to ticks, so always check yourself for these critters (ticks, that is!) after a spring or early summer ascent. Ticks are especially prevalent on Mount Lady Macdonald. See the "Hazards" section in the front of the book regarding tick-borne diseases.

On the summit ridge of Lady Macdonald in spring.

Access The Trans-Canada Highway runs through the middle of the Canmore Corridor, with Spray Lakes Road beginning within the town and travelling south. The north end of Kananaskis Valley is reached via Kananaskis Trail (Highway 40), which intersects the Trans-Canada 65 km west of Calgary.

Bow Valley Trail (Highway 1A), on the north side of the Bow River from Seebe to Canmore, accesses Mounts Yamnuska, Fable, Gap and Grotto.

Facilities Canmore offers all visitor facilities and is a major tourist hub. Bars, hotels, bed and breakfasts, fast food, laundromats and the like are in abundance. At Exshaw, on Highway 1A, a combination gas station, cafe and store is found—perfect for a fix of junk food or cold beer after a trip up Mount Fable.

Accommodation Any type of accommodation you might seek is available in Canmore. You can also find a rustic campground on the west side of the Spray Lake Reservoir across Three Sisters Dam, about 18 km from Canmore. Until recently this campground had been free, but in their continuing money grab, the Alberta government now charges for these primitive sites.

For a cheap sleep in Canmore, visit the Alpine Club of Canada Clubhouse, 2 km east of Canmore on Highway 1A at the foot of Grotto Mountain. Campsites, budget motels and gas stations are also found at Dead Man Flat east of Canmore.

Information Centres For general information, Tourism Alberta is at the west end of the gas station strip in Canmore near the west overpass. Trail and campground information is available at Kananaskis Country information in the Provincial Building across from the Rose and Crown Pub. There is also an information centre at Bow Valley Provincial Park near Seebe on Highway 1X.

Emergency The RCMP maintains a station in Canmore on the strip. In the event of a climbing-related accident, Kananaskis Country rangers would provide rescue assistance. As well as the information centre, a seasonal ranger is stationed at Three Sisters Dam on Spray Lakes Road.

HEART MOUNTAIN 2135 m

Difficulty Easy, with one moderate step via northwest ridge
Round trip time 3-6 hours
Height gain 875 m
Map 82 O/3 Canmore

Heart Mountain is close to Calgary, can often be ascended year-round owing to chinooks that blast the route bare, and has at least two variations for descent. Heart Creek parking lot once sat right at the foot of the mountain by the highway, and to climb this popular little peak you parked, tramped 10 m to the ridge and followed the beaten path to the top. Since then, the parking lot has been moved farther west. Despite a slightly longer approach, the ascent remains a favourite early season pilgrimage where you can reintroduce flabby muscles to the rigours of steep hiking. It also makes a fine after-work outing from Calgary.

Park at the signed parking lot for Heart Creek trailhead on the south side of the Trans-Canada Highway at Lac des Arcs interchange, 75 km west of Calgary and 36 km east of Banff.

From the parking lot hike the trail paralleling the Trans-Canada Highway and

cross Heart Creek to the foot of the ridge. The way up is obvious, even without all the markers. Follow the path as it climbs rapidly up the right side of the "heart" shape. Slabs on the ascent are a pleasant change from scree, while more exposed spots can be avoided by a short detour left into the trees. Two-thirds of the way up the ridge eases and to continue, you scramble up a steep 3 m-high wall identified by red metal markers. You need not bother looking elsewhere for an easier place to ascend as there isn't one.

You soon reach the first summit. Some people are content to call it quits about here and watch for the marmots that live nearby, but a higher second summit lies about 25 minutes beyond to the southeast (318550). Follow the trail.

From the true summit there are two options for the return trip. Most popular is the pleasant circuit that can be made by heading northeast along a rounded ridge. Descend a short grassy slope, tramp across a saddle and up to attain a minor high point (322554). This open ridge then begins to arc left, coaxing you along on a windswept northwesterly course that gradually descends into mature for-

The crux, complete with markers.

est toward the highway. The route is well used and easy to follow. Join up with Quaite Valley trail, which parallels the highway just a short way past the hydro line, and this will take you west back to Heart Creek.

An **alternate descent** lies on the west side of Heart Mountain at a point almost directly below the true summit. It is shown on the map as an intermittent drainage. Descend open slopes toward Heart Creek as they funnel down toward a short drop-off guarded by a rock wall on the right. Turn this drop-off easily and follow a game trail to the upper reaches of Heart Creek valley, then wander downstream to the multi-bridge (and often busy) interpretive path.

Another option for exploration is available. If you have reached the second summit at 318550, you can add an interesting extension along an open ridge leading southeast to twin high points (325537) overlooking Barrier Lake. The ridge descends gently, losing elevation, then climbs back up again. The crux of this extension is a drop-off about halfway between Heart Mountain and the two 2300 m (7500 ft. on the map) unnamed points. There is no way to avoid this brief test-piece—you must climb down here. The descent involves little more than 5 m of careful scrambling but it is much steeper terrain. You will be returning the

Northwest ridge from Heart Creek showing first summit.
Photo: Gillean Daffern.

same way, but climbing back up this rock step is a whole lot easier.

Between roughly 45 and 85 million years ago during the Late Cretaceous to Middle Eocene period, tremendous compressional forces folded the upper strata of Heart Mountain into a plunging syncline. When seen from across the valley at Exshaw, it forms a near-perfect valentine heart.

TRAVERSE OF MOUNT YAMNUSKA 2240 m

Difficulty From west, easy. From east, also easy with fixed cable at 5 m crux
Round trip time 3-6 hours
Height gain 900 m
Map 82 O/3 Canmore
(shown as Mount Laurie)

Yamnuska is a popular early season outing and usually bustles with activity. Easy access and a variety of routes attract rock-climbers, particularly when bigger peaks are snowbound. Scramblers will find the ascent a good conditioner. Owing to its easterly location, Yamnuska often escapes bad weather plaguing peaks to the west. The Yamnuska environs are well known for their diversity of plant life and, in early season, purple crocuses of varying shades carpet the south-facing hillside. An east to west traverse is popular and finishes with a rapid descent down huge scree slopes. Try this from about May on.

Mount Yamnuska was formed by a geological movement called the McConnell Thrust. Eldon limestone of the Cambrian period (the steep southeast face) was pushed up onto much younger and softer sandstones of the lower slopes. The usual younger-over-older sequence of stratification or "layering" was therefore reversed, resulting in a geologically disorganized mountain. The demarcation line is evident at the foot of the steep face.

From Seebe intersection (Highway 1X) on Bow Valley Trail (Highway 1A), drive east for 2 km, then turn left and follow the road 200 m to a parking lot in the trees below Yamnuska. The trail starts at the west end, crosses the quarry access road and rises through aspen forest east of the rock quarry.

At the first intersection along the trail the right-hand fork, shown for hikers and horses, is the least-steep (but longest) approach route. It wanders up to the crest of the shoulder just east of Yamnuska, then continues down to CMC Valley behind. From the shoulder simply hike uphill toward the peak. Most scramblers

The crux on east ridge showing three options.

Yamnuska's back side showing traverse. W west side, E east ridge, C crux.

and climbers, however, continue straight ahead on the path rising west. Upon reaching the next junction on the open slope, note that the trail continuing straight ahead leads west to massive scree slopes below the face and is normally used only for descent. The preferred way up is the trail that cuts back up to the right (east). Steep zigzags lead to the mountain's east end and the trail continues around to the northeast side. The path descends at a crumbly buttress, then traverses below it before rising more steeply toward the ridge crest above. Angle west along the trail across talus and toward a shallow gully leading to a small notch in a rock wall on the skyline. This is the easiest place; harder options exist some distance upslope.

The route is straightforward until you reach a drop-off above a gully. Here (crux), you have three options. You can either downclimb a steep 5 m groove toward the gully, or else start slightly downslope to gain a horizontal ledge (easier) with a fixed cable (as of 2002) and traverse into the gully. Others prefer to continue up to the ridge, then scramble down 10 m of short rock steps. Though the holds are good, the feeling of exposure while downclimbing is hard to ignore.

Immediately past this is a steep wall rising in front of you alongside a notch in the summit ridge, avoided by descending scree below and back up around it. Continue easily to the big summit cairn. Somewhere in the midst of this cairn rests an alien rockform from the Pamirs Range of Russia, brought back by Calgary climbers. It is not known whether hybridization of species is occurring, but the expanding size of the cairn seems suspicious.

On **descent**, a beaten path in fine brown shale gives way to a short section of slabs followed by coarser rubble as it winds down the west side and around to the west end. In early season, snow may persist on this aspect when the rest of the peak has dried off and this has surprised climbers with smooth-soled rock shoes. Once you are below the face again, hike east to huge scree slopes and make a beeline to tree line. The trail descends to the quarry.

MOUNT FABLE 2702 m

Difficulty Moderate via south slopes and west ridge
Round trip time 6-9 hours
Height gain 1325 m
Map 82 0/3 Canmore
(unmarked 242642)

Mount Fable is a shapely peak hiding north of and behind Grotto Mountain. Although its summit does protrude above adjacent peaks, it is not entirely evident. However, looking north from Heart Creek, it rises majestically up Exshaw Creek, in sharp contrast to Baymag plant's ugly smokestack. Mount Fable's climbing season is longer than many and some years is feasible by late May. It is far from crowded but does see regular activity. A long ridge traverse south to Gap Peak and the highway is also possible.

From the hamlet of Exshaw on Bow Valley Trail (Highway 1A), follow Windridge Road on the east side of Exshaw Creek for 0.8 km to Mount Lorette Drive. Park by the footbridge.

Mount Fable ascent route and the traverse as seen from Gap Peak. F Fable.

Mount Fable's west ridge route ascends scree, then follows skyline ridge to top. Traverse goes left.

Cross the bridge and follow the elevated waterline for 10 minutes to the now smoothed-over concrete dam and walk up over it. Follow the trail up Exshaw Creek and reach a major side valley (265622) in one hour. Although this valley does drain the south slopes of Mount Fable, there is very little water en route so carry enough with you. Hike up (trail in places) to the base of the mountain. Then you can either plod up brown scree to the west ridge, or, less tedious, scramble up to the right by the last rock step in the gully, following slabs immediately right of this brown scree. Traverse left onto more low-angled slabs to gain the ridge.

Once on the crest, various unnamed summits to the north encircling Cougar Creek are revealed, as are more familiar local peaks lying south. The ridge leads quickly to the top and if snowfree is straightforward except for a brief narrow part. **Descend** the same way.

The first attempt party in 1947 failed, and attributed it to having wasted time owing to bush. A subsequent party took up the challenge and returned victorious. Were the problems with bush a mere fable? The successful party thought so, and since then this name has gained local recognition.

TRAVERSE TO GAP PEAK 2440 m

Difficulty Moderate scrambling, slight exposure
Round trip time 11 hours, including an ascent of Mount Fable

Experienced parties may consider undertaking a high level traverse following a straightforward ridge system that arcs west from Mount Fable, then runs south-southeast toward Exshaw for 3 km. It parallels the approach up Exshaw Creek and ends at a small, unnamed summit

The traverse as seen from Grotto Mountain. G Gap Peak, D descent to upper Grotto Canyon.

above Highway 1A (at 246612). You then descend scree into upper Grotto Valley and hike out. John Martin, who may have first done this traverse, calls the unnamed peak "Gap Mountain," as it overlooks Gap Lake. Hopefully, he won't mind me referring to it instead as Gap Peak to avoid confusion with Gap Mountain at Highwood Pass.

From the west ridge of Fable, ascend west to a broad ridge that curves south, separating into two different ridge systems. The more westerly right-hand one is complex, joining eventually to Grotto Mountain, but it is NOT a scramble. Gable Ridge (Gap + Fable = Gable), the left-hand ridge, is simpler. You can see it gradually losing elevation for much of the way to Gap Peak, where it then rises. If you're up to it, this traverse is a fine but longer return trip with unrestricted views throughout. In case of bad weather, you could probably descend west into upper Grotto Valley without continuing to Gap Peak. Gable Ridge has a few steps in it but is not a difficult scramble.

From Gap Peak, the least problematic descents are down west and southwest-facing scree slopes to upper Grotto Creek valley. The rocky, undulating ridge descending south-southeast and the gully (which becomes a canyon lower down) south of the peak should be avoided. However, open slopes below the summit lead easily to upper Grotto Creek at 233612 and are straightforward. Better yet, continue three bumps south for about 15 minutes to the next scree slope. Leave the ridge near the left side of this slope (by rock outcrop), **descend** to tree line, then angle right and leave the drainage. Descend pine forest well right of the drainage to reach Grotto Creek at 235600, about 1.5 km downstream of the previous option. Hike down-valley and upon emerging from the canyon, go east (trail) to Grotto Pond day-use area. If you have a bike, stash it near here for retrieving your car at Exshaw. This excursion will be a full day for most parties.

EAST END OF RUNDLE 2590 m

Difficulty An easy scramble via south scree slopes
Round trip time 3-5 hours
Height gain 900 m
Map 82 O/3 Canmore
(unmarked 105598)

The East End of Rundle is a good early season objective that requires minimal effort. This is not, of course, Rundle's true summit, but the eastern extremity of the 12 km-long uplift. Steep, high faces above the canal host several rock-climbing routes; the gentle south slopes serve as a climber's descent route. It is also a popular jaunt for scramblers and hikers as the snow on it often disappears by mid-May.

Follow Spray Lakes Road from Canmore townsite past the Canmore Nordic Centre to Whiteman's Gap and Goat Creek parking lot, 8.6 km past the Bow River bridge.

From the parking area, hike back along the road and look for a man-made trail between the Bow Crow Forest sign and the second set of powerline poles. It leads easily through ever-thinning forest to tree line. You can then either angle left and aim directly for the high point, going through a rock band via a gully, or continue straight uphill, gain the skyline ridge and scramble up that way. The gully is preferable on descent. Above are two minor points five minutes apart. On one unforgettable occasion years ago, the higher

East End of Rundle showing ascent route from Whiteman's Gap.

point hosted two skimpily-clad, much-surprised female sunbathers. Sadly, not much has been seen of them since.

The lengthy traverse of Rundle is often started from this end and though initial stages are straightforward, sections toward the main summit become technical and require a rope.

GROTTO MOUNTAIN 2706 m

Difficulty Easy to moderate scramble depending on route
Round trip time 5-8 hours
Height gain 1425 m
Map 82 O/3 Canmore

Grotto Mountain is a Canmore landmark ascended regularly. Often as early as April the faithful begin the season with a pilgrimage. The short approach walk is pleasant and you can maximize the view by combining both routes described for a traverse.

Drive to Indian Flats Road 4.2 km east of Canmore on Bow Valley Trail (Highway 1A). It leads past Bow Valley Riding Association's stable to the Alpine Club of Canada clubhouse. Limited parking may be available at the Alpine Club of Canada parking lot or at the first bend in the access road.

Direct Route

The shortest and steepest route takes a direct line from base to summit, following close to the right edge of a massive gully system draining the southwest slopes. From utility sheds below the ACC clubhouse parking lot, notice an obvious man-made trail angling up to the right. Follow this to the ridge, then over to the crest of the next ridge to the right (east). You'll see the horse corrals below at this point. Immediately past here, just 15 minutes from the parking lot, notice an important split in the trail. The trail continuing straight ahead is the Northwest trail. For the direct route, take the right branch that angles down and crosses a streambed. The trail angles up to the right and crosses pasture and grassy terraced slopes. Aim for open flanks to the right of the massive gully on Grotto's southwest side at 192600. Travel is easy.

Keep to the left as you ascend. Occasional slabs provide a change of regimen, but as some are both high and steep, you can simplify matters by staying near the

huge gully. This avoids most problematic sections. Winding trails around obstacles prove that even bighorn sheep prefer easier terrain. From tree line, tramp up rubble to the cairn.

Northwest (ACC) Trail

An alternate ascent (or descent) route lies more toward the northwest end of the mountain. In the summer of 1995, volunteers from the Rocky Mountain Section of the Alpine Club of Canada completed a nicely-graded trail that cunningly dodges all cliff bands. Although not trail builders by trade (as far as I know!), this group did an admirable job carving the winding path into the hillside and creating switchbacks to ease the grade. Hopefully, parties descending will use common sense and avoid taking shortcuts that can so quickly ruin a trail.

This northwest route actually ascends the southwest flanks. In previous editions I described a route left of this new trail as the Northwest Variation—because that end of the peak is kind of northwest. Logically, this new route should be called the ACC trail. It too is left of the huge gully, but not as far left as the Northwest Variation. For the ACC trail, begin as for the direct route but do not branch right after 15 minutes, go straight. Stay on this obvious trail as it heads generally toward the huge gully first, then curves left aiming for open flanks of the peak. Cairns are evident and you'll have no problem following it as it winds to scree line. If descending it, watch for a big cairn at tree line.

A long plod up rubble leads to the ridge. Follow it past a false summit before finally reaching the true summit. If you walk along the crest of the ridge, you may not even notice the tunnel through the rock beneath, mere minutes before the true summit.

For anyone with energy left, the unnamed peak attached to and northeast of Grotto at 220620 presents demanding scrambling. Attack from the left side after descending scree to the intervening col, keeping in mind you must also slog back up this tedious slope. That is why few bother.

In 1858, Hector and Bourgeau of the Palliser expedition discovered a large cave or grotto in the mountain, for which it is named. Note: Apparently, the **easiest ascent route up Grotto** starts from a small roadside pull-out located 4.9 km east of Indian Flats road (see intro) below a quarry. The man-made trail is on the left

hillside and meanders up the south aspect of the peak.

Heading along the northwest ridge of Grotto, summit in background. Direct route ascends right skyline.
Photo: Gillean Daffern.

Grotto Mountain showing D direct route, NW northwest variation.

MIDDLE SISTER 2769 m

Difficulty An easy scramble from
Stewart Creek
Round trip tlme 5-9 hours
Height gain 1400 m
Map 82 0/3 Canmore

Like an in-between child, Middle Sister receives the least attention of the Three Sisters, or at least it used to. Since the first edition of this book in 1991, increased visits are improving the approach trail. Often, the route is in condition by late May, but you may still want to take an ice axe for lingering snow patches.

Stewart Creek on the east side of the peak provides access but to reach it you must now cross an area of development including a golf course just off the Trans-Canada Highway. The province has erected a 3 m-high wire fence along the highway that extended several kilometres east of the overpass, so when open, the most logical and direct route to Stewart Creek is from the golf course. Turn off the highway at the Bow River Campground overpass 5 km east of Canmore, 4 km west of Dead Man Flat and go to the golf course. Previous spokespeople

for the resort assured me that hikers would be allowed to cross the property and it is hoped this policy will continue despite a change of ownership. After all, today's scramblers may well be tomorrow's golfers (sigh).

Once you reach Stewart Creek, cross it to the west side and gain an old exploration road leading upstream. Along the way, you pass remnants of a collapsing trestle. Shortly beyond, the road crosses then goes up the middle of Stewart Creek before finally settling on the east bank. It

Original register on Middle Sister,
now missing.
Photo: Gillean Daffern.

Stewart Creek and Middle Sister from Wind Ridge showing ascent route. B Big Sister. Little Sister is to right.

ends on a steep hillside immediately east of Little Sister from where you see almost nothing of the upper valley.

Follow the creek, which soon forks; you should take the right branch. Some 10 minutes later, a major avalanche gully coming down from Little Sister meets the main drainage; continue straight ahead. The terrain is rocky and steep hillsides confine you to the drainage, but make your way along as best you can. Impatient parties have been known to dash for the summit as soon as they see a col on the right. This is the wrong col, the Little Sister/Middle Sister col. Control that eagerness and keep trudging on straight ahead.

The streambed curves right and climbs a little more steeply to escape tree line. As the simplest line to the Big/Middle Sister col is a rising angle from left to right, the farther up-valley you

wander, the more obvious the route becomes. You will be below and east of Big Sister at the point you begin angling up to gain Middle Sister. It seems like a long plod to here, but fortunately you have gained much of the total elevation already. After tramping up slabs and scree to the Big/Middle Sister col, the effort will be justified, giving you a fine view throughout the length of the Canmore Corridor, including the unprecedented development everywhere.

There are no difficulties for the remaining walk to the summit. Although Big Sister is close, it is clear there is no easy way up from this side. The normal ascent route lies on the south side and is approached from Spray Lakes Reservoir. Once you have admired the view and signed the summit register, **return** the way you came up.

MOUNT LADY MACDONALD 2605 m

Difficulty Final 50 m of route is difficult
and exposed
Round trip time 4.5-7 hours
Height gain 1300 m
Map 82 O/3 Canmore
(unmarked 179649)

Mount Lady Macdonald is a classic early-season conditioner with an exciting finish. Low snowfall and chinook winds make it feasible by April most years, and it is one of the most-frequented scrambles around Canmore. Most of it is a hike, but many parties find the final narrow ridge too exposed and do not actually reach the true summit.

Follow Elk Run Boulevard through Elk Run Industrial Park just east of Canmore on Highway 1A and park in the paved lot by Cougar Creek bridge across from Canyon Ridge subdivision.

From the parking area follow the trail upstream left of the deeply eroded creekbed. Almost as soon as you enter trees but before the canyon, follow the obvious beaten trail branching left. There once was a boulder dam in the canyon, but a heavy downpour completely obliterated it in 1990 and gave downstream homeowners a darn good scare.

The trail ascends the open hillside to the left immediately before the canyon. You will have no trouble finding this well-travelled track. Be sure you branch right at a fork after some 10 minutes where the trail angles up right. This is about the only place you could get off

Lady Macdonald from Cougar Creek. S summit, P plateau.

route. The path climbs steadily through forest granting increasingly better glimpses of the Canmore Corridor as you grunt upward.

It was not uncommon to see bighorn sheep on these slopes in the past. Barring dogs in the area or helicopters overhead, who knows, you still might see them too. Sheep like to loll in the spring sun, unwittingly offering woodticks a warm body to bite into. Lacking sheep, woodticks find an unwitting hiker even better fodder as there is less hair to contend with (usually)! Springtime is the worst—or the best, if you're a tick. Remember this as you unwittingly loll in the sun, and check for ticks afterward.

When I first ascended this peak in 1983, these were little more than forested slopes. By comparison, some parts have now become deeply rutted, testimony to the peak's popularity. Canmore Trailminders, a local volunteer group, has built a new section of trail to avoid the most eroded area, but in places may be hard to discern owing to a myriad of other trails.

Higher up the trail parallels slab forming a well-defined ridge and leads to a small open plateau below the summit scree slopes. At time of writing, construction has been halted on the teahouse for several years. As such, it is little more than debris and proof that Alberta's Conservative government favours development over environmental protection.

The most common finish to the top of the peak angles diagonally left across scree and slabs toward the highest point on the skyline. Watch for a good trail and at least one big cairn, but if still snowy, you can head directly up to the ridge above. Although the visible highpoint is not the true summit, it is close by. On the skyline ridge the terrain changes drastically. You must carefully follow a narrow, exposed ridge leading to the cairn a few minutes beyond. The final section is steep slab on the west side and overhangs on the east side. Most demanding are the 15 or so metres where the ridge descends slightly then rises back up to the true summit. The rock is firm and there are small footholds too, but most folks find themselves looking awkward at least partway. You can also backtrack and try from the scree slope below, climbing a 20 m-high groove in slabs, but most people prefer the ridge. There is no easier way, despite what earlier editions of this book suggested. If you do turn back, you won't be the first!

From the summit you can look east into the headwaters of Cougar Creek or enjoy the myriad of peaks lying south and west. Anyone who has visited the Robertson Glacier area might recognize Mount Sir Douglas: Look between Mount Lougheed and Big Sister. Mounts Temple and Hungabee of the Lake Louise group are visible to the northwest as well. Those who have scrambled up here regularly cannot help but notice the phenomenal pace of expansion and development, not only at the foot of the mountain, but throughout the whole Canmore Corridor.

Lady Susan Agnes Macdonald, wife of Canada's first prime minister, lent her name to this peak. Upon completion of the transcontinental railway, this adventurous lady insisted on riding on the locomotive's cowcatcher for better views as the train clattered from Lake Louise toward Golden. Sir John thought the idea "ridiculous." She, however, was undaunted and declared her vantage point "quite lovely."

SQUAW'S TIT 2500 m

Difficulty A moderate scramble with exposure and one harder step
Round trip time 4.5-7 hours
Height gain 1200 m
Map 82 O/3 Canmore
(unnamed point at 164660)

This politically incorrect and unofficial nickname refers to a small outlier of the Fairholme Range overlooking Canmore. It is the high point of a ridge jutting out west between Mounts Lady Macdonald and Charles Stewart. Despite its minor stature, the ascent offers interesting, exposed scrambling near the top, but sees far fewer ascents than its neighbours. Snowfree conditions are required; try from June on.

From the Canmore west overpass, reach the peak from either the east end of Bow River Drive in the hamlet of Harvie Heights, 2 km west of Canmore, or the shoulder of the access road into the hamlet. A drainage left of the peak reaches the access road; Squaw's Tit is obvious to the northeast.

Head through intervening forest to the base of the triangular mountain face, then hike uphill through thinning trees. The object is to gain the left-hand skyline ridge. Higher up this ridge becomes a little daunting with exposure and slabby sections until the angle eases near the

summit "nipple." At that point, close scrutiny will reveal all sides to be steep or overhanging, with the exception of the left (northwest) side. Conditions here, too, need to be dry, as you must traverse across steepish gullies until easier terrain allows you to scramble up and back to the right to reach the top. In case you are wondering, the higher point to the northeast does not have a name. Once you've enjoyed the view without the crowds, **return** the same way.

Squaw's Tit as seen from highway.
Route circles left at summit nipple.

HA LING PEAK 2408 m

Difficulty An easy ascent via southwest slopes
Round trip time 2.5-4 hours
Height gain 700 m
Map 82 O/3 Canmore
(unmarked 123573)

Overlooking Canmore, this ascent is short, simple and, since trail improvements, much less steep. It is a favourite pilgrimage of locals; paragliders sometimes use it as a launch when the wind cooperates. The referenced coordinates show the actual location of the mountain and it is this point that concerns rock-climbing enthusiasts and scramblers. A higher adjacent summit (2685 m) to the southeast, now called Mount Lawrence Grassi, may also be reached if you're good at routefinding. Ha Ling Peak is a popular season starter and should pose no problem from mid-May on.

From East End of Rundle, the back side of Ha Ling Peak is just a steep hike. Mount Lawrence Grassi is adjacent to right.

Follow Spray Lakes Road from Canmore townsite past the Nordic Centre to Whiteman's Gap and park in Goat Creek parking lot, 8.6 km past the Bow River bridge.

Cross the road and walk uphill to the bridge over the canal. Immediately behind a small building is a well-worn path beaten into thick moss. For years, this was the climber's descent route. In 1997,

On the trail near the top of Ha Ling Peak.

Canmore Trailminders, a group of hardworking local volunteers, reworked the trail and now it is a straightforward trek suitable for anyone who appreciates good views without technical difficulties.

Follow the path as it climbs lazily through thinning coniferous forest gaining about 400 vertical metres to tree line, whereupon the western panorama unfolds. The trail angles up to the right toward the ridge and then heads up and left to gain a final 300 m. The giddy drop down the northeast side is a real contrast to the gentler ascent slopes, but please don't roll rocks down this sheer precipice—there may be climbers coming up! Mount Temple is the highest peak visible to the west; part of the impressive Royal Group lies to the south and, should anyone care, smoggy Calgary huddles on flatlands to the east.

Although it is feasible to traverse over to reach Mount Lawrence Grassi at 127567, expect problematic routefinding between downsloping ledges. It is much more difficult than what you've just accomplished and requires a keen eye to discern the route. Apparently, many are unable to pick it out. Should you opt to try, you can easily walk-off from that summit to the canal via the west slopes. Otherwise, simply **return** the same way.

This mountain was called Chinaman's Peak until 1997, when a Calgary Chinese businessman found the name offensive and formally protested to the Alberta government. Much controversy ensued, but in 1998 it was officially changed to honour the Chinese miner who first ascended it back in 1886. Ha Ling was reputed to have made the round trip on a bet in six hours, and when skeptics couldn't see his summit flag, he made the ascent again with witnesses firmly in tow.

Opposite: Big Sister from Spray Reservoir. P pinnacles on summit ridge, D short downclimb.

BIG SISTER 2936 m

Difficulty A moderate scramble via southwest slopes
Round trip time 5-8 hours
Height gain 1200 m
Map 82 O/3 Canmore

Big Sister is the highest of the photogenic trio called Three Sisters, which rises gracefully above Canmore. It is an attractive mountain readily ascended by southwest slopes on the back side, and is downright enjoyable. Even with an ice axe, a steep snow patch that lingers along north-facing slopes near the top often foils those who attempt it too early in the season. Try from late June or July on.

Follow Spray Lakes Road from Canmore and park in the big gravel pit across from the dam, 17.3 km from the Bow River bridge in the townsite.

From the gravel pit you'll see a huge gully system that drains the back (southwest) side of the peak. Find the well-trodden ascent route that starts on the slope immediately left of the bottom of this gully. This path quickly gains elevation as it rises through forest, staying well above the leftmost branch of this gully system.

The route continues rising steeply through thinning forest and not until near tree line is there any respite. Now you have two choices. The simpler option is to descend the steep wall on your right. You will probably have to backtrack a short distance to find it (cairn). Notice the cavelike hole at the base of the wall where you descended. Continue up the slope now.

If you follow the ridge, you'll encounter more demanding slabby terrain. A downsloping 2 m-high slab (crux) soon confronts you. The two routes join near the big pinnacles along the final ridge. At this point, scramble down 5 m toward a notch, then continue along left of the pinnacles. If snowy, traversing this steep (50°) slope could be deadly. Even with an ice axe, a slight slip could become an involuntary glissade, and you would tumble hundreds of metres downhill.

When snowy, this bit is NOT scrambling, it is mountaineering. That is the key reason that this ascent is not recommended for early season trips. The remainder to the top is much easier.

A fine view of the Canmore Corridor awaits. Close by are Middle and Little Sister. While the latter is a technical climb, Middle Sister, too, is a scramble. "Three Sisters" first appeared on George Dawson's coal map in 1886. Before then, "Three Nuns" had been in use with individual peaks referred to as "Faith," "Hope" and "Charity."

MOUNT LAWRENCE GRASSI 2685 m

Difficulty Moderate scrambling at the top
Round trip time 4-6 hours
Height gain 945 m
Map 82 0/3 Canmore
(unmarked at 127567)

Now that this high point overlooking Canmore has been officially recognized and named, it bears inclusion as a separate peak. The ascent involves a bit of light bushwhacking but is otherwise straightforward. The summit gives a fine perspective of the Canmore Corridor and the northern end of Spray Lakes, but avoids the crowds of nearby objectives like the East End of Rundle.

Follow Spray Lakes Road from the Canmore townsite past the Nordic Centre to Whiteman's Gap and park in Goat Creek parking lot, 8.6 km past the Bow River bridge.

Cross the road and walk uphill to the canal bridge. Cross the canal and walk southeast along it. The peak is seen through a clearing in some 15-20 minutes and although you could probably head up there, we continued for another 15 minutes until just past the rockcuts in the hillside. Then turn left and go more or less straight up through the woods to tree line. Rubble slopes lead to a ridge and occasional slabs as you near the top. Don't expect too much in the way of difficulty; only near the top are there a few moves of hands-on scrambling. After enjoying the view of peaks like Mount Lougheed and Sparrowhawk or the ever-expanding Canmore townsite, return the same way.

Lawrence Grassi was a kindly, well-liked Canmore miner who had a great appreciation for the mountains. As an amateur guide he often took parties up his favourite peaks, one of which was Mount Louis at Banff. To make it easier for folks to reach the small ponds below Whiteman's Gap, he singlehandedly built a gently-graded trail, replete with wooden benches at strategic rest points. A pot of tea was usually ready for anyone who cared to drop in on the way past his home. He was a master trail-builder and further evidence of his skills is found in the many fine trails at Lake O'Hara. Unfortunately, his trail to Merlin Lake in the Skoki area of Lake Louise was never finished. The lovely pools below Whiteman's Gap, now known as Grassi Lakes, and the mountain that rises above them pay tribute to this good-hearted soul.

On the east summit of Mount Lawrence Grassi.
Photo: Gillean Daffern.

RIMWALL SUMMIT 2680 m

Difficulty Moderate scrambling
Round trip time 5+ hours
Height gain 1020 m
Map 82 J/14 Spray Lakes Reservoir

Rimwall is a local name for the north wall of an unnamed summit immediately west of West Wind Pass. This route goes up the easier backside. As seen from the Trans-Canada Highway near Dead Man Flat, Rimwall is a steep, formidable rampart at the head of Wind Valley, but from Spray Lake it is more mellow. Nonetheless, short cliff bands and routefinding add challenge. If you've done the local favourites, this one is feasible from about June on.

Follow Spray Lakes Road south from Canmore. Park on the south side of the road just west of signed Spurling Creek at an adjacent drainage, about 22 km beyond the Bow River bridge and 4.6 km past the dam. This is the unofficial trail to West Wind Pass (cairn).

The south side of Rimwall is a tamer prospect than the north side and the ascent slopes are visible from a kilometre or so south on Spray Lakes Road. From the parking spot, cross the road to the left side of a dry drainage. This is NOT the flowing stream, Spurling Creek. As you follow this (dry) drainage, the trail climbs onto the left bank above it and continues to the pass crossing steeper hillsides en route.

To ascend Rimwall (180506), there is no point in going all the way to West Wind Pass. Traverse left (west) from the trail near tree line or even sooner. Scramble over small east-facing rock bands but resist the urge to gain elevation. A major rock band is encountered and it is likely

Rimwall from Spray Road. P West Wind Pass, D drainage.

85

that you'll have to walk downhill alongside it until able to sneak around to its low point. Then you can head uphill on open rubble slopes toward the top. Scenery is better from the ridge to the right. If all snow has melted, the short rock band at the top can be bypassed by hugging alongside it to the right. Use caution; this side puts you above the vertical northeast face.

Perhaps most spectacular is the array of peaks bordering Spray Reservoir. Emerald green Wind Ridge and prairies provide a pleasant contrast to rugged profiles of Mounts Lougheed, Nestor and Buller. If the landscape fails to entertain, with binoculars you could always watch hikers below on Wind Ridge.

Either **return** the same way or head more directly to the road following a small drainage right (west) of the lower scree slope you ascended. This rather confined drainage descends waterworn bedrock slabs. A drop-off requires a brief detour left but otherwise, if dry, you can largely stay in the middle. This is more fun than steep, mossy slopes alongside. Unfortunately, as a descent neither option is a hands-in-pockets walk.

The Rimwall from the summit of Windtower.
Photo: Gillean Daffern.

MOUNT BALDY 2192 m

Difficulty One moderate (but avoidable) step via southwest shoulder; some exposure
Round trip time 3-5 hours
Height gain 800 m
Map 82 O/3 Canmore
(unmarked 369528)

Mount Baldy—not to be confused with Old Baldy farther south—is close to Calgary, close to the road and close to the ground. During World War II, when the nearby Forest Experimental Station was an internment camp, prisoners were occasionally allowed to make ascents of this mountain—if they promised to return. It is still a pleasant ascent, if you're allowed to go. Like Mount Yamnuska on a spring day, the precipitous lower cliffs abound with rock climbers while not far away, scramblers tramp to the top. Everyone has a good time. The ascent is often possible by mid-March and in a dry year, right through to November.

Park by a small stream on the shoulder of Kananaskis Trail (Highway 40), 1.6 km past Barrier picnic area turn-off at the south end of Barrier Lake and 12.7 km south of the Trans-Canada Highway.

From the stream, a trail angles up the gravel slope by a rock cut, goes a few steps right and enters pine forest. Continue on trails through forest toward the ridge. In the past, most parties followed the ridge up but it appears that today, many people bypass much or all of it along the right side on a well-trodden trail. Years ago, lacking a better objective, we traipsed up one cloudy spring day and found hardly a track anywhere. Compare that with its eroded condition today.

If you follow the ridge, the exposure on either side soon increases. Many peo-

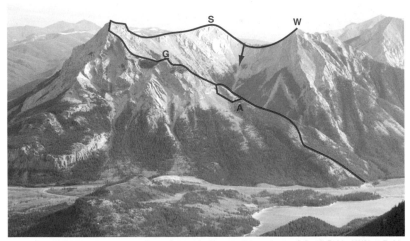

Photo: Kris Thorsteinsson.   *G gendarme, A alternate detour at crux, S South Baldy, W West Baldy.*

ple now detour around almost all of it to the right and plod up loose rubble instead, but if you enjoy a little challenge, here is what to expect. About two-thirds of the way up, a rock step requires a short exposed (but not steep) down-climb of 2 m. Many boots and hands over the last few years have improved it by cleaning off the loosest rock. Otherwise, you can avoid this short downclimb by backtracking a little way down the ridge and descend the northwest side to the rubble slope below. From there, angle up past the first slab, then scramble toward the visible dip in the ridge above—the rock step. Farther up the ridge, either ascend or bypass a slabby wall. Judging by the well-worn trail to the right, many seem to detour. The rest of the way is straightforward. Unless a traverse is in the plan (longer and more difficult), **return** the same way.

Beyond Mount Baldy

Round trip time 5+ hours
Map 82 J/14 Spray Lakes Reservoir

If you are confident of your scrambling abilities and the rock is dry, you can continue to South Baldy, 1 km south (372519). The trickiest part is getting down to the connecting ridge. From the summit, walk south toward the point where the ridge drops off abruptly. Look for a place to descend small, rubbly ledges by traversing back and forth on the left (east) side. Frequent use is making this route obvious. It is then largely a hike to South Baldy, from where West Baldy (higher) beckons at 368515, 0.5 km southwest. Once you hike over to it, the easiest way up is to go around the first

A figure nears the downclimb as he heads for South Baldy.

bump along the right, scramble up a gully, then work left at the top. Unfortunately, there is no direct way down to the highway from West Baldy owing to steep, high slabs on the west side. Probably the simplest and quickest **descent** is to retrace your steps just to the ridge between South and West Baldy, then descend scree slopes to the drainage between the three Baldy summits. It leads right back to the road and even offers a fairly decent trail.

SMITH-DORRIEN AREA

Mount Nestor	2975 m	moderate	p. 91
Mount Sparrowhawk	3121 m	easy	p. 93
Mount Buller	2805 m	moderate	p. 95
Mount Engadine	2970 m	difficult	p. 96
The Tower	3117 m	moderate	p. 98
Mount Galatea	3185 m	difficult	p. 101
The Fortress	3000 m	easy	p. 103
Mount Chester	3054 m	moderate	p. 104
Gusty Peak	3000 m	easy	p. 106
Mount Shark	2786 m	moderate	p. 107
The Fist	2630 m	difficult	p. 108
Mount Smuts	2938 m	difficult	p. 110
Commonwealth Peak	2775 m	moderate	p. 112
Mount Murray	3023 m	moderate	p. 114
Mount Burstall	2760 m	difficult	p. 115

Peaks in this chapter form a mountain corridor accessed by Spray Lakes Road and Smith-Dorrien Trail in Kananaskis Country. This area is south of Canmore, north of Kananaskis Lakes and is reached from either end via the 60 km-long gravel road parallelling Spray Lakes Reservoir.

In spite of the gravel road, this area is popular with hikers, climbers, fishermen and mountain bikers. Mountain structure is typical Rockies Front Range—limestone bedded with a noticeable southwesterly dip. The corridor sits at a higher elevation than Kananaskis Valley, one range east. Precipitation here is greater and the scrambling season is a little shorter. If weather is inclement, either Kananaskis Valley or Yamnuska may well be drier than what you'll find

here. Owing to heavier snowfall, some peaks may not be in good (snowfree) scrambling condition until July. North-facing slopes may harbour snow until August. The highest peak in the area is Mount Sir Douglas, but it is not a scramble. The surrounding Haig, French and Robertson glaciers are popular winter ski-touring destinations.

As with much of the Rockies, rock here is typically loose, shattered and downsloping. Mount Smuts, although limestone, too, boasts solid, steeply angled slabs and ribs. Since the first edition of this book, Mount Smuts seems to have become a testing ground for many scramblers. This airy ascent pushes the upper limit of what can realistically be called scrambling, but whether one uses a rope

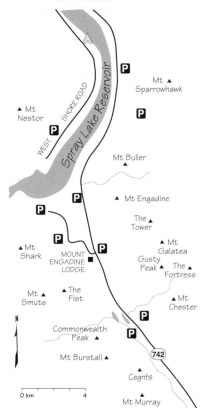

fers little commercial development but despite strong public opposition, many unwarranted schemes have been proposed. Hopefully, it will remain free of the fate that has befallen the Canmore Corridor. Paving the road would hasten the ruin as tour buses would follow in short order.

Access to the north end of Smith-Dorrien is best from Canmore via Spray Lakes Road that starts after the Bow River bridge. For the south end of Smith-Dorrien, turn off Kananaskis Trail (Highway 40) at King Creek, 50 km from the Trans-Canada Highway, then turn right in a further 2.5 km. Chester Lake is almost an identical distance from Calgary from either Spray Road and Canmore or via Kananaskis Trail. The latter is quicker owing to more pavement and fewer bends.

Facilities and Accommodation Fortunately, there are no hotels in the Smith-Dorrien corridor yet. Engadine Lodge, a small privately-owned inn, is 37 km south of Canmore and offers meals, rooms and licensed mountain guide service. Otherwise, visit Canmore for a roof over your head (or a beer in your hand!). Boulton Creek near Kananaskis Lakes has a small store and cafe. Campgrounds are at Kananaskis Lakes and on the west side of Spray Reservoir across Three Sisters Dam, 18 km from Canmore. Until recently, this rustic campground had been free. The oversight has since been rectified by government money-grabbers.

or not, it is an exciting outing. Judging by register comments of some 70 parties in six years, successful parties have thoroughly enjoyed it. Other routes in this neck of the woods are easier and include plenty of scree.

Chester Lake, the most heavily visited spot, is a favourite day trip for hikers and offers a few good scrambles. Overuse has damaged lakeshore meadows and overnight camping is no longer allowed at Chester Lake. This should not affect scramblers as access is quick anyway. As of 1998, the Smith-Dorrien corridor suf-

Information and a seasonal ranger station is at Three Sisters Dam in a small A-frame building called Spray Office. Hours are limited but an outside pay phone is available. Kananaskis Country information and RCMP are found in Canmore. See the Canmore chapter for additional details.

MOUNT NESTOR 2975 m

Difficulty A moderate scramble by south slopes; some exposure near the top
Round trip time 4.5-7 hours
Height gain 1250 m
Map 82 J/14 Spray Lakes Reservoir

Mount Nestor boasts an impressive view of the Spray Lakes vicinity and it is virtually impossible to get lost on the way up. While the east face of the peak hosts a much-frequented technical route, the south aspect provides the normal way off. This south route is also a pleasant, no fuss way to get up the peak and begins right next to the West Shore Road. Note: Owing to vandalism and partying, the last part of this road has been closed, necessitating a bike approach. Try from late June on.

From the bridge over the Bow River in Canmore, drive Spray Lakes Road for 17.3 km and cross Three Sisters Dam to West Shore access road. The closure is after this. Follow this winding gravel road for a further 13.4 km. At this point, the road makes a quick "S" turn as it rises up a small hill. Mount Nestor's south drainage is by the bend at the bottom of the hill—watch for flagging or a cairn.

At the base of the hill (cairn or flagging), there should be an animal trail that follows along the right side of the overgrown drainage just above thickets of willow and poplars. Within minutes you pass through these poplars and cross the drainage to follow up the left side until, within some 20 or 30 minutes of starting, you're out of the trees. South is an unrestricted view of Mounts Birdwood, Smuts and Sir Douglas.

Photo: Kris Thorsteinsson.

Opposite: Mount Nestor across Spray Lakes Reservoir. A variation can be taken on descent.

A roadside view of Nestor's ascent slopes. T trough.

Continue straight ahead past stunted krummholz and carpets of bearberry where greenery soon gives way to rubble. The route is evident. Geologists know this trough you are traipsing up as a syncline, caused by folding of rock layers. The trough widens significantly at the top where you attain the crest of a rocky ridge separating this trough from a much broader gully. Cross this broader gully and hike up onto a rounded shoulder on the skyline—the only logical place to go. The angle eases as you approach the summit ridge.

Near the top, you must descend about 10 m and cross a brief connecting ridge to the true summit, which is about 2 m higher. When I got to this point many years ago, one quick glance scared me off. Had I taken a closer look, overall lack of exposure and difficulty would have been

apparent and I could have saved a second trip. A couple of moves just past this ridge might seem mildly exposed to some people, however.

The summit does not offer much room for lounging about, but you can cozy up and admire the impressive skyline. Big peaks include Mount Sir Douglas, Mount Ball and the distant Goodsirs. As often happens, though, Mount Assiniboine steals the show.

On **return**, a pleasant variation is to descend the broad gully paralleling the one used for ascent. Near the bottom, it curves gently left and rejoins the route of ascent.

Ships involved in the Battle of Jutland have lent their names to many peaks in the Kananaskis area. Nestor was a destroyer that sunk during the conflict.

MOUNT SPARROWHAWK 3121 m

Difficulty An easy scramble via west scree slopes
Round trip time 6-10 hours
Height gain 1350 m
Map 82 J/14 Spray Lakes Reservoir

Mount Sparrowhawk provides an expansive view of Spray Reservoir. The west slopes are a giant heap of rubble, and you shouldn't have a problem ascending it. The peak was once touted as the downhill ski venue for Calgary's 1988 Winter Olympics, but nearby Mount Allan was chosen instead. The sole reminders now are a few discarded poles, snow-fencing and markers on the upper portion of the once-proposed runs. The ascent is worthwhile; plod up it from late June on.

Drive to Sparrowhawk picnic area, 26.3 km south of the Bow River bridge in Canmore.

Wind has reportedly blown deadfall across parts of the trail now so travel will be slower. Start across from the picnic area (181442). Sparrowhawk Creek, just metres south of here, is NOT the correct drainage, despite a trail along it. You want to end up alongside the next stream north (183450). It heads toward, then left of, the rock spur (Read's Ridge) at 207439, west-southwest of the top. There are other routes up the west slope, too, but Read's Ridge is not one of them. It ends abruptly in a drop-off.

Tramp up the scree and near the top, circle around the summit cliffs on the right (south) side to finish by trudging up the east side to the cairn. **Return** the same way.

Mount Sparrowhawk is not named after a bird, as you might expect, but rather a World War I battleship—which was probably named after the bird.

Summit bump on Mount Sparrowhawk.
Route circles to the right at
base of summit cliffs.
Read's Ridge is at the right of photo.
Photo: Kris Thorsteinsson.

MOUNT BULLER 2805 m

Difficulty A moderate scramble if upper slabs are snowfree and dry; brief exposure
Round trip time 5-8 hours
Height gain 1010 m
Map 82 J/14 Spray Lakes Reservoir

Mount Buller is readily accessible via a good hiking trail or an open gully. This Kananaskis peak is not likely to be crowded and the view warrants at least one visit. Try from about June on.

For the hiking trail approach, park at Buller picnic area on the west side of Smith-Dorrien Trail/Spray Lakes Road, 35.4 km south of the Bow River bridge in Canmore and 32 km north of the Smith-Dorrien Trail/Kananaskis Lakes Trail junction.

There are two approaches to Mount Buller's high col. Walk across the road and follow Buller Pass trail for approximately 30 minutes to a drainage coming off the south slopes. Now leave Buller Pass trail and head left (north) aiming directly toward a high col visible between Mount Buller and a subsidiary peak to the southwest. Ascend either lush green slopes on the left side or rockier, slabby terrain to the right. Don't wander too far right or you will reach uncomfortably steep slabs and will end up traversing back left anyway.

While this ascent to the col is straightforward in dry summer conditions, a fatality did occur here in April 1989, the result of rockfall released by snowmelt. Gullies are dangerous funnels in such conditions and should be avoided. Another approach to the col is up the open gully 3.5 km north of Buller picnic area. When dry it is a sure bet as you can't get lost.

From the col (181385) between Buller and the unnamed peak to the southwest, you have 350 vertical metres to go. A trail snakes up the scree but serves better on descent. Ski poles are definitely justified on this unpleasant, ball-bearing rubble. Near the top a peeling effect is particularly evident at a short, narrow friction slab. You do not want to encounter snow here because of the airy drop on either side. A slip would be fatal. This slab is the only interruption to the tedium. In 1996 a memorial register to the young man killed here was placed by friends, making two registers to sign.

Mount Assiniboine is the reigning summit to the west. The pointed peak left of it is Mount Eon—a summit of historical significance. It was first climbed in 1921 by Dr. W. E. Stone, a distinguished alpinist of the day. After ascending the summit chimney, he promptly plummeted back down and was killed. His horrified wife could only watch helplessly as the tragedy unfolded.

The **return** is via the same route. Henry Cecil Buller was a lieutenant in Princess Patricia's Light Infantry, killed in World War I.

Opposite: Telephoto view of ascent route from Buller Creek approach. B Buller Creek, C col.

MOUNT ENGADINE 2970 m

Difficulty A difficult scramble via west-northwest ridge
Round trip time 7-10 hours
Height gain 1170 m
Map 82 J/14 Spray Lakes Reservoir

Mount Engadine is one of the less-frequently climbed peaks bordering Spray Road and may appeal to the recluse. In 1987, it had seen five ascents in the previous 16 years, but it has seen many more since. Once you abandon the trail to gain the west-northwest ridge of the mountain, some tedious bushwhacking follows, but this is still the most direct way up. Try from late June on.

Drive to Buller picnic area on the west side of Smith-Dorrien/Spray Lakes Road in Kananaskis Country, 35.4 km south of the Bow River bridge in Canmore and 32 km north of the Smith-Dorrien/Kananaskis Lakes Trail junction.

Cross the road and hike Buller Pass trail for 15 minutes. Wade or hop Buller Creek and bushwhack for a half hour toward tree line on the south side. Walk along the base of high west-facing slabs signalling the start of the west-northwest ridge, and scramble easily up any of several rubbly gullies to gain the ridge crest.

If you stick to the ridge top, overhangs will necessitate a couple of easy detours to the right, but if you prefer scree and no exposure, you can also trudge alongside below the ridge. The remainder of the route is mostly an enjoyable scramble save for the final 200 m where rock dete-

Mount Engadine ascent route and optional descent.

Am I there yet? Along Mount Engadine's west-northwest ridge.
Photo: Kris Thorsteinsson.

riorates into tedious, treadmill rubble. If you steer to the right, a bit of slabby rib should still project above the debris and give more solid footing.

The view is spectacular, with Mount Assiniboine dominating row upon row of summits to the west. On the left skyline ridge of Assiniboine you'll notice a slight bulge at half height. Surprisingly, this is considered a separate peak, Lunette Peak, and is just over 3353 m (11,000 ft.). It really isn't separate at all, but it was named in 1901, when Reverend James Outram and his guides mistakenly ascended it in thick cloud thinking it was Assiniboine. They snagged the proper peak the next day, however.

On return we descended west-facing rubble, then continued down broad gullies, finally circling around back to the northwest to reach Buller Creek. It is now recommended that you **descend** the west-facing gully completely and make a direct line through forest back to the road. This descent is more popular, and there are apparently bits of animal trails en route.

The Engadine is a world-renowned tourist mecca in the Swiss Alps, however, it is named for a ship that played a small part in the Battle of Jutland.

THE TOWER 3117 m

Difficulty A moderate scramble by south-facing scree or snow slopes
Round trip time 6-10 hours
Height gain 1260 m
Map 82 J/14 Spray Lakes Reservoir (unmarked 205351)

In summer, The Tower and its companion valley to the south are one of the more pristine and less-visited spots along the Smith-Dorrien/Spray corridor. The ascent route is similar in character to Mount Galatea, although not as steep. With snow on the slope, the glissade descent can be a riot so take an ice axe. In dry years the peak may be in condition by mid-June, but with a late spring or heavy snowfall, July would be more appropriate. There are two possible approaches:

Usual Approach

Park on the shoulder of Smith-Dorrien Trail/Spray Lakes Road opposite Mount Engadine Lodge, 7.5 km north of Burstall Pass parking lot and 38.2 km south of the Bow River bridge in Canmore.

The trail starts directly across the Engadine Lodge turn-off, and follows south along an old logging road. At the first cutblock, angle uphill to the left on skid roads to the uppermost limit of the clearing. Continue through forest until the slope eases, and traverse south-southeast along a semi-open ridge (180330). This ridge becomes better-defined as you go, and you'll have no trouble following Rummel Creek to your left as it curves into the valley. This route is a popular winter ski trip. Idyllic Rummel Lake (200325) is a perfect place for a break before continuing past open meadows to the rocky upper valley.

Direct Approach

Park beside the cutline and sign for Peter Lougheed Provincial Park boundary on Smith-Dorrien Trail/Spray Lakes Road, 6.7 km north of the Burstall Pass parking lot and 39 km south of Canmore.

Head up this cutline. When finding the route becomes confusing at a logged cutblock, continue straight uphill. The cutline resumes once you reach the forest. Rising steeply, you soon gain the crest of the ridge traversed by the usual approach. Follow the cutline east down the hillside, across Rummel Creek and follow it to meet the other approach route at Rummel Lake.

Whatever your approach, resist the temptation to ascend the subsidiary peak west of The Tower. You can't connect to the main peak as deep notches bar the way shortly before the true summit. These notches and cliffs will force you to descend almost right to the valley bottom. Instead, wander past Rummel Lake and start the ascent just beyond the second lake (206336). As you clamber up scree slopes, you'll notice a third lake in a barren bowl to the northeast. Gradually work your way right and toward the ridge, then continue to the top.

A closer view of The Tower. Route steepens near the top.

Confusion surrounds the unofficial name. History recalls that Hans Gmoser's climbing party of 1957 called their first ascent "The Tower," but their photos clearly show The Fortress, some 3.5 km southeast. Apparently, over the years, strong southerly chinook winds have pushed the name north to this mountain. Although it doesn't resemble a tower, the name does have a better ring to it than "Unnamed 3117."

Opposite: South face route on The Tower from Galatea's ridge.

The steep-looking south face of Mount Galatea showing ascent route.

MOUNT GALATEA 3185 m

Difficulty A difficult scramble and/or steep snow ascent by the south face and ridge
Round trip time 6-10 hours
Height gain 1280 m
Map 82 J/14 Spray Lakes Reservoir

Mount Galatea is the finest viewpoint of the Kananaskis Range. Like adjacent summits, the approach is a popular hike visiting larch meadows and lakes. On a clear day you'll see peaks as distant as Mount Olive on the Wapta Icefields, Howser Towers in the Purcell Range, and at least 10 of the 18 peaks over 3353 m scattered around the southern Rockies. The upper section of the route is steep, but lower portions make for a good glissade if you have the right snow conditions and an ice axe. This ascent is more mountaineering in nature than simply scrambling and you should avoid it if much snow remains on the upper face. Try from late June on.

Park at Chester Lake parking lot on Smith-Dorrien/Spray Lakes Road in Kananaskis Country, 44 km south of Canmore and 20 km north of Smith-Dorrien/Kananaskis Lakes Trail junction.

Follow the well-used hiking trail to Chester Lake as for Mount Chester. Once you reach the lake, a good trail diverges left along the north shore, leading past Elephant Rocks and over a gentle rise into a pretty valley immediately north of Chester Lake. Continue up-valley past two small ponds to an obvious large scree pile at the base of Galatea's south face. Ascend this slope toward a small waterfall. Keep to the right as you ascend, using slabs where possible to reduce some treadmilling. This also avoids the fall-line of stones from eroding cliffs above you.

Continue along the ridge as it curves left near the top, moving onto the face if steps along the ridge present problems. The slope angle steepens noticeably here. When dry this is of small consequence, but if snowy, as is likely in June, it feels dicey to be out on this steep incline once the snow softens up. Even with an ice axe you must use caution along here. After a two hour plod up, however, the rapid 10 minute glissade down should be memorable if not apprehensive. Although this peak is easy to approach, it doesn't see that many visitors.

The summit of Mount Galatea boasts a far-ranging view and many happy hours could be spent here attempting to identify surrounding and distant mountains. It is common to see parties on Gusty Peak and Mount Chester nearby, as these also draw energetic outdoor folks. If you're interested in doing The Tower (3117 m) immediately north, this is an excellent spot from which to survey the line of ascent up the south slopes. Once the wind comes up and the Kananaskis rock has made a suitable impression on you, **return** the same way.

Galatea was a British cruiser engaged in the historic World War I Battle of Jutland; in mythology, her role as a beautiful sea-nymph was a decidedly less militaristic one.

The Fortress

The Fortress from Chester Lake approach. C Fortress/Chester col.

Photo: Gillean Daffern

L-R Summit view of Mount Assiniboine, Gusty Peak, Mount Galatea and The Tower.
Ascent routes for latter three are visible.

102

THE FORTRESS 3000 m

Difficulty An easy scramble via southwest ridge
Round trip time 5-8 hours
Height gain 1100 m
Map 82 J/14 Spray Lakes Reservoir

The Fortress is the second most popular scramble in the Chester Lake area. For variety, you can combine two approach op-

tions to make a loop, visiting entirely different valleys complete with exquisite alpine lakes. From Highway 40, the towering 600 m north face above Fortress ski area does present a fortress-like appearance. Even the turrets are evident. That perspective gives no hint of a gentle shoulder leading easily to the top. Note: Camping is now prohibited at Chester Lake. Try this ascent from July on.

Park at Chester Lake parking lot on Smith-Dorrien/Spray Lakes Road, 44 km south of Canmore and 20 km north of Smith-Dorrien/Kananaskis Trail junction.

Headwall Lakes Approach

An approach from Headwall Lakes, although longer, may be the preferred direction. The scree up to The Fortress/Chester col serves better on ascent, while loose rubble on the Chester Lake side makes for a better descent. Most parties do not use this approach, though.

The easiest route to Headwall Lakes is via the colour-coded ski trails. On the south side of the parking lot, find the ski sign and follow the blue loop. Turn left onto a road marked blue/yellow in 1 km, then in less than 1 km you reach a junction and a blue loop lies to the left. Keep right, angling up a long hill flagged with yellow markers. Upon reaching the logged area on a ridge, continue on the yellow road until it fords Headwall Creek. Many people follow the stream to the upper valley from this point. If you continue uphill and look along the edge of the cutblock, a better trail can be found that leads through forest to the first meadow.

Wander farther up the valley passing two sparkling lakes separated by a waterfall. Continue beyond into the stony up-

per reaches of the valley and ascend to the Chester/Fortress col. Although the summit appears close from this point, allow a full hour to the top as there are still some 325 vertical metres to gain.

Surmount the summit block easily on the left (northwest) side. Far below the sheer north face lies Fortress Lake and an awe-inspiring amount of atmosphere lies between the two. Mount Galatea, the dominant peak to the northwest, is another pleasant scramble, as are adjacent Mount Chester and Gusty Peak to the east and north of you, respectively.

Chester Lake Approach

Hike the well-used trail to Chester Lake as for Mount Chester. Once you reach Chester Lake, follow the left shoreline and trails around to the waterfall and into the upper valley. At first there are meadows, mosses and a bubbling stream, but this jumbled landscape of boulders becomes increasingly barren farther back. Shortly before a tiny pond, angle up talus slopes on your right to gain the Chester/Fortress col. Snow often lingers on this shadowy slope and may allow a fast and exciting descent if you've brought along an ice axe. From the col, the route coincides with that of the Headwall Lakes option.

MOUNT CHESTER 3054 m

Difficulty A moderate scramble via scree and slabs of southwest side
Round trip time 4-7 hours
Height gain 1150 m
Map 82 J/14 Spray Lakes Reservoir

Mount Chester offers fine scrambling beginning in alpine meadows near a popular lake. The ascent gives an excellent return for the effort and is a personal favourite of

mine. If you go, please treat this fragile area with care. Scars from big boots do not heal quickly in the harsh climate found at this elevation, and this ascent is now one of the most popular in Kananaskis. Heavy visitor use has damaged the lakeshore meadows, and as a result, camping is no longer permitted. Regardless, the outing is a fine day trip and is possible from about July on.

Park at Chester Lake parking lot on Smith-Dorrien Trail/Spray Lakes Road, 44 km south of Canmore and 20 km north of Smith-Dorrien/Kananaskis Trail junction.

Follow the popular hiking trail to Chester Lake. This path begins as an old logging road and later dwindles to a footpath as it enters forest. Within an hour you emerge into open alpine terrain and larch meadows alongside the stream draining Chester Lake.

Minutes before reaching the lake, cross the creek and wander south across flowery meadows toward the col immediately west of Mount Chester. Hike up the broad gully to this saddle. It is also possible but less direct to gain this col from Headwall Lakes to the south, or to use that valley as an optional exit. During prime season, late July to mid-August, you may discover a profusion of wildflowers eking out a fleeting existence on these harsh slopes. After basking

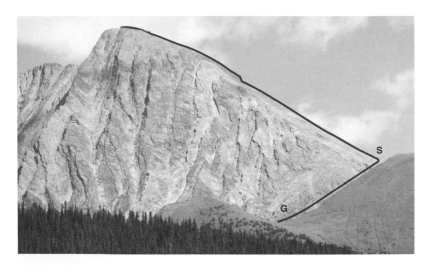

Photo: Kris Thorsteinsson.

From Mount Chester, T The Tower, GA Mount Galatea, G Gusty Peak and F The Fortress.

in a view of the western skyline, turn your gaze eastward. Firm, knobbly slabs give an enjoyable scramble to the summit 300 m above. If you prefer scree instead, more is found farther right.

Although this point is a little lower, the summit panorama is as good as that seen from nearby Mount Galatea. On a sunny summer day, it is most likely that others will be enjoying the spectacle as well. Fifteen people sharing the summit on a sunny Sunday is not unheard of on Mount Chester. Peaks such as Farnham Tower, shaped a bit like a smokestack, are visible 90 km west in the Purcell Range. Loftier, closer peaks include Mount Assiniboine—the "Matterhorn of the Rockies," Mount Sir Douglas and Mount Joffre, all of which soar to more than 3353 m (11,000 ft.). This vantage point also affords the opportunity to study the equally-easy ascent routes for The Fortress and Gusty Peak northeast and north of you, respectively.

Chester, Galatea, Engadine, Indefatigable, Shark and several other peaks in this area borrow their names from cruisers and destroyers involved in the Battle of Jutland. This was a notable conflict fought during World War I, and its significance is two-fold. It was the only period in which both the entire British and German fleets were engaged; furthermore, it ended in a stalemate.

Opposite: Mount Chester from Smith-Dorrien Trail.
S saddle, G gully.

GUSTY PEAK 3000 m

Difficulty Easy ascent via south scree slopes
Round trip time 5-8 hours
Height gain 1100 m
Map 82 J/14 Spray Lakes Reservoir (unmarked at 227322)

Gusty Peak is another easily-ascended peak near scenic Chester Lake and it sits close to Mounts Chester, Galatea and The Fortress. Many more parties ascend it these days but it is still noticeably less crowded than Mount Chester. The view is fine and problems are few. Try from July on.

Park at Chester Lake parking lot on Smith-Dorrien Trail/Spray Lakes Road, 44 km south of Canmore and 20 km north of Smith-Dorrien Trail/Kananaskis Lakes Trail junction.

Hike to Chester Lake. Once you reach it, follow the left shoreline and trails around to the waterfall and into the upper valley to the northeast, as described for The Fortress. Go almost to the Chester/Fortress col and along the west shore of a tiny pond. Gusty Peak is on your left. Facing it (north), angle up diagonally to the right on scree slopes, following the tilt of the strata that should lead right toward the main summit at the easternmost end. The foreshortened view fools folks into believing the high point sits directly above, but this line instead leads to steep terrain and the lower west peak. Traversing between the two is unpleasant and unnecessary.

If free of snow, this ascent is little more than a steep trudge up (and back down!) a rubble slope, and the only stumbling block is the abundant loose limestone variety underfoot. This rock, from the Banff Formation of 360 million years ago, is prevalent throughout the Front Ranges and sharp eyes might find horn coral fossils here and in similar areas.

Gusty Peak is an unofficial name given by the first ascent party of Alpine Club members from Calgary in June 1972. High winds accompanied their ascent and snow persisted underfoot. Spring was late that year and by mid-month, runoff records were set on many major rivers both in British Columbia and Alberta.

Ascent route angles up scree slopes to top.

MOUNT SHARK 2786 m

Difficulty Moderate scramble via the
north ridge; brief exposure
Round trip time 6-9 hours
Height gain 1000 m
Map 82 J/14 Spray Lakes Reservoir

In spite of its lower elevation, Mount Shark
is an excellent vantage point and a pretty
decent scramble. Technical difficulties are
few, but lack of a recognizable path beyond
Karst Spring probably dissuades the curious wanderers from exploring much farther. Try from July on.

*Mount Shark from the east side. The peak is normally
ascended via the north (right skyline) ridge.*

Drive to Mount Shark/Engadine Lodge
access road on Smith-Dorrien Trail/Spray
Lakes Road, 6.4 km north of Burstall Pass
parking lot and 38.2 km south of the Bow
River bridge in Canmore. Follow this
road to its end where there is a parking
area and trailhead.

From the parking area hike or bike the
wide trail 4 km to Watridge Lake. Continue on foot around the lake and up to
Karst Spring below the north ridge, the
normal route of access. Head straight up
the hillside and work your way left.
With a little persistence and the odd hint
of an animal trail, you steadily leave the
din and the crowds below. This short
stretch of bush up to the ridge is unpleasant but necessary.

As you gain tree line, feathery-needled
Lyall's larch replace scattered patches of
spruce. Head left to gain the ridge. Soon
you're enjoying pleasant scrambling up
angular, slabby limestone typical of the
Front Ranges. On a calm day, Spray Lake
mirrors Mount Lougheed in deep shades
of aquamarine. Just when you're having a
good time, the ridge narrows. Ah, this
mountain will not be won so easily after
all! Depending on your exact route, challenges will vary, but this section should
never actually be difficult. Brief exposed
sections of the crest can often be bypassed
on the right. After a couple of false summits and rotten rock, you finally reach the
crumbling summit. "Superb" only begins
to describe the view. Lush, green valleys,
sparkling lakes and icy, precipitous faces
meld into a magnificent landscape.

The **return** is via the same way. Once
you reach tree line, you can simply head
down through bush toward noisy Karst
Spring. You'll find bushwhacking downhill to be much easier.

THE FIST 2630 m

Difficulty Difficult scramble with loose rock and brief exposure
Round trip time 5-7 hours
Height gain 770 m
Map 82 J/14 Spray Lakes Reservoir (unmarked 149301)

Shaped like a clenched fist thrusting skyward, this unofficially-named craggy little peak boasts an exciting finish. The imposing vertical rock walls on the east side impart an air of futility, despite its comparatively low elevation. The secret lies in hiking around to the south flanks—hidden from the road—to an easier, more reasonable line of ascent. Since the first edition of this book, the summit now sees much more traffic and has somewhat less loose rock as a result. A helmet is advisable in case of stonefall from other parties. Try from late June on.

Drive to Mount Shark/Engadine Lodge access road on Smith-Dorrien/Spray Lakes Road, 6.4 km north of Burstall Pass parking lot and 38.2 km south of the Bow River bridge in Canmore. Follow this road west for 0.9 km crossing Smuts Creek en route and take the first left turn onto an old logging road. Park here.

From the parking area a few metres off Mount Shark access road, walk south along an old logging road. Within some 30-35 minutes, just before the road drops to Commonwealth Creek, bear right on another logging road, well-trodden and usually flagged, which leads toward the noisy stream. A rough path on the north (right) side of the creek continues into Commonwealth Valley.

Hike along the trail for about an hour to open, marshy meadows and wide avalanche slopes below the peak on your right. These open slopes provide access to the connecting ridge between The Fist and its westerly neighbour, Mount Smuts. The most direct (and least bushy!) route is to follow the small drainage up the avalanche slope. There should be smatterings of a trail here. You will have gained most of the required elevation for the as-

The Fist from Commonwealth Creek, showing ascent route from Smuts/Fist ridge to gully.

The Fist from Mount Smuts. Route normally goes left of fin, then to notch, or turns left just before notch.

cent upon reaching the Smuts/Fist ridge, and this is a good spot for a break before proceeding.

From the ridge, a trail continues up scree toward the peak heading for the gully to the left of the big freestanding rock fin. While you can go up either side of this fin, the left side is the logical choice. If you choose the right side, you'll have to scramble over a dividing wall higher up anyway.

There are two ways to reach the summit from within this gully. Option one is to continue all the way up the gully to a skyline notch at the end. Here, above a steep drop down the east side, make a sharp left turn and scramble up onto airy ledges and rubble for the last few metres.

This bit has less loose debris than in years past, but is still exposed. A slip would likely be fatal. Alternatively, a short distance before the skyline notch, you can climb a steep (2 m) wall on small holds to gain a gully on the north side. This rubbly gully quickly widens and leads easily to the top. Fortunately, these two options are only minutes apart if you want to compare or try each.

When I first ascended this peak, an inquisitive old mountain goat peered down at me from above, watching with smug amusement. My slow, cautious movements no doubt allayed any apprehensions, and, oblivious to the terrific drop below, he scampered away, completely unfazed by the exposure.

MOUNT SMUTS 2938 m

Difficulty Difficult climbers' scramble via the slabby south ridge. One of the most difficult ascents in this guide.
Round trip time 6-9 hours
Height gain 1075 m
Map 82 J/14 Spray Lakes Reservoir

Mount Smuts presents demanding scrambling on steep, slabby limestone ribs. Sections of the route are also exposed—"ex-hilarating" comes to mind. Some parties don a climbing rope; many others probably wish they had one available for at least one section. Capable climbers and scramblers will find it unnecessary IF the rock is dry, but only a few parties make the summit each year. Many back off and some have required rescuing. Several pitons are evident on the route now. Try from July on or whenever all snow is gone.

Photo: Leon Kubbernus.

Drive to Mount Shark/Engadine Lodge access road on Smith-Dorrien Trail/ Spray Lakes Road, 6.4 km north of Burstall Pass parking lot and 38.2 km south of the Bow River bridge in Canmore. Follow the access road west across Smuts Creek for 0.9 km, and make the first left-hand turn onto an old logging road and a parking area.

From the parking area, walk south along the old logging road. After some 30-35 minutes, just before the road drops down to Commonwealth Creek, bear right and follow the well-trodden trail that leads back into the valley. A rough path on the north side continues upstream.

Hike alongside meadows and beaver ponds passing The Fist and continue toward Smuts Pass. This is the high saddle at the west end of the valley between Mounts Smuts and Birdwood. Just a wee bit before the pass, on the north side of the valley, ascend a large scree-cone toward a scree gully above. Although you can't tell by the foreshortened view up this gully, the summit of Mount Smuts lies to the right. Trudge up this gully; it narrows higher up before the left wall finally peters out completely. Now you must ascend the slabby right-hand wall—look for a cairn. From here, near-vertically tilted ribs of firm Palliser limestone rise directly to the summit, alternating steep rises with stretches of plodding.

Once you begin the real scrambling there is little variation possible. As well, upon gaining the slabby right-hand wall above the gully, you'll quickly realize whether it is to your liking. Remember, you may have to descend the same way and it is more difficult to downclimb. The crux is a short, smooth slab with a giddy drop on the east side.

Opposite: The exciting south ridge of Mount Smuts—no place for novices.

Typical scrambling on Mount Smuts.

If the north ridge is free of snow, it offers an easier descent route. Descend this ridge to the first big promising looking gully on your left. Scramble (grovel) down it until it steepens. At this point it becomes obvious that it would be easier to simply traverse out of the gully on ledges to your left (south) and reach easier terrain. Angle down rubble and scree slopes below, then turn left and hike south down the drainage toward Birdwood Lakes, small ponds immediately west of Mount Smuts and Smuts Pass. From the lakes, go left (east) up over Smuts Pass to the foot of your ascent ridge again. Jan Christiaan Smuts was an exemplary statesman and general of the Union of South Africa.

COMMONWEALTH PEAK 2775 m

Difficulty Moderate scramble via southwest face
Round trip time 5-10 hours depending on return route
Height gain 850 m
Map 82 J/14 Spray Lakes Reservoir

Commonwealth Peak, shown only on newer maps, will never be an all-time classic scramble, but as a getaway from the crowds, it is worth ascending. The view of the Kananaskis Range is excellent, and an alternate exit exists to extend your day if desired. Take runners for the boggy approach and a bike saves about an hour if returning the same way. Carry an ice axe for early summer visits. Try from about July on.

Park at Burstall Pass parking lot on Smith-Dorrien Trail/Spray Lakes Road, 44 km south of Canmore and 20 km north of the Smith-Dorrien Trail/Kananaskis Lakes Trail junction.

Hike (or bike) 3.5 km along Burstall Pass trail to where it becomes single track (leave bikes here), then descend to the gravel outwash flats. The hulking mountain on the skyline northwest of you is Mount Birdwood. Pigstail is the pointy

peak immediately east and unimposing Commonwealth Peak (165275), your objective, is right (east) of Pigstail. The ascent route goes up the broad avalanche gully to the col between these latter two peaks.

Slosh across the flats toward the ascent gully fording braided streams and calf-deep bog. The least bushy choice is to stay toward the left side of the avalanche slope right next to mature forest (goat trail). From the col, a perfect view of The Fist and Mount Smuts is revealed, and you'll probably decide to have a bite while eye-balling just where to go next. If you wander out on the cornice, the decision will be made for you. You'll plummet straight down.

The ascent route follows a big scree ramp above the col that angles up and to the right of steeper rock, aiming for the right-hand skyline. Treadmill up this rubble, whereupon a trail leads around into a wide gully cunningly tucked behind. Thrash up this loose gully as it rises to the left, staying to the left as you go. After narrowing, this gully spits you out on open slopes of blocky, broken rock almost directly above the col. Turn right and scramble (yes, actually scramble!) up some 15 m of rock to the summit ridge. As much of the rock is loose and crumbly, steeper variations are not advisable on the ascent.

Ascent route from the col, seen from Pigstail. G gully.

Although you are a little lower than most nearby peaks, the view is nonetheless remarkable, especially the panorama from Mounts Nestor to Chester. Notice Commonwealth Lake far below deep in the forest immediately north. If you depart via the alternate (longer) exit, you will pass by this tranquil pond.

There are three options for the **return**. Fastest is via the same route and the loose rubble works wonderfully well going down. Otherwise, you can descend north from the col (steep initially, and ice axe may be required) and continue out to Commonwealth Creek valley. Then turn right and follow the trail on the north side of the creek east to logging clearcuts. Continue through forest and ford Smuts Creek to reach Smith-Dorrien Highway.

Option three: From the col, descend snow or scree slopes on the north side until you can contour right and by gaining a small amount of elevation, hike up over a col (162282) on the north side of Commonwealth Peak. Once over the col, drop down into a meadowy, secluded valley strewn with massive boulders. A faint trail leads north to Commonwealth Lake, and beyond, a much better trail continues to a logging clearcut. Follow old logging roads leading east and north. When you reach Commonwealth Creek crossing, do not cross, but hike downstream through more forest and clearcuts. Ford knee-deep Smuts Creek to reach Smith-Dorrien Highway. A bike stashed 4 km north of Burstall parking lot would be an ideal finish. Expect a full day for either of these latter two options.

Opposite: Scrambling up to the summit ridge with the col far below.

MOUNT MURRAY 3023 m

Difficulty A moderate scramble via north ridge to southwest side
Round trip time 7-10 hours, including ascent of unnamed (Cegnfs)
Height gain 1135 m
Maps 82 J/14 Spray Lakes Reservoir
82 J/11 Kananaskis Lakes
(unmarked 205230)

Mount Murray in the rugged French Creek area is a straightforward scramble with the best part at a short rock band near the top. You ascend an unnamed smaller peak along the way. Most editions of maps do not yet show Mount Murray by the road at coordinates 205230 (bottom of map 82 J/14), and this overlooked peak sees comparatively little activity. Try from July on.

Park at Burstall Pass parking lot on Smith-Dorrien Trail/Spray Lakes Road in Kananaskis Country, 44 km south of Canmore and 20 km north of Smith-Dorrien/Kananaskis Trail junction.

From Burstall parking lot, hike the old logging road west past silty Mud Lake. When the trail curves to the right at the top of the first hill, continue straight ahead on another old logging road. Either wade French Creek and continue along the road, or hike up the right side toward the first waterfall, cross on downed logs

and then regain the road. **Note:** This first waterfall is invisible from the old road. Before reaching the second waterfall (10-20 m high), follow the high-water trail left into the forest. The waterfall is not visible from here. Cross a gravelly drainage and minutes later at the next drainage (which joins the big waterfall now below you), go left. Evergreens soon give way to widespread gravel washed down a gully in 1995. Cegnfs is above at 205242; ascend slopes to the right of the gully to the top.

Descend easily to the col and scramble toward Mount Murray, traversing around the north and west sides below the summit rock band. Circle around until near the southwest ridge where a brief scramble completes the ascent.

On your **return**, don't descend from the col to the valley as many unseen cliffs are below. Although it is not necessary to plod all the way back up Cegnfs, you do have to contour far enough around to outflank rock bands just above tree line meadows.

General Sir A. J. Murray was chief of the Imperial General Staff, 1915 and general officer commanding in Egypt 1916-17. Cegnfs is an unlikely and unofficial acronym derived from the initials of the first ascent party. Pronounce it however you like.

From Mount Burstall, C Cegnfs, M Murray and G gully.

MOUNT BURSTALL 2760 m

Difficulty Difficult, exposed scrambling for final 100 m of east ridge
Round trip time 4-7 hours
Height gain 890 m
Map 82 J/14 Spray Lakes Reservoir

A short, simple approach makes this minor summit a logical choice when ambition, good weather or time are lacking. The view is rewarding and includes big peaks around French and Robertson glaciers. The route is largely straightforward but the exposed and loose summit ridge keeps the crowds at bay. Try from about mid-July on.

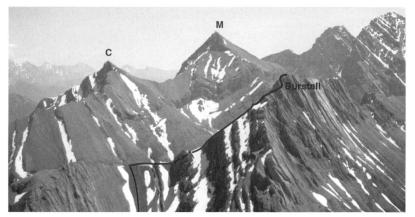

Upper part of Burstall ascent route. C Cegnfs and M Murray behind.

Park as for Mount Murray.

Follow the Burstall Pass trail for about 30 minutes. Five minutes past a massive boulder lying squarely on the path, turn left and hike up the right-hand edge of a logged slope to the wide avalanche gully, which takes you directly up to the east ridge. From this ridge, the summit is 300 vertical metres above. After admiring Mounts Murray and Cegnfs to the southeast, turn right to follow sheep/human trails up the grassy hillside. Tedious rubble leads to the final ridge from where the large summit cairn is visible. This last section is shattered and may look scary, but fortunately, much of the route stays

below the ridge traversing ledges to the right. Care is required because of the loose rock and exposure.

Ledges below the crest lead toward a broad slab in a corner capped by a large overhanging block. The obvious route is a well-trodden but narrow gully/crack line angling up right to regain the ridge. The summit is just beyond. If desired, you can continue to the lower west end of the mountain, but expect one tricky exposed bit at a notch. Most folks don't bother. Once your senses have been suitably sated, **return** the same way. Just so you're not left hanging, H. E. Burstall was a Canadian lieutenant-general of World War I.

115

Scrambling along the south section of Nihahi Ridge.

ELBOW/KANANASKIS VALLEY

Mount Fullerton	2728 m	moderate	p. 120
Mount Remus	2688 m	moderate	p. 122
Mount Romulus	2832 m	moderate	p. 125
Mount Glasgow	2935 m	moderate	p. 126
Banded Peak	2934 m	easy	p. 128
Cougar Mountain	2863 m	moderate	p. 130
Nihahi Ridge Traverse	2530 m	moderate	p. 132
Compression Ridge	2500 m	difficult	p. 134
The Wedge	2665 m	difficult	p. 136
Opal Ridge	2575 m	moderate	p. 138
Mount Kidd South Peak	2895 m	easy	p. 141
Mount Kidd	2958 m	moderate	p. 142
Fisher Peak	3053 m	difficult	p. 144
Mount Bogart	3144 m	moderate	p. 147
Mount Lawson	2795 m	moderate	p. 148
Grizzly Peak	2500 m	easy	p. 150
Gap Mountain	2675 m	moderate	p. 152
Tombstone South	3000 m	moderate	p. 154
Mount Hood	2903 m	moderate	p. 156

Peaks in this chapter are found in two specific areas in the Front Ranges of the Rockies. These areas are Little Elbow Recreation Area and Kananaskis Valley. Owing to their proximity to Calgary, both are extremely popular with city dwellers, especially on weekends.

The two locales are more or less adjacent and topography is similar to other areas within the Front Ranges: long limestone ridges, strata dipping to the southwest. In the Opal Range, strata are tilted up until nearly vertical. Snowfall is comparatively light, as is rainfall, making for a long scrambling season. Kananaskis Valley is unique in that its alignment is northeast to southwest and, for reasons that I don't completely recall, this alignment tends to make valleys slightly warmer. It may be that this orientation allows the mountains to funnel warmer west or southwest winds (such as chinooks) along the corridor's length rather than act as a windbreak. In any case, the phenomenon makes for good scrambling but poor skiing. Like the Canmore Corridor, these areas offer fine early season objectives.

Kananaskis Country has been under a constant threat from developers for years and Kananaskis Valley is no exception. At present there is a proposal for a development at the Evan-Thomas Creek that would block an important wildlife corridor and also alter access to Mount Fisher. At time of writing, a large scale public consultation on the future of K Country is underway. Previous polls have proven that the public neither needs nor wants increased commercial development in Kananaskis. Unfortunately, this wish conflicts with the goals of both money-hungry developers and the Alberta Tories, neither of whom seem able to grasp the importance of leaving large areas in their natural state. It is possible that the future of Kananaskis will never be satisfactorily settled unless the desires of the average

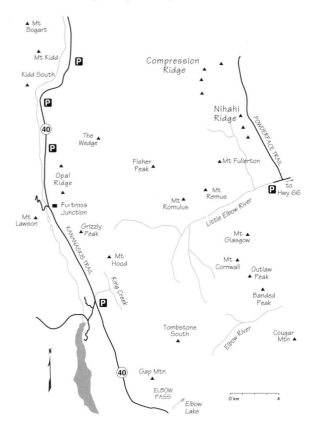

hiker or low-impact recreationists were to suddenly coincide with goals of those trying to line their pockets.

Access The Little Elbow Recreation Area is reached from the village of Bragg Creek, 40 minutes southwest of Calgary. Elbow Falls Trail (Highway 66) leads west to the recreation area. This road is closed at Elbow Falls from December until mid-May. The area features several hiking, biking and equestrian trails and a large campground. Kananaskis Valley is reached via Kananaskis Trail (Highway 40) from the Trans-Canada Highway, 65 km west of Calgary. This road continues south, crosses Highwood Pass and travels east through the foothills past Longview to meet Highway 2 eventually.

Facilities Canmore offers the best selection of facilities and services and is the major tourist hub of the area. Located east of Highway 40 junction on the Trans-Canada is Chief Chiniki restaurant (store and service station also). Bragg Creek east of Little Elbow Recreation Area has an ever-expanding number of shops, restaurants, stores and services, too. In Kananaskis Valley, limited groceries are available at Kananaskis Village Centre near Nakiska Ski Hill. What is left is largely hotels and bars. Mount Kidd RV Park just south has a small store. Gas and a reasonable selection of food and campers needs can be found at Fortress Junction farther south. Boulton Creek Trading Post near Kananaskis Lakes has a cafe and store.

Accommodation Canmore offers the most complete range of accommodation. Hotels and Ribbon Creek hostel are at Kananaskis Village and while K Country has many campgrounds, expect most to fill by early afternoon, especially on Fridays. Mount Kidd RV Park in Kananaskis Valley is the most decadent campground to be found; showers are available, too. A large campground can be found at Little Elbow Recreation Area. For affordable accommodation in the company of fellow climbers and hikers, check out the Alpine Club of Canada Clubhouse. It is 2 km east of Canmore on Highway 1A at the foot of Grotto Mountain.

Information Centres In Kananaskis Valley, information is available at Barrier Lake and at the visitor centre in Peter Lougheed Park. Other information centres are at Elbow Valley on Elbow Falls Trail and at Bow Valley Provincial Park near Seebe on Highway 1X.

Emergency Park Rangers are stationed at Elbow Ranger Station and Boundary Ranger Station by Ribbon Creek, which also serves as the Emergency Services Centre. RCMP are in Canmore and at the Ribbon Creek Emergency Centre.

MOUNT FULLERTON 2728 m

Difficulty A moderate scramble via northeast slopes and ridge. Good routefinding required on more challenging southeast ridge.
Round trip time 6-11 hours
Height gain 1050 m
Map 82 J/15 Bragg Creek

Mount Fullerton is one of the Front Range peaks that comes into condition comparatively early in the season, making it a good May starter. Depending on whether or not you enjoy testing your routefinding skills, there is a choice of routes that can be combined into the traverse. A bike is a time-saver on the approach.

Park at Little Elbow Recreation Area west of Bragg Creek on Highway 66. Unless you are a registered camper, the parking area is to the left of the campground entrance.

Northeast Ridge

Walk or cycle west through Elbow campground to Little Elbow trailhead. Little Elbow trail was once a driveable road and is well suited to mountain bikes for the 3.5 km to Nihahi Creek. Allow 40 minutes on foot to reach this point. At Nihahi Creek a signed trail to the right

leads you into a broad, alluvial streambed—typically bone dry—running north between Nihahi Ridge on the right and Mount Fullerton on the left.

After approximately 1-1.5 hours from Little Elbow trail, the main branch of the valley turns abruptly westward and circles around to the north side of the objective. At this point you can either follow the small, rocky drainage that emanates from an amphitheatre at 445320 on the northeast side of Mount Fullerton and gain open slopes on the right, or you can cut directly through trees to this open northeast ridge. The way up then becomes obvious. Only near the top at a few short rock steps is this route a hike, and before you know it, you're on the summit. A lower, unnamed point to the west is a 20 minute walk away.

If you choose to ascend by the more challenging southeast ridge, this northeast ridge route makes for a no-nonsense descent. The stony plod back along Nihahi Creek can hardly be called inspiring though.

A group begins descending the northeast ridge.

Photo: Clive Cordery.

Looking west to Mount Fullerton from along Nihahi Ridge. N NE ridge, S SE ridge.

Southeast Ridge

The long southeast ridge is a much more challenging undertaking. You can gain it at Little Elbow trail just west of Nihahi Creek, or, to avoid the first two hours of forest, continue part way up Nihahi Creek. Ascend open slopes and dry drainages at any of several places on the east side of Fullerton to gain the southeast ridge. Continue north, passing two lesser but well-cairned summits along the way to where real routefinding begins.

Contrary to more typical Front Range topography where strata are bedded with a noticeable dip to the west or southwest, the rock layers here dip to the east. This geological anomaly presents a challenge. Beyond the second cairned high point the ridge narrows and ends abruptly in a 5-10 m drop. As you look farther ahead, successively lower strata rise ramp-like, only to drop off in a similar manner. The test is to find a practical descent route down to successively lower ledge sys-

tems so you can progress westward to the summit. Some of these ledges are easier to descend on the left (south) side; at least one is downclimbed on the north side. Snow lingers on the north side and adds to the difficulty, so save this route until June at the earliest.

It is not necessary or advisable to traverse along the narrow "neck," which appears to connect to the main summit mass. It is simpler if you're a couple of ledge systems below and left of it. A few small cairns lend hope. Once you turn a particularly large skyline buttress on its left side, you have pretty much passed all obstacles. Finally, circle around to a more southwesterly aspect and hike to the summit. **Descend** via the easier northeast ridge.

C. P. Fullerton, for whom the mountain was named, was once chair of Canadian National Railways.

MOUNT REMUS 2688 m

Difficulty Difficult via chimney, moderate by north slope
Round trip time 6-8 hours if approaching by bike
Height gain 1050 m
Map 82 J/15 Bragg Creek

Mount Remus, pint-sized brother to adjacent Romulus, is a logical trip for shorter days of autumn when Little Elbow River is low enough to wade. A bike for the approach, old runners to wade the river and ski poles for the scree are all useful for this ascent. This mountain has been largely overlooked in the past but is a pleasant change from more often-visited destinations.

Park at Little Elbow Recreation Area west of Bragg Creek on Highway 66. The parking area is to the left before the campground entrance.

From the gate at the west end of the campground, follow Little Elbow trail for 6.6 km (some 45 minutes by bike) to a wide flat spot on the shoulder. This once-driveable road is perfect for mountain bikes, but watch for hikers and horse riders too. If you meet horses you should get off your bike until they pass. At 6.6 km you will be directly across from an obvi-

ous wide scree gully leading up to the skyline ridge of Mount Remus. From late August on, Little Elbow River is typically calf deep and is an easy, if chilly, ford.

After sloshing across, head briefly through trees to the drainage gully and traipse up rubble sporadically carpeted with patches of juniper and bearberry. Mount Glasgow rises behind you. Higher up, the gully diverges into two or three drainages before the ridge. Either branch to the left will do. The waterworn bedrock in the gullies degrades to loose talus for the last section.

Mount Remus seen from Mount Glasgow. D optional descent.

The summit block. C chimney route, N north side ascent route (easier).

Amble west along the ridge to the summit block where the only challenge awaits. There are two choices. You can climb the facing cliff band by a chimney where the cliff is least high. Slog up scree to its narrow mouth. Though near-vertical, there are acceptable holds for climbing the chimney, especially on the left wall. The total chimney height is about 5-7 m, but without a rope is unnerving and is harder when wet. An easier option, assuming the north side is dry, is to traverse around to the right and scramble up rocky slopes to the top. A short walk leads to a large cairn on the broad summit plateau.

To the west the most recognizable peak is Mount Blane, sporting a tall knife-shaped feature on the south ridge called "The Blade." Glasgow, Cornwall and Banded Peak lie straight south of you.

Return the same way, or better yet, traverse farther east along the ridge toward a minor summit. Then you can angle directly down massive slopes of brown shale below for a quick descent back to the main ascent gully.

Remus and Romulus were twin brothers and founders of Rome; Mount Romulus rises straight west of Mount Remus and displays an impressive escarpment. Beginning farther up-valley, it, too, is a scramble.

View of scree basin and south ridge of Mount Romulus. D drainage, B basin, S summit.

Looking along the ridge toward the summit of Mount Romulus. Mount Remus is to the right.

MOUNT ROMULUS 2832 m

Difficulty Moderate scrambling; mostly a hike
Round trip time 5-7 hours from campsite to summit; 1 hour to campsite by bike
Height gain 1230 m
Maps 82 J/15 Bragg Creek
82 J/14 Spray Lakes Reservoir

With a mountain bike for the 11 km-long approach, Mount Romulus is a pleasant way to wind down the scrambling season. You are unlikely to find a beaten path or crowd on this peak. Between the long approach and the river crossing, you may have it all to yourself, despite a nearby campsite. Try from mid-June on.

Park at Little Elbow Recreation Area west of Bragg Creek on Highway 66. The parking area is to the left before the campground entrance.

From the gate at the west end of the campground, follow Little Elbow trail for 10.8 km to Romulus backcountry campsite. This once-driveable road is perfect for mountain bikes (watch for hikers and horse riders), and most parties will choose to cycle if given the option. If you meet horse riders you should get off your bike until they pass.

Enter Romulus campsite and ride to the back of it to wade the river. An old pair of runners or shoes is handy for the crossing, best done later in summer. Once the feeling returns to your feet, head into the trees and up the hillside along the base of Mount Romulus. The idea is to get into a large drainage coming off the south end of the peak at 408253 and later gain the south ridge. If you're lucky you may stumble across a good hiking trail that wanders along through the forest into the north fork of Elbow River. Whether you find the trail or not, head west along the foot of the peak. Angle up into the big drainage on the

south side just before the river emerges from a canyon.

Follow the drainage up into a big scree basin. The ridge above on the left leads to the summit that lies some distance east, and there are a few places to get on it. Either one of two gullies on the left close to or beyond the last little trees offers a way through rock bands and onto the ridge. Otherwise, you can also continue straight ahead up loose brown scree toward a col and reach the ridge from there. This involves a lot more traversing hillside on rubble.

You cannot get lost once you're on the ridge. It is not narrow and is largely a walk, although it does have an annoying habit of going down when it should be going up. The summit gives a close view of Romulus' adjacent counterpart, Mount Remus, and the vertical walls guarding it. Distant peaks like Mount Rae are also visible. Like many ascents in the Front Ranges, however, the absence of glaciers and craggy summits renders the landscape a bit drab, with muted shades of gray, brown and dark green predominant. Once the scene becomes too melancholy, **return** the same way.

MOUNT GLASGOW 2935 m

Difficulty Moderate scramble via snow/
scree slopes and west ridge
Round trip time 7-12 hours
Height gain 1310 m
Map 82 J/15 Bragg Creek

An ascent of Mount Glasgow offers a close look at a notable tetrad of Front Range peaks that includes nearby Mount Cornwall, an unofficially-named summit called Outlaw Peak and lastly, Banded Peak at the southeast end. The most identifiable feature of the group may be the east aspect of Mount Cornwall. This scree slope holds snow like moss holds moisture. By midsummer it usually displays about the only snow on the horizon. Two summits to the south, Banded Peak's triangular shape, accentuated by a conspicuous horizontal band just below the top, further contributes to the group's unique appearance. With mountain bikes and proper logistical planning, the general cluster can be conquered in a long day. Try from mid-June on.

Drive to Little Elbow Recreation Area west of Bragg Creek on Highway 66. Unless you are a registered camper, parking is to the left of the campground entrance.

Walking the initial 1.5-2 hours is drudgery, so I suggest you cycle it. Almost everyone else will probably be cycling along this old road, too. From the parking area follow the road through Little Elbow Campground past the gate and continue along Little Elbow trail. Once you cross the river to the south side on the blue bridge, watch for the first drainage that crosses the trail at 443271, 7.2 km from the gate. This is a seasonal stream and may not even be flowing, so watch carefully (cairn if you're lucky!). Emanating from a stony valley between Glasgow and an 8900 ft. (2700m) outlier (460258)

All the rubble you can stand. The NW side of Mount Glasgow showing route from Little Elbow trail.

Photo: Kris Thorsteinsson.

The south ridge of Mount Glasgow from the north end of Mount Cornwall.

to the north, the drainage gives access to easy west-facing slopes leading to Glasgow's barren summit.

Hike along the left side of the drainage, keeping above it for the first part where it becomes a narrow canyon. Once this chasm peters out you can boulder-hop straight up the creekbed. At the far (southeast) end of the valley, turn right and outflank steep walls via a long scree slope (snow-covered during June and later). This takes you around onto the rubbly west ridge and the summit. There are no difficulties, but this route is a strong argument for using ski poles on scree. With an ice axe, you can glissade any snowy bits on return.

Ambitious folks will note the possibility of extending the trek south to Mount Cornwall, then southeast to Outlaw Peak (455205), and finally over to Banded Peak. Only the descent of the ridge from Glasgow towards Cornwall presents any challenge. You can then hike out down the east fork of a southeast-trending drainage (462195) between Banded and Outlaw peaks to reach Big Elbow trail at 478178. You intercept this trail at the second drainage past (southwest of) the bridge that crosses over to the north side of Elbow River (15.2 km from the trailhead). To do this rambling traverse, parties have approached opposite ends of the circuit on mountain bikes, then swapped for the return pedal back to Little Elbow Recreation Area. Naturally, the long daylight of June and July is preferred for this lengthy undertaking.

Glasgow and Cornwall were cruisers that played a prominent role in the 1914 Battle of the Falkland Islands.

BANDED PEAK 2934 m

Difficulty An easy scramble via southwest scree slopes
Round trip time Allow a full day even with a bike approach
Height gain 1310 m
Map 82 J/10 Mount Rae

For folks who aren't interested in the entire Glasgow to Banded traverse, Banded Peak alone is a worthwhile outing. Driving west toward the Rockies, this summit is recognizable by its pyramidal shape accentuated by a horizontal rock band near the pointy top. Much of the approach uses an old road and without a bike it is not logical as a day trip. Try from about mid-June on.

Drive to Little Elbow Recreation Area west of Bragg Creek on Highway 66. Unless you are a registered camper, parking is to the left of the campground entrance.

From the parking area follow the road through the campground and branch left onto Big Elbow trail, immediately crossing the bridge over Little Elbow River. Cycle along this road (watch for horses and hikers) for 15.2 km from Little Elbow

bridge, at which point you should be close to the drainage at 478178. The road rises slightly up a small hill here; the correct drainage is immediately past this rise. This drainage emanates from the south side of Banded Peak and provides access to the easy southwest slopes.

Stash your bike and head up along the right side of the creek. Later in the summer this will be dry. Look for an animal trail on the hillside above the creek to

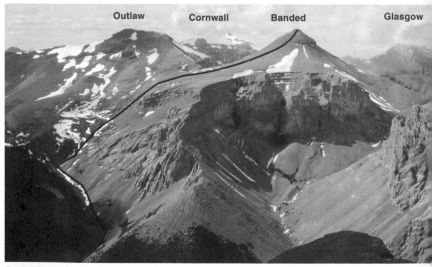

Outlaw   Cornwall   Banded   Glasgow

Banded Peak route from Cougar Mountain.

128

A sunny day on Banded Peak. Outlaw Peak to the left, Mount Cornwall to the right.

Photo: Gillean Daffern.

The final pyramid of Banded Peak from above Outlaw/Banded col.

avoid bushes in the drainage. The streambed soon opens up and you will have little problem reaching the basin below the peak at 463193; just be sure to follow the right-hand fork. The basin is open and you can easily tramp up to the top of Banded Peak on your right or Outlaw Peak rising straight ahead. The summit has a view of prairies in the east and larger peaks to the south and west, most notably, Mount Rae (3218 m). Vast amounts of rubble comprise this part of the Rockies. If the rest of the province ever runs out of scree, this area will be worth a mint. Unless you are traversing to Mounts Cornwall or Glasgow, **return** the same way.

COUGAR MOUNTAIN 2863 m

Difficulty Moderate scrambling and much scree via northeast ridge
Round trip time 7-11 hours
Height gain 1250 m
Map 82 J/15 Bragg Creek

Cougar Mountain sees few visitors but because of its location in the drier Front Ranges, you can ascend it when bigger

peaks are snowbound. Like other peaks in the Little Elbow Recreation Area, a bicycle is the sensible option for the 12 km approach. The ascent is straightforward, and offers a fine view of the steep east faces of Mist Mountain and Mount Rae, big peaks like Mount Assiniboine and peaceful, rolling prairies to the east. Try from mid-June on.

Cougar Mountain as seen on approach. Only the false summit is visible here.

Drive to Little Elbow Recreation Area west of Bragg Creek on Highway 66. There is limited trailhead parking by the bridge over Little Elbow River in the campground, otherwise, unless you are a registered camper, parking is to the left of the campground entrance.

Cross the suspension bridge over Little Elbow River and cycle the old road for about 12.3 km. This is a multi-use trail so please be cautious and courteous. When meeting horseback riders you should get off your bike, move to the side and let them pass you. As you ride along the road

toward the objective there are good views of Cougar Mountain from several points. The side facing you is the ascent route although the true summit isn't visible. After you cross the bridge to the south side of the river the road climbs, dips slightly, and rises again all within about 0.5 km. The northeast ridge of the mountain, the ascent route, is above on the left. Allow 1-1.5 hours by bike to here.

Hike up through forest and talus slopes to the open ridge above. Continue along this broad ridge, which rises and

Descending the easy lower slopes of Cougar Mountain.

becomes more clearly defined as you near some rock steps. While they may look questionable, these bands are easily surmounted except for the highest step, where you detour around to the left on a beaten sheep path. Apparently this peak does see visitors after all.

Above these rock steps the ridge again broadens and levels off. Behind you is a fine view of Threepoint Mountain, Mount Rose and Big Elbow River. Trudge up to the high point above, from where you will see the true summit just west. Down over the south side lies a beautiful little turquoise lake not shown on the map. This false peak is a good spot to have a drink and study the final ridge to the summit.

Walk down scree to the col and scramble up the ridge to the top. In general, you can stay close to the crest and only minor detours to the left are necessary. A couple of steps are steep, but they are short and are not exposed.

The top is the ideal location to view the Banded/Cornwall/Glasgow traverse, especially the approach to Banded Peak. Far off Mount Assiniboine is also apparent, and to the west, a green carpet dotted with puddles of blue leads your eye to steep, gray walls of Mount Rae. Rolling prairies disappear in haze to the east. After you've seen enough scree, scree and more scree, **return** to your bike the same way.

NIHAHI RIDGE TRAVERSE 2530 m

Difficulty Moderate scrambling
Round trip time 8-10 hours to traverse
Height difference 930 m between
highest point and start
Map 82 J/15 Bragg Creek

The south end of Nihahi Ridge is a popular hike, but of the myriad hikers who set off, few parties undertake the entire 7 km-long traverse. When dry, much of this trip is merely traipsing along a breezy, rocky ridge, but occasional slabby places and short sections of downclimbing add challenge too. The view includes foothills, prairies and bigger peaks in the Kananaskis Front Ranges. This ridge is often in condition by late May and for a season starter, it's worth the effort at least once.

Park at Little Elbow Recreation Area west of Bragg Creek on Highway 66. The parking area is to the left before the campground entrance.

Walk west through Elbow Campground past the gate and follow Little Elbow

Approaching Nihahi Ridge's high point at the north end.

trail. One kilometre past the gate, Nihahi Ridge trail heads off to your right through forest to the south ridge. The hiking trail runs below the east side of the ridge for a distance before gaining the crest. Scramblers can gain this crest earlier to enjoy a panoramic view sooner. Scramble up at a point just past the first rock bluff.

Much of the route is little more than hiking. Periodically you'll encounter rock steps that require a short scramble to descend while the odd slabby spot adds further variety. It is straightforward when dry but harder when snowy. To the west, scramble routes up Mount Fullerton are visible and Mount Fisher protrudes beyond it. To the east, Powderface Ridge and sprawling Moose Mountain intervene before prairie.

The traverse has its ups and downs, and as a result, you must repeatedly lose and regain elevation. Although the highest points near the north end register about 900 m above the trailhead, you actually gain significantly more than that. If you tire of the whole game, descend easy slopes west to Nihahi Creek at any one of several points and hike back to Little Elbow trail.

*Nihahi Ridge as seen from
Powderface Ridge to the east.*

Allow 5-6 hours to the north end high point at 458360, from where you have two possible **descents**. One is via west-facing scree slopes to the small, partly treed basin lying southwest. This is the source of the usually-dry north fork of Nihahi Creek. You'll see other obvious descent routes just west of this high point also. Then a long but worry-free trudge leads down dry Nihahi Creek to Little Elbow trail. Just before a canyon, the trail rises on the left over a shoulder. From Little Elbow trail it is about a 40 minute walk back to the campground.

Another exit from the north end of Nihahi Ridge is to descend north to Prairie Creek basin and hike east to Powderface Trail. Though lacking an established trail, it is a shorter return but requires a second vehicle at Prairie Creek, 9.5 km north of Highway 66/Powderface Trail junction. Nihahi is a Stoney Indian word for rocky, which aptly describes all 7 km of this ridge.

Crux downclimb along the traverse.

COMPRESSION RIDGE 2500 m

Difficulty Difficult scrambling in places
Traverse time 11+ hours, a long day
Height difference 940 m higher than Nihahi trailhead

Compression Ridge is the twisted sister to arrow-straight Nihahi Ridge. Only true masochists will consider continuing from Nihahi Ridge to traverse horseshoe-shaped Compression Ridge. This long, tiring scramble is for experienced, capable parties with routefinding skills, not for those who require a trail. Two cars are necessary, as are dry conditions, good weather and long daylight. Try from June on.

Park a second car near Canyon Creek on Powderface Trail, 14.5 km north of the Powderface Trail/Highway 66 intersection. Be sure to study Compression Ridge's northeast slopes for a descent route toward Canyon Creek and the road.

From Nihahi Ridge, problematic sections of Compression Ridge occur just prior to the highest point at 436380 and east of there at a series of pinnacles. These are visible to the north across Prairie Creek basin from Nihahi Ridge. Continuing beyond Nihahi Ridge, travel is initially easy and promising. If you're lucky, you'll find a welcome snow patch for water. Soon past the first major high point at 439364, difficulties begin. Turn a steep rotten wall with a slight drop immediately beyond by descending rubble on the left. Then a narrow but solid ridge leads to the highest point, 7-8 hours from Elbow Campground.

Typical scrambling along Compression Ridge traverse.

Beyond (east of) the highest point, steep steps and pinnacles appear, and, like unruly drunks at a party, are best avoided. Do this by descending and traversing scree and slabs on the right (south) side. Of note is a rock wall straddling the ridge displaying a large window clear through it. Skirt below this. Problems then diminish and just a long, tiring plod follows. If necessary, you could descend south slopes to Prairie Creek, but this would leave you many kilometres from either vehicle.

As you reach the final high point at the north end, you will notice scree slopes leading west to a side drainage of Canyon Creek. These would suffice as a descent, or, if you've checked from the road, descend the east side of the ridge. Just past the high point, drop down onto grey rubble followed by brown rubble. Near tree line, a belt of slabs, unseen from above, can be descended

Inspecting the window.

in a couple of spots toward the treed knoll (458408). Steep cliffs block Compression Ridge's north end.

It is an hour along typically-dry Canyon Creek to your car. We took 11 hours for this trip in optimum conditions. With any snow remaining on narrow parts of Compression Ridge, it would NOT be a scramble. The outing could also start at Canyon Creek and would be much the

same level of difficulty. If travelling in that direction, you could always finish by walking out Nihahi Creek instead of traversing Nihahi Ridge if desired.

Compression describes the forces that created the upthrust strata, tight folds and the snaking "S" shape of this particular ridge. If straightened, it might be as long as Nihahi Ridge. Maybe even longer.

THE WEDGE 2665 m

Difficulty Moderate scrambling with a short difficult spot along summit ridge
Round trip time 5-9 hours
Height gain 1100 m
Map 82 J/14 Spray Lakes Reservoir

In the past, parties have usually climbed The Wedge by steep technical routes on the west side while the northeast ridge and face are used for a straightforward descent. Surprise! This moderately-angled face makes an enjoyable scramble up, with the most fun occurring along the summit ridge. An acceptable approach trail leads to tree line and much route variation is possible once you reach the rock. Try from about June on.

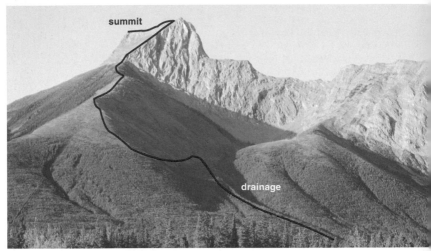

The Wedge as seen from near Wedge Pond.

Drive to Wedge Pond in Kananaskis Country, 30 km south of the Trans-Canada Highway on Kananaskis Trail (Highway 40).

The best way to reach the peak is by following a good trail on the left side of a watercourse that drains a small basin below the steep north face. It is important to find this drainage. You can recognize it from the road as a winding line of lighter coloured poplar trees, which prefer streambeds, growing amid evergreen-clad slopes between Wedge Pond and the mountain. From the parking area, walk a short way along the lakeshore and watch for a trail heading into the trees near a single culvert. Farther upstream there will be water flowing in this stream early season, but it seeps underground before reaching the lake.

A trail along the left bank leads to open slopes below the northeast ridge. After hiking up the grassy hillside to the crest of this ridge, Fisher Peak is immediately apparent to the southeast. As you tramp along the open ridge crest toward the northeast face of The Wedge, bleached and weathered wisps of tree trunks mingle with newer growth. According to Ruth Oltmann's *The Valley of Rumours...the Kananaskis*, in the scorching hot summer of 1936, a careless camper's fire at Kananaskis Lakes ignited the tinder-dry woods. The resulting inferno burnt much of Kananaskis Valley, including this area.

As you reach the northeast face, the route is clearly more laidback than suspected and you can follow any number of lines to the ridge above. It works well if you move toward the right edge of the rubbly slope as soon as possible. You may even find a cairn or two.

Scrambling along the summit ridge.

Expect no difficulties to the summit ridge, but the challenge increases as you scramble to the true summit, 15 minutes south. For a few metres, the ridge is narrower, more exposed and loose—the crux.

From the top, you'll see Mount Joffre's snowy face to the south while nearby lies the long, gently curving mass of Opal Ridge, yet another scramble. When you've seen enough, **return** the same way.

Assuming you know ice axe self-arrest, in early summer you can sometimes glissade from near tree line down into the basin below the peak's north end.

If you missed the approach trail, you might think "The Wedge" describes the difficulties of squeezing through tightly-knit lodgepole pine trees, however, the mountain's suggestive shape is the true explanation.

OPAL RIDGE North Peak 2575 m

Difficulty Moderate scrambling
Round trip time 4-7 hours
Height gain 870 m
Map 82 J/14 Spray Lakes Reservoir

Opal Ridge is an 8 km-long ridge parallelling Kananaskis Trail between Rocky and Grizzly creeks. Perhaps Opal Ridge's most noteworthy features are tightly-folded strata visible in the steep west flanks above the road. These are particularly noticeable at the south end of the ridge as you drive north. For scramblers, this mountain offers variety, a view and easy access. You can ascend it from either end, midway along or traverse it. The traverse is recommended for competent scramblers. Owing to its location and orientation, snow clears off quickly, and you can sometimes head up as early as mid to late April. Take an ice axe in early season.

North End Approach

Park about 1 km south of Rocky Creek bridge on Kananaskis Trail (Highway 40), and 35.7 km south of the Trans-Canada Highway. This is just south of Eau Claire Campground.

Opal Ridge sits right above where you have parked. Rather than fight through close-knit pines and scrub bush infesting the lower north end of the ridge, it is preferable to scramble up open, steeper slopes right above the road. This avoids much of the feisty flora. Once on the ridge, continue south, rising through thinning evergreens. This forest leads to scree slopes below steep, grey walls that guard the north end of Opal Ridge. Behind you, The Wedge rears skyward.

Traverse around to the right for a short distance where a wide gully on the west side breaches the cliff band. Above the gully, go up over a bit of a shoulder, plod up more scree. A quick scramble then dumps you on the surprisingly flat top. The highest adjacent point lies slightly south and to reach it you'll first scramble up a short 3 m-high wall. Here you will probably opt to sprawl out and enjoy the scenery before contemplating the southerly traverse. Mount Fisher dominates the eastern horizon, while the popular bowl route up Mount Kidd is evident to the northwest. Unless you plan to do the traverse, **descend** the same way.

North end of Opal Ridge as seen from the road.

Looking north along Opal Ridge.

Opal Ridge Traverse

Difficulty Difficult scrambling, some exposure
Traverse time 6-10 hours

Traversing Opal Ridge makes for a long but fulfilling day. Several high points along the way offer interesting challenges plus a little routefinding; other parts vary from tedious trudging to pleasant walking. One cliff band requires a significant loss of elevation to continue. The view throughout is terrific.

It is preferable to travel north to south as a couple of the trickier places are easier ascended than descended. Exposed sections are few and short, and while some difficulties are turned either left or right as required, others must be

met head on. The north end is more involved. It is pointless to describe the whole trek in detail, but there are sections worth noting. Part way along, a high wall blocks the entire ridge. This requires a substantial descent toward the highway before you are able to finally overcome the troublesome rock band. This is the low point, both figuratively and literally. You must then trudge all the way up to the ridge again. If you've had enough fun by this point, this also looks like a feasible spot to bail out and descend to the road. Otherwise, the remainder of the traverse gradually shifts to enjoyable hiking as you approach the 2590 m-high point (315275) directly above Fortress Junction Service Station.

This is a fine rest stop. Kananaskis Lakes shimmer to the south with Mount

South section of Opal Ridge above Fortress Junction from Fortress Road.

Joffre's icy north face rising above a cluster of summits beyond. This panorama looks sublime in the gentle light of evening, and it could well be this late once you are here. Conversely, should afternoon thunderstorms be building, everything may be looking far too dramatic and have you worrying about getting down. Either way, most parties will be happy to head down here, especially if they have remembered to bring money.

Descent is easy. Backtrack north toward the next bump, then charge down huge shaley slopes, aiming for open terrain to the right (north) of the drainage. You can see these slopes plainly from the highway. The line of big rock pinnacles along the ridge poses no barrier, however, do not go into the drainage. The abrupt drop-off where the waterfall iceclimb "Solid Cold" forms each winter will stop you short. Instead, keep right

(north) and descend various trails to Fortress Junction. You may want to stash a bike to avoid the anticlimactic roadside plod back to Rocky Creek.

For anyone wanting to scramble up to this 2590 m-high point from the highway, simply reverse these directions. The proper drainage is just north (left) of the service station.

Diehards wanting to push on past the 315275 high point and continue to the far south end can do so. Grizzly Creek (unmarked at 311251, immediately west of Mount Evan-Thomas) affords a feasible route back to the road, but is not nearly as fast as the shale slopes at Fortress Junction.

According to *Place Names in the Canadian Rockies* by Boles, Putnam, Laurilla, Dr. George Dawson of the Geological Survey found quartz crystals coated with Opal while prospecting nearby.

MOUNT KIDD SOUTH PEAK 2895 m

Difficulty Easy to moderate scramble
via southwest slopes
Round trip time 5-9 hours
Height gain 1290 m
Map 82 J/14 Spray Lakes Reservoir

The south peak of Mount Kidd is a pleasant
outing, easily ascended from Galatea
Creek trail and unlikely to be crowded.
There are few problems. Try from June on.

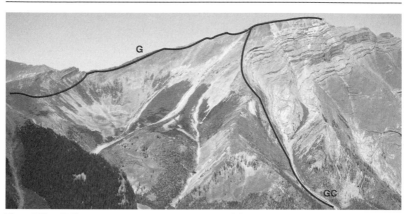

Photo: Gillean Daffern.   *G Guinn's Pass route, GC Galatea Creek route.*

Drive to Galatea Creek parking lot on
Kananaskis Trail (Highway 40), 32.7 km
south of the Trans-Canada Highway.

From the parking lot, follow the trail left
at the T-junction as for Lillian Lake. After
about one hour of steady walking, past
the canyon, the trail leaves coniferous
forest and enters an avalanche area of
willows and poplars (cross six bridges
total). This is just one minute before the
seventh bridge that crosses to the
stream's south (left) bank. Here the path
is very close to the hillside. Watch for
cairns marking a good trail heading
upslope at the edge of the taller evergreens. The obvious trail ascends a steep,
grassy hillside and a broad avalanche
gully (250365). Continue up this gully

through stunted poplars and bits of slab.
Higher up, you should stay left and gain
the ridge on your left. Skirt a couple of
brief but steep rock bands near the summit ridge on the left, then slog up coarse
rubble the last way. A few notches interrupt the ridge but you can bypass these
on the right (south). The top lies only
minutes away.

An **alternate** and more scenic ascent
route is viable from Guinn's Pass. Head
east from the pass traversing below the
ridge crest on the south side until well
beyond the first high point (237374). If
you don't, a steep drop-off will require
much elevation loss and backtracking
to circumvent it. The two routes join
higher up.

Return via the south slopes.

MOUNT KIDD 2958 m

Difficulty A moderate snow/slab/scree ascent via southeast bowl
Round trip tlme 5.5-9 hours
Height gain 1350 m
Map 82 J/14 Spray Lakes Reservoir

Mount Kidd has become very popular of late. It is a steep, unrelenting grind best done about late May or June when compacted snow allows step-kicking going up and glissading on descent. Otherwise, expect heaps of loose scree. Knowledge of ice axe self-arrest is imperative during prime months. Your safety also depends on accurate assessment of snow clinging to the steep walls above the bowl. As much of the route is visible from the highway, most parties prefer to wait for a major or climax avalanche to occur before heading up. This is evident by large amounts of avalanche debris compacted into the lower third of the bowl and below the waterfalls.

If unsure of conditions, you should postpone the attempt until later when the climb merely involves tedious scree and a bit of slab.

Drive to Galatea Creek parking lot on Kananaskis Trail (Highway 40), 32.9 km south of the Trans-Canada Highway.

From Galatea parking lot follow the hiking path down the hill and across the suspension bridge over Kananaskis River. Continue for a few minutes through trees and over Galatea Creek to a directional sign and a T-junction. Take the right-hand fork for Terrace trail. Follow the trail as it parallels Kananaskis River on the east side of Mount Kidd, reaching a streambed in 20 minutes. In spring this icy cold brook is an ideal place to chill victory drinks for the return. Have a look—maybe you'll find some!

Leave Terrace trail and follow a beaten path along the right side of the stony, often-dry streambed toward the huge bowl draining the peak's east side. Scramble up the right-hand side of the waterfalls on firm rock ledges that lead into the wide bowl. This bowl is a classic example of a syncline, which here identifies the northern end of an ancient upheaval called the Lewis Thrust. The leftmost gully above is simplest and least steep. The next gully to the right is similarly easy once you're in it, but you must traverse steeper slabs to reach it. A line of pinnacles separates these two routes. Though slabs and scree present few obstacles, the angle is unrelenting. Carry an ice axe if there is snow on this slope, and, if new snow has fallen just prior to your attempt, you should probably go elsewhere. Slabs are slick when wet.

Be aware that snow-covered sections of this route may hide rock bands. Water flowing over these steps can weaken the overlying snow, and there is a very real hazard of falling into an icy, wet chasm between the rock and packed snow. Be watchful. A similar occurrence on Mount Niblock in June 1989 resulted in a fatality.

Although the incline is better suited to staring groundward, you may notice the peculiar window near the base of a high buttress along the skyline ridge connecting north and south peaks. While the south peak is also attainable from a different approach (described separately), this buttress along the intervening ridge prevents any possibility of traversing the two summits.

The southeast bowl route on Mount Kidd. S streambed, G gully.

Upon topping out of the ascent gully, Mount Bogart rears up just across Ribbon Creek. A 10 minute walk up a stately ridge leads east to the true summit where now sits a telecommunications repeater. In early season, be wary of the massive cornice just beyond the cairn.

John and Stuart Kidd once ran a general store and trading post at the nearby settlement of Morley; the mountain was named for the latter.

Chugging up the big gully in prime glissading conditions. The Wedge rises behind.

FISHER PEAK 3053 m

Difficulty Difficult and exposed downclimbing near the summit; a climber's scramble
Round trip time 10-14 hours with mountain bike approach
Height gain 1570 m
Map 82 J/14 Spray Lakes Reservoir

Mount Fisher is a high sprawling mountain dominating the headwaters of Evan-Thomas Creek in Kananaskis Valley. As seen from the road, the long north ridge rises in a graceful arc to a series of three distant small bumps, the leftmost being the summit. Even the most direct route is long and has a difficult 25 m step (see photo on page 10). Compared to Mount Smuts, this crux is just as difficult but very different. The alternative is even longer with more rough biking plus bushwhacking. This makes a long day longer yet. Most parties will prefer using a bike for one-day ascents of this peak. If you would like to add your name to the register, try from July on.

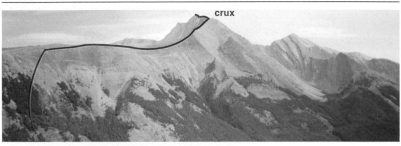

Fisher Peak from the McKay Hills. Crux is at the summit bumps.

Drive to Evan-Thomas parking lot in Kananaskis Country some 28 km south of the Trans-Canada Highway on Kananaskis Trail (Highway 40). Mount Fisher sprawls in the distance to the southeast as you near the parking area.

From the parking area, the wide trail is relaxed pedalling initially but narrows and roughens just past an intersection—keep left here. Before long you cross a stream, then the road curves left back toward Mount Fisher. Many sections are rough because of horse traffic and water erosion, so most folks will be pushing up some hills. As you approach Fisher's north ridge the road crosses a side stream coming in from the left (356346). A couple of skinny logs are usually in place here. The road immediately rises and then parallels the north ridge. Gill Daffern advocates heading up through forest near a campsite at 8 km; we continued up the road until about 9 km. To continue farther it would have been necessary to cross Evan-Thomas Creek to the west side, either wading or rock-hopping. Finding your bike here should be easier. Allow 1.5 to 2 hours by bike to this point.

Head up through open forest crossing boulder fields to the broad ridge. This plateau hosts mosses, meadows and flowers—a pleasant surprise after the acres of debris! Wander south toward the summit mass. The plateau descends a bit, then rises into a better defined rocky ridge with an increasing drop on your left. The crux step is unseen from here.

Seeing this step may leave you feeling disappointed, but look carefully, it can be downclimbed. First descend a short distance close to the crest, then traverse a few metres back to the left (as you face inwards) more toward the south side. Descend a steep 3-4 m-high wall in a corner. Arm strength and a good long reach are assets here. This is the crux; easier terrain leads to the ridge. Note that a short rappel would simplify matters. As you continue to the summit, one other shorter notch must be downclimbed. Allow about seven hours to the top.

From the summit, most striking is the substantial distance between you and the parking lot: Good thing you brought that bike after all. The **return** is via the same route. Climbing the crux will be much easier, but finding your bicycle again may be tough. On the way out, remember, horse riders use the road, too, so please be courteous. Given the rough road it is unlikely you will be speeding, but watch for them and dismount until they pass.

Although I have not personally tried this next and longer option, I will attempt to describe it for those disliking the harder route. You must go far enough up Evan-Thomas Creek that you can gain a gully (more like a small valley) curving around the southwest side of the peak. This gully at 375302 separates Fisher Peak from an unnamed peak 1.5 km due south. Then, if you tramp far enough around, you can slog up easier terrain (a scree gully) and gain the summit ridge past the crux step.

First you must find the best spot to gain this gully. It is unseen from the road owing to trees. At about 10.5 km the road splits. The right fork rises to MacKay Hills, and the left (your route) descends to another

Ascending a step on return. The crux step rises behind.

creek crossing. At about 11 to 11.5 km, a big, steep, rough hill will require pushing your bike. This hill immediately descends steeply (splitting into two separate trails partway down) losing every bit of hard-won elevation. The top of this hill seems a logical point to head into the trees to gain the big gully. Shown as an intermittent stream on the map, it should become recognizable farther up. If in doubt, work your way right as you ascend. A direct line will merely put you on the summit ridge before the crux step. This step is the circular contour line at 382310 on the map. Expect a good long day.

John A. Fisher served as sea lord of the British Admiralty, among other postings, and that was enough to have his named stuck onto a mountain forever. Only in Canada, you say—pity.

Photo: Gillean Daffern.

One heck of a trudge! The normal route on Mount Bogart begins above Ribbon Falls.
The only challenge is a rock band near the top. R Ribbon Creek, B basin, C crux.

MOUNT BOGART 3144 m

Difficulty A moderate scramble by south slopes from Ribbon Creek
Round trip time 7-11 hours
Height gain 1650 m
Map 82 J/14 Spray Lakes Reservoir (shown incorrectly in edition 2, should be 1 km southwest at 235412)

Mount Bogart, the second highest point in the Kananaskis Range, is one of the more recognizable peaks as you approach the Rockies from Calgary. The prominent triangular summit often holds snow when nearby mountains are bone dry. Although the view is excellent, the outing is long and uninspiring at times. Difficulties are few, however. Try from late June on.

Drive 23.4 km south of the Trans-Canada Highway on Kananaskis Trail (Highway 40). Turn right and follow signs to Ribbon Creek parking lot.

From Ribbon Creek parking lot, follow the popular hiking trail beginning on the north side of this swift stream. This is normally a busy trail but for this ascent you'll probably be starting early enough to beat the rush. Continue along the wide path for 11 km to Ribbon Creek Falls. Beyond the campground the trail angles up from the base of the falls and switchbacks to cross a rock slide.

Leave the hiking trail once you reach the small stream coming down from a high valley at the south end of Mount Bogart (235395). This watercourse may not always be flowing. Follow goat trails up green slopes on the left-hand side of the drainage until it becomes simpler to cross over it. A bit of scrambling on ledges and up a gully leads through the rock band to an unexpectedly large, meadowy cirque complete with various alpine flowers and a tiny pond.

This basin offers a perfect opportunity to relax and contemplate the rest of the ascent. Don't be fooled by the foreshortened perspective of the route. The summit is farther away than it looks. After a couple of hours of slogging up a treadmill of scree, it will have become painfully obvious just how deceptive the earlier view really was. Upon reaching the rock band guarding the top, scramble up a narrow but prominent gully. This is the crux, so persevere, the end is in sight. Once you overcome this gully the terrain eases to a mere plod.

The summit vista includes many familiar nearby peaks in Kananaskis and on a clear day, visibility extends more than 100 km to the Purcell Range of British Columbia. Closer at hand, a short hike along the ridge gives a bird's-eye view of the three Memorial Lakes lying one airy kilometre below. These three ponds are the ultimate source of Ribbon Creek's north fork.

Return the same way. Mount Bogart is named for geologist Donaldson Bogart Dowling, who explored the area for the Geological Survey of Canada in 1904.

MOUNT LAWSON 2795 m

Difficulty A moderate scramble via east-facing rubble slopes
Round trip time 5-7 hours
Height gain 1240 m
Map 82 J/14 Spray Lakes Reservoir

Mounts Lawson and Inflexible parallel Highway 40 forming a continuous 8 km-long escarpment of the Kananaskis Range. Although ignored for years, Mount Lawson sees regular visitors now, despite the intervening kilometre of dense pine forest between road and peak. With an ice axe, early season trips frequently grant a good glissade on the descent. Mount Inflexible (3000 m) can be reached as well, but this extension has not proven popular. As viewed from Fortress Junction, a deep basin carved in the escarpment separates these two, with Lawson to the left. The first drainage left of the basin with the waterfall below it grants a direct line of access to Lawson's summit. Carry an ice axe as approach slopes are steep.

Access is via Fortress Ski Area access road, 41.8 km south of the Trans-Canada Highway on Kananaskis Trail (Highway 40). Park at the first switchback beyond the bridge.

From the first switchback where you park, the initial test is to get into the correct drainage. It will be the second one you come to after leaving Fortress road. It is worth taking a compass bearing on the peak before diving blindly into the forest, and I certainly wished I'd followed my own advice last time. The first drainage, the larger of the two, flows well down into the trees. Cross this to the second drainage; smaller, overgrown and dry until you advance well upstream. It will require some 25 minutes to reach this drainage from your car. As you progress up the streambed, a couple of waterfalls encountered can be scrambled around to the right. Shortly after, the alpine zone of larch-treed slopes is reached. Now you are granted an uninterrupted view down Kananaskis Valley against a backdrop of serrated Opal Range peaks.

Above tree line the slope feeding the ascent drainage is moderately angled and presents no problems. From the road this section appears steeper than it actually is. Farther left, the angle steepens giving more interesting scrambling, but it is not without the ubiquitous rubble. Toil up oodles of debris and short bluffs of broken, angular limestone to the wide summit ridge. The highest point sits a few minutes south.

Looking west is a hidden valley complete with a tarn tucked between parallel ridges of Mounts Lawson and Kent. Much farther south and west are impressive forms of Mounts Joffre, King George and Assiniboine, all over 3353 m. Determined souls can traverse north along the ridge toward Mount Inflexible (3000 m), but expect loose rock and several spots that require climbing down and back up overlying steep, rubbly slabs. Significantly more difficult, it adds about 300 m elevation gain just getting there. Most people don't bother, and of those who have, apparently few have enjoyed it. I didn't think it was that bad, but it does add four hours and much more elevation. For a simpler return from Inflexible, some parties have descended west toward the hidden valley, then climbed back up to the low point of the ridge, adding yet more elevation, but most

Don't let a few trees deter you! Route starts from Fortress Ski Area access road.

would likely be happier simply ignoring the traverse. Enough said.

On the **return**, if you have your ice axe there may be an opportunity to glissade. With optimum snow conditions, an exhilarating sitting glissade of more than 500 m is possible, a quick and cheeky way of losing both elevation and excess body heat. Be sure you know how to control your speed and perform self-arrest: There has already been one glissading accident on this slope.

Major W. E. Lawson was a topographer with the Geological Survey of Canada; Inflexible was a battle cruiser engaged in the Battle of Jutland. Kent was a newspaper reporter.

GRIZZLY PEAK 2500 m

Difficulty An easy scramble via south and east slopes
Round trip time 4-6 hours
Height gain 900 m
Map 82 J/14 Spray Lakes Reservoir (unmarked at 328249)

This small summit sitting by Grizzly Creek is unnamed on maps, but Grizzly Peak bears inclusion for accessibility and the view alone. West of Mount Evan-Thomas and beside the road, it offers an outstanding view of the Kananaskis Valley, vertically-tilted Opal Range summits and the Elk Pass area. Sitting right above Kananaskis Trail, the steep, slabby west aspect looks daunting and reveals nothing of the easier backside. That side can be seen from a few kilometres farther south or along the south end of Smith-Dorrien Road. Sheep trails offer a reasonable approach. Try from about mid-June on.

Park on the side of Kananaskis Trail (Highway 40) at Ripple Rock Creek (unsigned)1 km south of Grizzly Creek and 46 km south of the Trans-Canada Highway. This stream is midway between Grizzly Creek and Hood Creek, both of which are signed and are 2 km apart.

Above the stream on the left (north) side you'll find a well-used animal trail parallelling the drainage and heading up the steep, open hillside. Start off on this. Don't hike alongside the creek as it is confined and bushy. Contour on hillside around the south side of peak above the creek, but not so high as to encounter summit cliffs extending down. Some trails lead up into

Grizzly Peak seen from the south. Ascent route sneaks around to the backside. Kananaskis Trail is to the left.

Enjoying a fine view of Kananaskis Valley from Grizzly Peak.

steep scrambling terrain and this is where folks can go wrong. The correct route may be steep sidehill, but if travel isn't technically easy, try lower down.

Make your way around the peak, crossing open slopes of scree and vegetation, then angle up toward the high saddle tucked between Grizzly Peak and Mount Evan-Thomas when it becomes visible. If you're hoping for a nice level spot for a snack, you're out of luck until this saddle. Until this point, terrain is relentlessly steep. If not for well-established grasses and small plants, it would surely have eroded away eons ago. Almost everywhere back in this basin are steep, grassy slopes. No wonder so many bighorn sheep are attracted to the area.

Once you reach the broad saddle, it is an easy 15 minute hike to the top. You might notice a lonely little larch tree that by some quirk has taken hold on this slope and managed to survive where none other has. From the top, there is a fine view of the Kananaskis Lakes with snowy Mount Joffre behind. Nearby Opal Range peaks like Evan-Thomas, Packenham, Brock and Blane are easily studied from here, and to the north you can see The Wedge.

Deep rubble gullies on both the south side and the west face appear to be possible descent routes, however, I would not recommend trying these. Opal Range summits, because of their vertical bedding of strata, sometimes lure gullible parties down innocent-looking scree gullies only to end in vertical drops. Once you've seen enough, **return** the same way.

GAP MOUNTAIN 2675 m

Difficulty A moderate to difficult scramble via east side. Loose rock and exposure
Round trip time 3.5-6 hours
Height gain 780 m
Map 82 J/11 Kananaskis Lakes

Gap Mountain is indisputable proof that bigger isn't always a better viewpoint. This little peak is close to the road and over half the elevation is gained merely by hiking. Because of the exposure and steep slopes of loose rock, this scramble is recommended only for small parties of experienced, competent scramblers. An early start is not required for this little peak but a helmet is worthwhile. Try from July on.

Park at Little Highwood Pass day-use area at the east end of Valleyview Trail, 6.4 km west of Highwood Pass and 10.6 km southeast of Kananaskis Lakes Trail/ Kananaskis Trail (Highway 40) junction.

From the parking area, walk west along Valleyview Trail about 300 m and head off to the right into forest. You should be close to either one of two gullies that drain from an open pass set between Mount Elpoca to the east and Gap Mountain to the west. Gain this pass, which then provides access to the east side of

Telephoto view of Gap Mountain's east side. P pass.

So little effort, such a fine view! Beautiful Kananaskis Lakes from Gap Mountain.

Gap Mountain. Travel through forest is easy, and occasional sheep trails aid your short approach.

The pass is a fine viewpoint and an ideal spot for a break. Here you can admire the hidden alpine basin feeding Elpoca Creek tucked below vertical walls of Mounts Elpoca and Jerram. Beyond, jagged Opal Range peaks parade northward. You can also study the route up the east side of Gap Mountain, although the perspective does suffer from foreshortening. From where the ridge abuts the mountain, a bit of trail leads up slab and rubble toward the first steep wall. Now angle left to gain a much broader gully. A brief exposed traverse takes you around a corner crossing downsloping rock above a deep, steep gully. It is only about three or four moves but a fall would be deadly. Parties have scrambled up almost directly above the abutting ridge and also from points farther to the right.

Continue up steep rubble and shattered, downsloping slabs. Terrain to the left is easier angled. Care is needed as the rock is extremely loose in places and rubble lies on slabs and ledges. By now it should be evident why this is not a good group objective: dislodged debris falls straight onto parties below. Once you get onto the ridge above, the slope lays back and the fabulous Kananaskis Lakes panorama unfolds. The rest of the way is obvious and you can either continue up the ridge crest or along scree to the top.

Major peaks on the skyline include snowy Mounts King George, Sir Douglas and Assiniboine, with snowcapped Mount Ball farther north. Behind, the road winds east up to Highwood Pass. With binoculars, you may even see tiny people trudging up the summit ridge of Mount Rae, or perhaps tiny people on Mount Rae staring with binoculars toward Gap Mountain. Whatever the case, on a clear day, the top is an excellent viewpoint. Resist the urge to descend gullies on the west side. West-facing gullies on Opal Range peaks usually end in vertical drops and therefore do not make good descent routes. **Return** the same way.

153

TOMBSTONE SOUTH 3000 m

Difficulty Moderate scrambling via the south ridge, possible exposure
Round trip time 7-11 hours
Height gain 1020 m
Map 82 J/11 Kananaskis Lakes

The 82 J/11 map edition 2 incorrectly shows Tombstone Mountain at 407165. Tombstone Mountain has a double summit and is actually 1.5 km northwest. This scramble ascends the peak at the above coordinates, unofficially called Tombstone South.

Tombstone South, tucked behind the Opal Range, sits in lovely subalpine surroundings not far from ever-popular Elbow Lake. The readily-approached south ridge is an enjoyable scramble, and much of it on delightfully firm slabs. At time of writing, the register recorded only three ascents in 13 years, despite ease of approach and its proximity to popular backpacking, hiking and mountain biking destinations. The summit view is excellent, surroundings are serene and bush is minimal. Although sections of the approach are rough, a mountain bike does save time. Try from July on.

Drive to Elbow Lake trailhead on the north side of Kananaskis Trail (Highway 40), 12.3 km southeast of Kananaskis Lakes/Kananaskis Trail junction.

From the parking lot, a steep trail ascends the hillside, gaining elevation quickly. Bikers will probably push up this bit. The trail soon eases and reaches Elbow Lake in a mere 1.3 km, where you'll find a backcountry campsite along the right (south) shore. This campsite is an ideal base for day trips to this peak, Tombstone Lakes and hikes nearby. Continue down the left (north) shore past the lake in wide open subalpine surroundings. Mount Elpoca, with its towers high above, is along your left side and to the right is Mount Rae and tiny Rae Glacier. Tombstone South lies pretty much straight down the valley and the right-hand ridge is the route of ascent.

Nearing the true summit.

At a point about 4.5 km from the parking lot you should be almost directly across from the peaks' south ridge. Stash your bike, perhaps in mats of ground-hugging krummholz, and boulder-hop or wade Elbow River. "River" is a definite stretch of terminology here. Although the intervening distance from road to ridge is short, you may find yourself briefly entangled in densely-knit alpine firs before escaping the forest for open ridge.

Once on the ridge, the best scrambling follows the crest up firm slabs much of the way. Loose scree is absent until higher up, while exposed spots can usually be detoured to the left. Behind in the distance is Mount Tyrwhitt, while all about you a luxuriant carpet of green unfurls. Higher up a rock band bars the ridge and you should angle across the scree to a low point where it is easily overcome. Head back up on loose rubble toward the ridge and soon reach the false summit. The connecting ridge makes a slight descent before reaching the true summit, minutes away.

Peer carefully over the east side: The gut-wrenching drop to Tombstone Lakes will snatch your breath away. The jagged Opal Range, not typically viewed from an easterly aspect, juts skyward to the west. Mount Jerram, in particular, looks impressive. Neighbouring Tombstone Mountain was named by George Dawson for rock pinnacles near the summit that resemble tombstones. Mighty Mount Assiniboine pierces the skyline to the northwest, while the glaciated east face of Mount King George identifies the Royal Group.

You may have noticed the apparent ease of **descending** the southwest-facing slopes beneath the summit. They converge into a gully at the bottom. Coarse rubble with stretches of slabs comprises this descent and much variation is possible. With luck you will strike a well-beaten trail at tree line leading around the base of the peak. When appropriate, simply shortcut through the forest again to reach Elbow trail.

Opposite: The approach view showing ascent and descent routes.

MOUNT HOOD 2903 m

Difficulty Moderate scrambling via west slopes and south ridge
Round trip time 6-10 hours
Height gain 1300 m
Map 82 J/11 Kananaskis Lakes

Mount Hood is one of the less conspicuous peaks in Kananaskis' Opal Range. Despite the lack of technical difficulty, it is not a high-traffic mountain. The bushy approach discourages the casual wanderer, and because it is not evident from the road it does not attract as much interest. Most Opal Range summits require roped climbing, but this is one of the few viable scrambles of the group. Try from late June on.

Drive to King Creek, 52.5 km south of the Trans-Canada Highway on Kananaskis Trail (Highway 40).

The approach to Mount Hood can be as involved as the actual climb. Although you can reach the peak via Hood Creek farther north, it is preferable and less problematic to approach from King Creek, despite additional distance.

Follow the trail through King Creek Canyon. Heavy rains in 1995 washed out the many bridges, so depending on when they're rebuilt, you may get your feet wet. When the stream forks, follow the left branch that leads north below steep, grassy avalanche-prone hillsides, the realm of bighorn sheep and the occasional grizzly. Since the 1995 washouts, this part is tougher, but there may be a sheep trail higher up on the east side of the creek. Continue up-valley to the headwaters to gain the broad saddle between Mount Hood and a long unnamed ridge to the west.

From the saddle, turn right and scramble up a gully to the col between Mounts Hood and Brock. The rubble and the steeply-dipping, shattered rock on Hood's south ridge are typical of most south ridges in the Opals. All peaks here have the same pronounced tilt, but some peaks are harder than others. Fortunately, this is not one of them. Continue up the ridge to the top. **Return** via your ascent route.

Sir H. L. A. Hood was rear admiral and commander of the ship Invincible, which was sunk at the Battle of Jutland.

Ascent route showing G gully, C col and south ridge to summit.
Photo: Gillean Daffern.

KANANASKIS LAKES AREA

Mount Warspite	2850 m	difficult	p. 160
Mount Indefatigable	2670 m	difficult	p. 162
Mount Northover	3003 m	difficult	p. 165
Mount Sarrail	3174 m	easy	p. 167
Warrior Mountain	2973 m	easy	p. 168
Mount Cordonnier	3021 m	easy	p. 169
Mount Fox	2973 m	difficult	p. 170

This small but spectacular area lies within the confines of Peter Lougheed Provincial Park.

Situated at the south end of Kananaskis Valley and encompassing several high peaks, this locale records considerably heavier precipitation than areas farther north such as Canmore. Because of this greater precipitation, these scrambles are typically mid to late summer outings. While Fox, Warspite, Indefatigable and, to a lesser degree, Sarrail are done as day trips, the remaining three summits are located in the backcountry around Aster Lake and are overnight trips.

Ever since the first edition of *The Kananaskis Country Trail Guide* some 20 years ago, Aster Lake has continued to attract more backpackers and mountaineers seeking unspoiled wilderness. There is significant glaciation on Mount Joffre, the highest peak in the area. Mount Joffre has long been a lure to mountaineers and, while not particularly difficult, the need to ascend this fairly extensive glacier along with a moderately angled ice/snow slope prevents its inclusion as a scramble. Several other summits in the area are worthwhile

scrambling objectives, though, and as a total backcountry experience, these outings have their own unique appeal.

While Mount Indefatigable uses a maintained trail, the path to Aster Lake has been left unmaintained to limit overuse and is subsequently more rugged. An overnight permit must be purchased at a visitor centre, a quota has been set and random camping is not allowed. Food storage lockers are provided at the campsite. Please practise "no trace" camping in these pristine surroundings and keep it as untouched as possible for others to enjoy, too. To some folks, camping is synonymous with campfires, however, even if you could find enough wood, fires are NOT permitted at Aster Lake. That is precisely why so little environmental degradation is evident.

Not surprisingly, grizzlies sometimes pass through the Kananaskis and Aster lakes area. Visitors should observe and follow all precautions for travelling in bear country. Make noise, stay alert, keep a clean camp and store your food in the lockers provided at Aster Lake. Read the section on "Hazards" in the front of this book.

View toward the Royal Group from Mount Northover.

Access Kananaskis Lakes and Peter Lougheed Provincial Park are reached by Kananaskis Trail (Highway 40), which leaves the Trans-Canada Highway 65 km west of Calgary and runs southwest for some 52 km. Alternatively, you can follow the gravelled Smith-Dorrien Trail/Spray Lakes Road that begins in Canmore and runs south for some 60 km to intersect Kananaskis Trail.

Aster Lake Trail

To reach Aster Lake drive to the far (southeast) end of Upper Kananaskis Lake parking lot in Peter Lougheed Provincial Park. The lakeshore trail begins here; the approach is as follows.

Walk south along the lakeshore trail for about 1.5 hours passing Rawson Lake

trail. Watch for a well-used branch diverging left. This trail to Aster Lake is unimproved and unmarked. The only sign nearby shows the lakeshore trail continuing on beyond this spur. Take this spur—it enters a small open meadow immediately, then continues to Hidden Lake and along the east (left) shore to the southern end.

Until mid or late August, the water level in Hidden Lake, en route to Aster Lake, is too high to permit shoreline walking. Then you must follow a rough trail through the woods, but owing to deadfall, this route takes two or three times longer than the pleasant 30 minute stroll along the shoreline. Then, a mere 30 minutes of grassy shoreline walking will see you around the pond.

Past Hidden Lake the path enters mature forest and the flat section ends. From this point, elevation gain is rapid as you crawl under and over rotting fallen logs, then slog across a scree slope below the northwest outlier of Mount Sarrail. After the trail levels out above cliffs and you've passed a high waterfall, you'll see the remnant northwest glacier of Mount Sarrail above, global warming notwithstanding. Undulating ribs of limestone extend down from the west ridge of Mount Sarrail right to trailside and the west ridge is visible on the skyline. This is a good spot to go up if you're ascending Mount Sarrail. Otherwise, pass a seasonal pond, whereupon larch forest leads to open alpine at Aster Lake.

A trail continues up and over a series of ridges, reaching the lake in less than an hour. A seasonal ranger MAY be stationed in the cabin at Foch Creek. This is tucked just off the trail (to the left) before Aster Lake. However, scramblers visiting Aster Lake should note that it is back-country and in the event of an accident or emergency, rescue assistance is considerably farther away than more heavily-visited "roadside" ascents.

Facilities Boulton Creek Trading Post near Kananaskis Lakes has a store and cafe. For a wider selection, Canmore is your best bet, although Fortress Junction offers a gas station with a small store. Limited groceries are also available at Mount Kidd RV Park and in Kananaskis Village, farther north on Kananaskis Trail. There are absolutely NO facilities at Aster Lake.

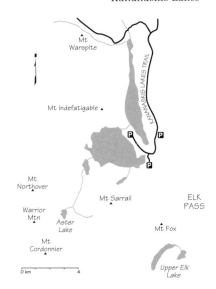

Accommodation Drive-in campgrounds are found at Kananaskis Lakes. These are popular and tend to fill up quickly. Farther north on Kananaskis Trail are Mount Kidd RV Park and several hotels in Kananaskis Village. Canmore is your other alternative.

Information The Kananaskis Visitor Centre is located in Peter Lougheed Provincial Park.

Emergency Park Rangers (and RCMP) are stationed at Boundary Ranger Station at Ribbon Creek on Kananaskis Trail, which also serves as the Emergency Services Centre. A seasonal ranger may be in residence at Aster Lake.

MOUNT WARSPITE 2850 m

Difficulty Difficult scrambling, exposure, loose rock, routefinding and possible steep snow slopes; a climber's scramble
Round trip time 8-12 hours
Height gain 1160 m
Map 82 J/11 Kananaskis Lakes

Mount Warspite is occasionally ascended as the finale by climbers when traversing from either Mount Indefatigable or nearby Mount Invincible, with the described route being used for descent. As the route ascends a long, steep, north-facing slope, unless free of snow it will require step-kicking and perhaps crampons. In these conditions, which may well persist into late July or August, it is not simply a scramble but is a mountaineering climb. Rock scramblers should then avoid it. Unlike nearby more popular peaks with well-travelled trade routes, you will probably be alone on Mount Warspite. Parties should be competent in routefinding, scrambling up loose rock and using an ice axe. You'll be amply rewarded with a fine view of the Smith-Dorrien Valley, Haig Glacier and Elk Pass. Although near a road, this trip imparts a feeling of isolation. Try from about late July on. Helmet and ice axe recommended.

Drive to Black Prince Cirque parking lot on Smith-Dorrien Trail/Spray Lakes Road, 11.7 km south of the Burstall parking lot.

From the parking lot, follow the wide interpretive trail to Warspite Lake. Upon reaching the lake, search around to find a good trail along the right (west) side of the lake. Once you find this unmaintained

Mount Warspite as seen on approach.
C col, S summit.

path, it leads through forest and up onto open avalanche slopes to the right of the Warspite Cascades. These falls tumble from the hanging valley below Mounts Warspite and Black Prince. Unless you enjoy heavy bushwhacking, don't circle around the left side of the lake. (I learned this after a mere two visits!)

Once you reach the hanging valley, hike past pretty little larch meadows and cross oodles of rock debris toward the brooding north end of Mount Warspite. Notice that below the peak, a traverse up steep slopes rising from left to right above the first cliff band leads to a high col (257157) at the northwest end of the objective. This col is the key to the ascent. Ideally, snow will have melted back and scramblers will be able to stick to rock or rubble. Those proficient at step-kicking and use of an ice axe will probably choose the snow. Note that failure to self-arrest a slip here would launch you over cliffs. Similarly, hugging close under the face exposes you to occasional rockfall (helmet). As you gain height, tiny Black Prince tarns under Mount Black Prince appear. Finally, the slope eases and the col gives you a chance to take a breather while contemplating the remaining 100+ m elevation.

This west side of the mountain is comprised of steep walls and rocky towers above rubbly slopes and short rock bands. Head directly up the northwest corner of the peak from the ridge, climbing a steep step left of a chimney. There is significant exposure on your left for a couple of moves and the rock is loose. Caution is required. Continue up treadmill rubble and a couple of short rock steps as you approach two steep towers above. Near the base of these towers, traverse right, going below a high, narrow

Steep terrain on Warspite's northwest corner.

chimney to a wide, easy slope of scree and small slabs. Grunt up this, angling left near the top. A crumbly bit of ridge leads quickly to the shattered summit.

Mount Warspite is connected to Mount Invincible by a long ridge trending southeast that continues on to Mount Indefatigable. The section from Warspite to Invincible is within the realm of any competent scrambler. From Mount Invincible, with a bit of diligence, you can reach Gypsum Mine road, which winds up the treed hillside northeast of that peak. With a bit of routefinding one can also descend east from this connecting ridge near either the two bumps between Warspite and Invincible and drop down to the valley. Be prepared to wade Smith-Dorrien Creek. This adventurous extension makes for a long day, which leaves you far from your vehicle. Most people will probably be content to **return** the same way via Black Prince Cirque. Like nearby peaks, Warspite was yet another ship involved in the Battle of Jutland in World War I.

MOUNT INDEFATIGABLE 2670 m

Difficulty A pleasant hike to the south peak; north summit and traverse involve moderate scrambling with brief exposure
Round trip time 4-5 hours for south peak; 5-7 hours for entire north to south traverse
Height gain 1000 m
Map 82 J/11 Kananaskis Lakes

In a superb setting above Kananaskis Lakes, this strangely-named peak lends itself well to a traverse in either direction. North to south is easier and preferable. Right from the beginning the view is expansive as you rise along an airy precipice overlooking Upper and Lower Kananaskis Lakes. Ascending either summit is popular and well worth the effort. Try from late June on.

Park at North Interlakes parking lot at the far end of Kananaskis Trail in Peter Lougheed Provincial Park.

South Peak

From North Interlakes parking lot, walk along the gravel lakeshore trail and across the dam. Almost immediately you should branch off to the right on Mount Indefatigable hiking trail. After passing through shady forest, this popular path quickly gains the open escarpment along the east side of the mountain. To ascend the south peak, watch for a well-used trail

diverging left about one hour along Mount Indefatigable hiking trail. This fork is right before a sign showing that the hiking path continues directly ahead. Follow this side trail as it climbs steadily up east-facing slopes of meadow followed by talus as it heads toward the south summit and a repeater tower above.

The attraction of an easily-attained summit draws many people away from the comfortable grade of the hiking trail, so the top can be a busy spot on a sunny day. Enjoy the view, but expect company. A short jaunt along the ridge usually provides more elbow room.

Typical parking lot view of south peak. S south summit.

A well-trodden route leads to the North Peak.

North Peak

To ascend the north peak, continue farther up the Mount Indefatigable hiking trail. Once you pry yourself from the strategically-set viewing bench, continue straight ahead on a well-used path. The trail enters larch forest and in about 25 minutes emerges unexpectedly at a beautiful alpine tarn high on the east side of the peak (303123).

Continue past this tarn and wander up grassy, flowered meadows to the east ridge, which leads directly to the north peak, the true summit. The route is becoming popular and a clearly visible path has now been beaten into the dirt and rubble along the way.

As you ascend, keep just left of the ridge to get into a broad gully, which you scramble up for the final 50 m. Although not difficult, this is the crux. The rock is notably loose for this final bit and dislodges easily so if you value your head, you probably won't want to be below anyone else here, even with a helmet. On one ascent, I was blissfully unaware of a localized thunderstorm brewing on the west side of the peak. I thought I was toast when lightning suddenly struck the cairn some 50 m above, causing me to beat a frantic, but temporary, retreat.

The summit panorama is truly magnificent, but the head-on perspective of the ridge connecting to the south peak suggests difficulties. A good part of the traverse, however, is mainly hiking, and takes about half an hour to the south peak. The rock is firm where needed and a few of the exposed sections can be skirted on scree on the west (right) side. One fatality has occurred here, apparently owing to a fall over the exposed east side, so use caution. When through admiring the Royal Group, glaciated Mount Joffre and the Opal Range, walk south for about 200 m past the tower to an obvious path descending the east side. This rejoins the Mount Indefatigable hiking trail.

Traversing from the south to north peak.

MOUNT NORTHOVER 3003 m

Difficulty Difficult scrambling with severe exposure; a climber's scramble
Round trip time 5-7 hours from Aster Lake outlet
Height gain 700 m from Aster Lake
Map 82 J/11 Kananaskis Lakes

Mount Northover is probably the most challenging scramble near Aster Lake. It is similar in character to the airy south ridge of Mount Smuts and about as demanding. While many parties would appreciate the security of a rope and some protection, those with solid rock-scrambling or climbing skills and comfortable with exposure will find this an exciting route when it is dry. It is possible to traverse the mountain, too, but an ice axe may be needed for snow patches. Apart from falling off, there is no quick way down from this south ridge. Don't confuse this serious scramble with the popular Aster Lake to Three Isle Lake hiking route: It is also called Northover Ridge, but travels below the peak along the southwest side.

From the outlet of Aster Lake, hike around to the gravel flats and braided outwash streams at the opposite side of the lake. This is near the south (left) end of Mount Northover. The ascent ridge is clearly visible as you approach and it looks daunting. Clamber easily to the ridge and away you go.

Initially the undertaking is simply good fun until you reach a steeply tilted slab, the first significant challenge. You can detour along the left side on small ledges and cracks rather than ascend it directly, but it is still exposed. The route then eases again, but the most intimidating part is yet to come.

The difficult south ridge route of Northover.

A small rise right before the summit is a logical spot to stop and study the crux. At this point, a fabulous view of glaciated Mount Joffre, behind you, is a temporary escape from reality. A steep, slabby wall guards the summit, and the only possibilities appear to be a few high-angle cracks. The steep, obvious crack directly beneath the top appears overhanging and is NOT the best choice. I started up a narrower crack to the left, then moved left again aiming for the lowest angled, least-slabby area. The hardest bit is maybe 6-8 m high, but the rock is solid. Note well, however, that a slip would result in a deadly plummet completely off the ridge. Conditions must be dry: use care. Descending this section would likely require a rope.

Assuming you've made it, breathe deeply, relax and enjoy a rest on top before checking out the north ridge **descent**. In late summer there should be little if any snow on it. While much shorter, it is still steep and notably looser than the south ridge. If snowy, it could require a rappel. Climb down carefully and when feasible angle left (west) across short slabs to scree slopes. The rounded scree ridge west is the Northover Ridge hiking trail that connects Three Isle and

Close-up of the finale. C crux.

Aster lakes. Turn left and go home—well, back to camp, anyway.

People have died on this mountain. It is a serious scramble with no room for mistakes as you are a long way from help. Unless conditions are ideal (bare and dry with good weather), consider a less-committing ascent in the area.

Lieutenant A. W. Northover was a member of the Canadian Expeditionary Force.

Descent route from Northover Ridge hiking trail. Ascent route is beyond right skyline.

MOUNT SARRAIL 3174 m

Difficulty Easy scrambling, mild exposure
Round trip time A long day from Upper Kananaskis Lake parking lot; 5-7 hours from Aster Lake
Height gain 1475 m
Map 82 J/11 Kananaskis Lakes

Mount Sarrail's northeast escarpment is the most commonly seen aspect, glowering far above Upper Kananaskis Lake. This face presents a forbidding proposition. By comparison, the west ridge is a kinder, gentler side and is accessible from the currently unmaintained Aster Lake trail. When free of snow, most of the west ridge is little more than a steep hike. Although feasible as a long day trip, many parties camp near Aster Lake and take two days.

The west ridge from near Aster Lake.

The simplest way to gain the west ridge of Mount Sarrail is right near the undulating ribs that extend down to trailside. (See Aster Lake trail description.) You can also head up anywhere near the seasonal pond a little farther along, although the scree up to the ridge from there is tediously loose.

The ridge angle is moderate with much pleasant hiking and a wonderful view of Mount King George ruling the Royal Group to the west. Toward the top are short, exposed stretches of slab and caution is also required where the small, steep pocket glacier abuts the ridge on the left. Stick to the rock ridge here.

As you reach the summit, stay well back from the cornice that often overhangs the vertical northeast face. If you squint carefully, the smokestack-shaped mountain way off to the west-southwest is Farnham Tower in the Purcell Range of British Columbia. Nearby is adjacent Mount Foch, apparently first ascended by Swiss guide Walter Feuz with client Katie Gardiner, after descending to the col. How the duo accomplished this some 60 years ago is not clear, as massive down-sloping slabs overlain with ball-bearing rubble must be negotiated. More than a few hopeful parties since have considered it unfeasible.

Place Names of the Canadian Alps by Boles, Laurilla and Putnam, explains that General Sarrail was a commander at Verdun. He later held a more peaceful position as high commissioner to Syria.

WARRIOR MOUNTAIN 2973 m

Difficulty A mountaineering scramble
requiring a short glacier crossing, but
otherwise easy
Round trip time 5+ hours from Aster
Lake outlet
Height gain 630 m
Map 82 J/11 Kananaskis Lakes

Warrior Mountain has a highway-width
scree slope to its summit and the ridge
over to Mount Cordonnier is only slightly
more difficult. There is just one obstacle:
A very small section of remnant glacier
lies along the east side of the two peaks.
This puts it into the realm of a mountaineering scramble. For those that are familiar with straightforward glacier travel,
this brief section will be no obstacle at all.
Far below these summits is Joffre Creek
and recently-created Height of the
Rockies Provincial Park. Alternatively, a
miserable and less direct tramp over
much morainal debris and boulders
avoids the glacier crossing entirely. Take
an ice axe, and perhaps crampons and a
rope, depending on route choice.

If you are properly prepared, cross the
short bit of glacier at the base of Warrior,
heading straight toward the low point of
the Warrior/Cordonnier ridge close to
Warrior's summit. Old moraines and rubble lead to this remnant glacier—more
like a snowfield now—and it takes 30
minutes to cross. Personally, I doubt if
there are any crevasses. Probing with a
long pole revealed none on the straight
line I chose, but this is certainly no guarantee. Normal glacier travel precautions
dictate roping up, so I recommend doing
just that.

Once you're back onto the rock, hike to
the top in less than an hour. In contrast to
the tamer east aspect, the west side of the

mountain drops abruptly to Joffre Creek
1500 m below. Small tarns at timberline
nestle against flanks of Shatch Mountain
immediately south, while to the northeast you can see clear across Kananaskis
Lakes to the serrated Opal Range. Not
surprisingly, it is Mount King George and
his Royal companions that are most
humbling. Waka Nambe, the impressive
rock spire rising skyward just west, takes
on an entirely different shape here compared to the overhanging tower seen
from Aster Lake.

Warrior Mountain and the glacier from Aster Lake.

MOUNT CORDONNIER 3021 m

Difficulty Easy scramble, brief exposure
Ascent time 1.5 hours from the top of
Warrior Mountain
Height gain 250 m from Warrior Ridge;
700 m from Aster Lake

To continue to Mount Cordonnier from Warrior Mountain, just follow the connecting ridge. At one spot it narrows where it crosses the top of a steep 20 m-high slab angling down to Mangin Glacier. Farther on, past a chockstone, again expect slight exposure but no real difficulties. If conditions are dry, anyone with glacier experience will probably not even notice these minor interruptions. The only surprise is that the summit is a wee bit farther away than you'd expected.

The entire route up Mangin Glacier to Mount Joffre is readily studied from Cordonnier. Below you to the south are the seldom-visited larch meadows spread about Sylvan Pass. It is possible to descend (or ascend) Cordonnier without crossing any glacier via a steep north-facing snow slope at 255015 where the ridge begins to rise and curve right. Expect miserable trudging over great masses of knee-wrenching debris and boulders. These were carelessly strewn about by Mangin Glacier as it beat a hasty retreat. Most peaks in Kananaskis commemorate World War I military leaders or ships, as does this one: Emilien Victor Cordonnier was a French general.

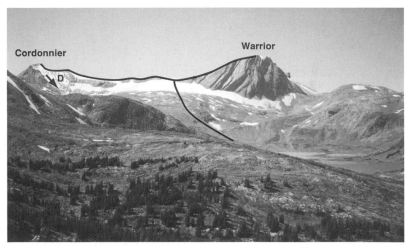

Aster Lake view of the peaks. D optional descent.

169

MOUNT FOX 2973 m

Difficulty Difficult, committing, exposed scramble
Round trip time 7-12 hours
Height gain 1240 m
Map 82 J/11 Kananaskis Lakes

Mount Fox grants a fabulous view of the Kananaskis Lakes and Elk Pass and will appeal to competent scramblers. Almost half the elevation gain requires hands-on rock scrambling and there is no quick way off. Although not as technically difficult as Mount Smuts, loose rock and the overall length make this route at least as serious. With good weather it is suitable for experienced, capable parties. Try from July on if the east ridge is snowfree. This ridge is visible from the highway by King Creek, appearing as an uninterrupted line angled at 40° from Elk Pass to the summit. An ice axe is useful.

Approaching the exciting east ridge of Mount Fox. P pinnacles. Frozen Lake to left.

Drive to Elk Pass trailhead on Kananaskis Trail in Peter Lougheed Provincial Park.

You can mountain bike most of the 5.8 km to West Elk Pass. From the parking lot the trail goes up over a ridge under the powerline, then descends to Fox Creek. Turn right at the junction after the bridge over Fox Creek and follow the trail alongside the creek as it continues south. The trail reaches an open boggy area (one hour from car) and then continues straight ahead rising over a slight hill. Five min-

utes farther, pass a picnic table, and ignore the ski trail branching right. Continue ahead, south, on the footpath that in minutes heads gently right into forest and soon reaches the information sign at the Elk Lakes Provincial Park entrance. Beware of porcupines at Elk Pass that may chew bike panniers, tires, etc.

From the information board start out on the path "Upper Elk Lake via Fox Lake," then diverge right and continue on Frozen Lake trail crossing boggy meadows and following the provincial

On the east ridge of Mount Fox.

boundary cutline directly toward Mount Fox. You'll pass concrete marker M2 delineating the B.C./Alberta border, after which the trail rises steeply to reach Frozen Lake. Allow two hours on foot from car to lake.

Frozen Lake is a pristine and lovely pond, especially if it has thawed. You'll probably appreciate a breather once you reach its peaceful shoreline. To ascend Mount Fox, hike north along the shore and up the steep open hillside to gain the east ridge. Stands of alpine larch quickly give way to checked and shattered grey limestone, terrain not unfamiliar to those who have ascended other Kananaskis peaks.

The angle is surprisingly constant, but you can sometimes avoid occasional steeper sections of the ridge by climbing left or right. While the route is not especially narrow, a slip would still be deadly and care is required throughout. You should watch the weather; descending this ridge is not much faster.

The crux awaits near the top. Cruxes are almost never at the beginning. Upon reaching a couple of pinnacles you must climb through a chimney in the larger one. It looks worse than it is, but the rock is extremely loose in places. Once past here, just plod up scree to the top.

The summit is spacious and affords a magnificent view in all directions. Kananaskis Lakes, Mount Sir Douglas and Haig Glacier look particularly fine. Notice that the west slope is scree to the basin near timberline. Although you could descend this side to reach Upper Elk Lake, it is hard to imagine circumstances dire enough to justify it. For a view of Lower Elk Lake you can scramble over to the sub-peak to the south in 20 minutes. It is not just a walk, though. One brief, exposed place rivals any part of the ascent route.

Return the same way. Although it is not much harder to descend the ridge, it is time-consuming. Wet rock would make it downright unpleasant. If you lose the trail below Frozen Lake, remember, the boundary cutline runs directly up the east ridge of Mount Fox and you should head that direction to get on track.

THE HIGHWOOD

Mount Tyrwhitt	2874 m	moderate	p. 174
Mount Pocaterra	2934 m	moderate	p. 176
Storm Mountain	3092 m	moderate	p. 177
Mount Storelk	2867 m	difficult	p. 178
Mount Rae	3218 m	moderate	p. 180
Mount Arethusa	2912 m	difficult	p. 182
Mist Mountain	3140 m	moderate	p. 184

Peaks in this chapter are found adjacent to a 5 km-long section of Kananaskis Trail (Highway 40) running southeast from Highwood Pass in Kananaskis Country toward Highwood Junction.

The usual Rockies Front Range topography is evident here; long limestone ridges aligned northwest-southeast. If one looks back millions of years, these limestone peaks were once horizontal layers of differing sediments under a great sea. The sediments had been collecting for perhaps 1.5 billion years. Gradually, two crustal plates collided, and over some 75 million years, slowly pushed the sediments up into waves of rock. This is a simple explanation of how the Canadian Rockies were formed. In this area, a noteworthy geological movement called the "Lewis Thrust" occurred and this event further uplifted and tilted peaks through here. The strata of these peaks have been so tilted by compressional forces that many now stand almost vertical.

With such steeply angled strata, one frequently finds faces that are steep on the west side and sometimes overhanging on the east. Erosion has played an important role in shaping these peaks, too. Pinnacles are sometimes encoun-

tered along seemingly plausible routes, formed by a result of weathering away of softer shales sandwiched between harder rock layers. This can add unexpected challenges to route shortcuts and variations. The ridgelike nature of the ranges, however, often allows relatively straightforward travel along the spine of the uplift once upon it.

The highest peak around Highwood is Mount Rae (3218 m). Mount Rae along with nearby Mount Tyrwhitt see most of the foot traffic. The Highwood area is comparatively dry, although snow tends to linger around Highwood Pass well into July. Underbrush is virtually absent and, given the relatively high roadside elevation, these ascents are tailor-made to our instant gratification society—quick and rewarding! Similarly, a late September ascent in this area is a real treat with golden larch trees in abundance. In a dry year, ascents are possible into November, long after the crowds have retreated indoors.

The abundance of small, meadowy alpine valleys and cirques seems to have a definite attraction for grizzly bears, too. Over the years, many have been trapped and collared for research projects. It is not uncommon for hikers to encounter these beasts on occasion and in fact, sometimes specific trails may be closed temporarily by authorities if warranted. Even the visitor driving through in early evening may see a bear wandering and browsing along the roadside. Ptarmigan and Tyrwhitt cirques in particular seem to have a high level of bear appeal. Be sure to make noise as you walk.

Access Highwood Pass is reached through Kananaskis Valley via Kananaskis Trail (Highway 40) starting 65 km west of Calgary. This road continues southeast reaching Longview and eventually Highway 2 south of Calgary. Highwood Pass is closed each year from Dec. 1 to June 15 from Peter Lougheed Park to Highwood Junction.

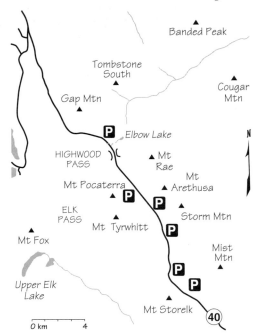

Accommodation Camping is available (if you arrive early!) at Kananaskis Lakes and farther north at Mount Kidd RV Park. Kananaskis Village has several hotels and nearby Ribbon Creek Hostel, while to the east the Longview area offers motels and camping.

Information is available at Kananaskis Visitor Centre in Peter Lougheed Provincial Park. A park ranger is stationed at Highwood Junction on a seasonal basis; others are found at Boundary Ranger Station in Kananaskis Valley. RCMP are in Canmore and Turner Valley.

Facilities Limited supplies are available at Boulton Creek near Kananaskis Lakes, at Fortress Junction, Mount Kidd RV Park, Kananaskis Village by Ribbon Creek and at Highwood Junction. Otherwise, visit either Longview or Canmore.

MOUNT TYRWHITT 2874 m

Difficulty A moderate scree/slab
scramble via east side
Round trip time 4-7 hours
Allow 1-2 hours up from Grizzly Pass
Height gain 650 m
Map 82 J/11 Kananaskis Lakes

Mount Tyrwhitt offers an easy approach, an
interesting scramble and minimal elevation gain. The starting point in delicate larch
meadows is an inspiring beginning. In autumn, brilliant golden larches make the
approach especially scenic. This ascent is
very popular, and rightly so. The views is

nothing short of outstanding. Available
options include a return loop or a ridge
traverse to a higher unnamed peak, depending on your level of energy. Please
walk softly through the meadows as this
fragile alpine terrain is easily damaged.
Years pass before plant life recovers from
big boots, so please use existing trails to
reduce your impact. Two things are desir-
able for this ascent: Clear weather so you
can enjoy the panorama and a helmet for
the steep rubble slope on return. Try from
July on.

Drive to Highwood Meadows parking lot
at Highwood Pass on Kananaskis Trail
(Highway 40). **Note:** Road closed Dec. 1
to June 15.

The photogenic rock arch on the east ridge.

From the parking lot start on the interpretive trail and head toward the first platform. Just before this path heads right
(two minutes maximum), branch left toward a draw to follow a trail past a
sinkhole and a big boulder on the right. A
beaten trail then leads you through forest
and up over a ridge before descending to
a small pond. Continue on the trail to the
open basin of Pocaterra Cirque, the headwaters of Pocaterra Creek's southwest
fork. An obvious path to the left leads up
and traverses scree slopes toward Grizzly col, the low saddle on the left (east)
side of the objective. The col separates
Mount Tyrwhitt from an unnamed point
immediately east, but is unmarked on
map 82 J/11. This saddle is an ideal place
to pause before trudging up the remaining 250 m to the top.

Grizzly col sits squarely atop the
Lewis Thrust, a geological event that
pushed massive sheets of older Rundle
limestone from the west over younger
and more easily eroded shales and
sandstones. Running northwest to
southeast, the fault line extends from

Mount Tyrwhitt ascent route. Mount Pocaterra is farther right. G Grizzly col, A arch.

Glacier Park in the United States north to Mount Kidd. This explains the abrupt transition between gentler shale slopes east of the col versus higher-angled grey limestone on Tyrwhitt.

About halfway up, close to the ridge, is the unique 5 m-high window formed by a rock arch. Resembling an inverted wishbone, it nicely frames multi-pinnacled Mount Elpoca to the north. If you look closely, this arch is visible from the highway at a point just northwest of Highwood Pass.

The view from the top is spectacular toward Kananaskis Lakes and Mount Joffre, and you really have to see it for yourself. If you find the outing too short,

two extensions are available. You can continue to Mount Pocaterra or for a longer, more scenic return, traverse the ridge northeast of Grizzly col back to your car. This traverse does involve a fair bit more elevation gain and loss. At one point you may have to descend some distance on the right to overcome a steepish, downsloping rock band, then regain much elevation. Farther along, you pass thin coal seams, representative of massive beds lying south in Crowsnest and Elkford. From the last high point above the parking lot, descend north and return to your vehicle. Sir R. Y. Tyrwhitt was the leader of the British destroyer flotillas during World War I.

Approaching the summit of Mount Pocaterra amid spectacular scenery.
Mount King George at far left, Mount Sir Douglas at far right.

MOUNT POCATERRA 2934 m

Difficulty Moderate scrambling with exposure
Round trip time Allow 3-4 hours from Mount Tyrwhitt
Map 82 J/11 Kananaskis Lakes (unmarked at 395070)

Mount Pocaterra is an unofficial name for a higher unnamed peak to the north at 395070 that is connected to Tyrwhitt by a spectacular exposed-looking ridge. Despite its appearance, you can scramble the length of this ridge without great difficulty. This does require quite a loss of elevation to a low point, then you must steadily regain every bit and even more. Once you leave Tyrwhitt, much of the first half or more is easy going along the crest, although the drop on the east is terrific. Only toward the finish does it become a bit more challenging. The few exposed spots can usually be avoided by dropping down on the west side; a towering gendarme also requires scrambling down on the left.

The second of the two summits appears to be marginally higher. As of 1997, both had a register and the mountain had seen few ascents. If you're looking for a longer outing offering an incredible view the entire way, this extension will do it. Note that no easy descent exists down the east side to Pocaterra Cirque. You must **return** via the ridge. The west slopes, though easy scree, would leave you in Elk Valley, a substantial distance from the road and your car.

STORM MOUNTAIN 3092 m

Difficulty A moderate scramble via southwest slopes
Round trip time 4-6 hours
Height gain 1050 m
Map 82 J/10 Mount Rae

Storm Mountain is a popular outing with a short, easy approach through larch meadows. A high starting point in the dry eastern Front Ranges eliminates bushwhacking or plodding through forest to attain the summit. Try from July on.

Park at Lost Lemon Mine information sign, 4.4 km south of Highwood Meadows parking lot on Kananaskis Trail (Highway 40). **Note**: Road closed Dec. 1 to June 15.

Two valleys access the peak. The narrower valley 0.5 km north of the parking area (455045) is where the descent route emerges, but the recommended approach enters the next valley south (460042) and offers the easiest route up. From the highway pull-off by the Lost Lemon Mine sign, follow the left side of the drainage (cairn). Then, at the last bit of meadow, ascend the scree slope on your left to the start of the ridge.

From the high point at the south end of the ridge (461052) you should immediately descend to a wide ledge 5 m lower on the east side. This conveniently avoids the narrow, scary crest. Still, this shaded ledge exposes you to an airy drop on the east side and if snowy, as it is sometimes, can be serious going. It is best when bone dry. Once you get past the low point, scramble back up to the ridge crest and to the top. There is a fine view to the west of Mount King George (3422 m),

the monarch of the Royal Group and Mount Sir Douglas (3406 m) rising skyward to the northwest.

For a rapid **descent** I used the west ridge, crossing a tricky, but short, connecting ridge across a notch. Others have descended from right below the notch, too. The west ridge leads to scree and slabs that take you quickly down to valley meadows. As you exit this valley a good trail heads left, traverses open slopes above tree line back toward the approach valley, then descends to the road.

Geologist Dr. George Dawson, a topographical surveyor and director of the Geological Survey of Canada, named the peak for storm clouds observed on the summit.

Photo: Gillean Daffern.

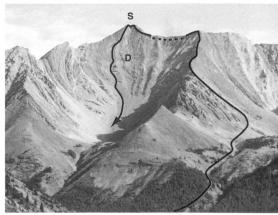

Storm Mountain ascent and descent routes. Route follows a ledge below ridge on east side. S Storm Mountain, D descent route.

MOUNT STORELK 2867 m

Difficulty Difficult scrambling with exposure; routefinding required
Round trip time 6-8 hours
Height gain 915 m
Map 82 J/10 Mount Rae

Mount Storelk is the next summit south of Mount Tyrwhitt on the long ridge known as the Elk Range. As of 1998, this peak had seen very few ascents despite ready access from the road. The suggested route involves sections of steep, exposed scrambling and your routefinding ability will largely dictate just how much fun or fear you'll experience. On a clear day, the summit view of Elk and Kananaskis lakes areas is magnificent. In autumn, when larches flaunt their golden splendour, this outing is a fine getaway from crowds at Mounts Rae and Tyrwhitt. Dry conditions are required for this ascent; try from July on.

Ascent route as seen from the road.

Drive 6.5 km east of Highwood Meadows at Highwood Pass and park on the side of the road. The peak and much of the route is visible at km 5.5. **Note:** Highwood Pass is closed from Dec. 1 to June 15th.

Below and east of Storelk's summit lies a small basin cradled between two east-trending ridges. An obvious drainage empties this cirque toward unseen Highwood River. The right hand of these two ridges rises directly to the summit, but is definitely too steep for scrambling.

However, the left-hand ridge on the south side of the basin reclines at a more reasonable angle. Your goal then, if you decide to accept it, is to hike into this basin, gain this easier ridge and follow it to the top.

Head off through the woods toward the drainage (compass bearing helpful). A short way in, circumvent a small pond, then descend to wade or hop Highwood River. High banks border the river in places here; you should find an animal trail at one of the better crossing points.

Close-up of ridge above basin.
Route shown is inexact.

Continue west until you reach the afore-mentioned drainage, which flows well into autumn, then find a good animal trail above it on the left side that leads you into the pretty, larch-filled cirque. More animal trails continue up and left passing through brief meadows to gain the the the open saddle at the low end of the ascent ridge. Grassy south-facing slopes nearby are ideal for resting and to scope out potential ascent routes ahead. The ridge probably looks steeper than you expected.

There is no advantage in following the crest of the lower part of the ridge as the steeper section that follows requires that you be left of the crest anyway. We traversed diagonally across broken rock and short slabs to gain a narrow gully that breaks through the steepest terrain. This is the first weakness left of the ridge crest. This particular gully then turns right and after further steep scrambling, you should reach easier angled rock partially overlain with rubble. This allows you to traverse right and then scramble directly up the crest to the spine of the peak. Many variations are possible but remember, easy-looking parts will be harder

than expected; steep parts may be scary or impossible. The rock is generally sound, but the descent is via the same route, so note your route well, whether it be to retrace it or to avoid it entirely!

Once you top out, turn right and scramble/hike north along the ridge to Storelk's summit some 25-30 minutes away. As you climbed from the cirque, the view of Highwood Valley continued to improve but now the entire Elk Valley, too, unfurls at your feet. And see how disgustingly easy this ascent would be from the west—a mere walk-up! North of the summit, the ridge continues north in a lazy arc to far-off Mount Tyrwhitt. Popular peaks like Mist and Storm are close by, while to the west lie peaks of the Italian Group and Mount Joffre, which you may not even recognize from this angle. Just look for the Petain Glacier around its flanks. When you've found it and have eaten all your goodies, **return** the same way—that is, unless you stumble upon a better descent!

Mount Storelk is so named because it lies between Storm Creek and Elk River.

MOUNT RAE 3218 m

Difficulty A moderate scramble via south slopes and ridge
Round trip time 5-9 hours
Height gain 1000 m
Map 82 J/10 Mount Rae

The foreshortened roadside view of Mount Rae renders it neither striking nor beautiful. Nonetheless, at 3218 m, it is one of the highest peaks in either the Front Ranges or the Kananaskis region. Combined with the easy approach, its height guarantees it a popular ascent, regardless of the scree involved. Narrow sections of the ridge from the col to the summit are dangerous if snow remains and accidents have occurred in the past. Carry an ice axe; try from about July on. **Note:** Gaining the once-popular SSE Ridge (King's Ridge) from the cirque's back right corner has become more difficult owing to exposed slabs.

Drive to Highwood Meadows parking lot at Highwood Pass on Kananaskis Trail (Highway 40). **Note:** Road closed Dec. 1 to June 15.

Cross the road and follow Ptarmigan Cirque trail. This popular little hike leads quickly past alpine meadows to Mount Rae's normal route. At the rear of the cirque veer left on the path and churn your way up a wide scree gully to a col between Mount Rae and an unnamed point at the

Mount Rae as seen from Tyrwhitt. P pinnacle.

Photo: Clive Cordery.

pinnacle

Typical terrain on Mount Rae's upper ridge.

9900 ft. (3018 m) contour line (428089). The left side of this chute is a little less tiring. As you top out, the view to the north bursts forth, and here you'll probably be about ready to snack and ponder the upcoming section. A minuscule glacier directly below you is the ultimate source of the Elbow River and Calgary's drinking water—mind where you pee! In early snowfall years before winter road closures, this secluded pocket of ice is popular with eager telemarkers. The sheltered north aspect holds snow well.

As you continue up the ridge, small gendarmes (pinnacles) can be easily skirted until a threateningly large one, which looks like it might even be the summit, straddles the entire crest. If snow is on the north-facing slopes to the left of this pinnacle, it is possible to circle around to the right to get up it. Climb a

small slab into a chimney beneath a monstrous chockstone. In dry conditions the logical way is to detour left onto scree and ledges high above the glacier and regain the ridge farther along. Otherwise, the next gendarme on the ridge crest will require some awkward moves. You can avoid most obstacles including the narrow summit ridge by keeping left.

The view from the top is impressive and encompasses both prairie to the east and many recognizable peaks to the north, west and south. The **return** is via the same route.

James Hector, surgeon and geologist of the Palliser Expedition, named Mount Rae for fellow surgeon John Rae. Rae was, among other postings, a doctor on a Hudson's Bay Company ship and he also helped in the search for the lost Franklin Expedition.

MOUNT ARETHUSA 2912 m

Difficulty Difficult scrambling via south slopes and southeast ridge
Round trip time 3-5 hours
Height gain 750 m
Map 82 J/10 Mount Rae

Mount Arethusa is a short but exciting scramble in the scenic Highwood Pass area. The ridge-like shape of this peak does not suggest any great challenge, but the route is exposed in several places and requires dry conditions. It is therefore rated "difficult" compared with the "moderate" grading given neighbouring Storm Mountain and Mount Rae. Like adjacent peaks, though, the high starting elevation makes for an easy approach and a short day. The optional descent route, with its few brief challenges, shrinks the return time by half. Try from July on.

Park 1.3 km south of Highwood (Pass) Meadows parking lot on Kananaskis Trail (Highway 40). **Note:** Road closed Dec. 1 to June 15.

From the parking area follow the left-hand side of the drainage through open forest. Wasting no time, this quick approach soon leads to alpine meadows of the upper valley with Arethusa's summit lying directly north. Toward the south end of the peak are several places where the horizontal cliff band has eroded away, and you can gain the ridge crest without any problem. From there, continue north along this interesting crest making short detours as required until you reach a point where you must descend a step in the ridge. This bit is the crux and needs to be snowfree.

Photo: Kris Thorsteinsson.

Ascent route gains ridge at right-hand end near low point in the ridge, then follows close to the crest. Summit lies at left-hand end.

Photo: Gillean Daffern.

Close-up view of Mount Arethusa. C crux, D descent.

Carefully scramble down an exposed 5 m chimney on the east (right) side. If snowy, it may not be feasible and could also be dangerous. Once down, you should immediately go over to the easier left (west) side to avoid the narrow, rotten ridge crest ahead. There are no further difficulties past here. The crux section is visible from the road as an obvious notch followed by a succession of small pinnacles.

If all the snow has melted, the west ridge gives a quick (but steep) **descent** route and is shorter than retracing your ascent route. From the summit, traverse ledges and short slabs diagonally for about 50 m to a deep notch. This notch can be seen from the highway. A curving gully leads steeply back to your left (south) to open meadows and your approach route from the road. Note that snowy or wet conditions would make this descent gully more than just a scramble. Tattered rappel slings in two steep spots bear testimony to the difficulties experienced by previous parties.

Arethusa, a woodland nymph in Greek mythology, was changed into a stream to escape her pursuers. In yet another surprising but more recent transformation, she became a ship, a British Light Cruiser, to be specific. Her final transformation occurred when she was sunk by a mine in 1916. She has been sorely mythed ever since.

MIST MOUNTAIN 3140 m

Difficulty Moderate scrambling by northwest ridge with brief exposure; more difficult from Mount Lipsett col
Round trip time 6-10 hours
Height gain 1050 m
Map 82 J/10 Mount Rae
(Mount Lipsett unmarked at 470013)

Although overshadowed by nearby Mount Rae, Mist Mountain is still one of the loftier viewpoints in Kananaskis. Located alongside Kananaskis Trail in the dry Highwood Pass area, it readily lends itself to a traverse. The most direct approach is from the north end and uses broad gullies to gain the northwest ridge. Try this ascent from July on.

Park at Lost Lemon Mine information sign, 4.4 km south of Highwood Pass Meadows parking lot on Kananaskis Trail (Highway 40). **Note:** Road closed Dec. 1 to June 15.

North Ridge Route

From the parking area, cross the road and follow a game trail along the left bank of the stream (451028) to avoid bush until you can reach open slopes. It is not necessary to go very far up the creek; the widest and perhaps easiest gully leading to the northwest ridge is one of the first that you reach (462027). Many adjacent gullies also offer potential scramble routes to the ridge above; you can study these at your leisure from the road. Most of the elevation gain occurs in reaching the northwest ridge. From there it is preferable to tramp alongside of rather than tiptoe along the crest. Expect an exposed bit near the top. At the summit you'll find a commemorative plaque.

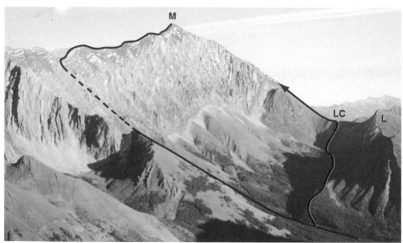

Two routes on Mist Mountain allow a traverse. L Mount Lipsett, M Mist Mountain, LC Lipsett col.

Photo: Gillean Daffern.

View from summit looking along NW ridge.

Lipsett Col Route

An ascent from the col between Mount Lipsett and Mist Mountain offers more challenge, particularly if you choose to scramble up ridges and ribs instead of toiling up rubbly gullies.

To reach Lipsett col, follow the stream as above but continue right to the headwaters, then scramble up wherever you like to gain the col between Lipsett and Mist. You could also hike straight up steep open slopes above the road to Mount Lipsett, but this would involve extra gain and loss of elevation. From Lipsett col many places exist to gain the south ridge of Mist Mountain. Some rock ribs and pinnacles overhang on east-facing aspects and may require some backtracking, other sections are surprisingly firm and offer delightful scrambling. It is short-lived, though, and quality quickly deteriorates as you reach the southeast ridge. Loose, frustrating scree concludes the ascent. Lacking a paddle, ski poles are probably best for this tedious terrain. You can combine these two different routes to do a high-level traverse while bagging unobtrusive Mount Lipsett (2482 m) as well.

Mist Mountain was named by geologist Dr. George M. Dawson for, not surprisingly, mist on the mountain—mist that might have come from small hot springs lying just east of the peak. It is also possible that he may have named it when naming nearby Storm Mountain, in which case the phenomenon would likely have been weather-related. Mount Lipsett is named after Major General L. J. Lipsett, C. M. G., Canadian Expeditionary Force.

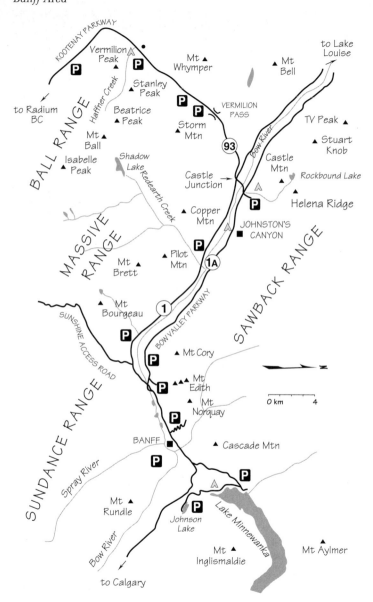

BANFF AREA

Mount Inglismaldie	2964 m	moderate	p. 190
Mount Aylmer	3163 m	moderate	p. 192
Cascade Mountain	2998 m	moderate	p. 194
Mount Rundle	2949 m	easy	p. 196
Mount Norquay	2522 m	difficult	p. 198
Mount Edith	2554 m	moderate	p. 201
Mount Cory	2802 m	easy	p. 203
Mount Bourgeau	2930 m	easy	p. 204
Pilot Mountain	2935 m	difficult	p. 206
Mount Brett	2984 m	difficult	p. 207
Copper Mountain	2795 m	moderate	p. 208
Castle Mountain	2766 m	easy	p. 209
Stuart Knob	2850 m	moderate	p. 211
Helena Ridge	2862 m	easy	p. 211
Television Peak	2970 m	easy	p. 212
Mount Whymper	2845 m	moderate	p. 213
Storm Mountain	3161 m	moderate	p. 215
Mount Ball	3311 m	moderate	p. 216
Stanley Peak	3155 m	difficult	p. 218
Vermilion Peak	2622 m	moderate	p. 220
Isabelle Peak	2938 m	difficult	p. 222

Banff and Bow Valley

Peaks described in this section occupy the area near Banff townsite, west along the Trans-Canada Highway to Castle Junction and in nearby Kootenay National Park. Banff National Park is undeniably the most popular of the four contiguous mountain parks, with the town of Banff hosting most of the influx. Backcountry destinations are similarly busy. This area boasts several Rockies' "postcard peaks," where camera-laden tourists record classic shots like Castle Mountain, Cascade and the great uplifted slab of Mount Rundle. To many roadside visitors, these three peaks epitomize Banff National Park. Coincidentally, each of these has a popular scramble route to the summit, each sees a large number of mountain ascents and occasional mishaps. Each scramble in this chapter can be done as a day trip, although Mount Ball, the highest scramble included in this area, is better under taken as a two-day trip.

Most of these peaks still fall (or rise!) within the Front Ranges and not until Castle Mountain do you reach the Main Ranges. Cambrian age rock, the oldest rock in the Rockies (600-800 million years old), is found in this latter range. So, too, are the highest peaks. Topography changes near the Continental Divide and is quite evident if you know what to watch for. Tilted, dip-slope mountains in the east give way to less disturbed mountains that are vertically-uplifted and deeply eroded. Soaring walls and steep buttresses guarding Castle Mountain are prime examples.

Unless close to or west of the Continental Divide, underbrush in this area is seldom problematic. Nonetheless, areas west of Banff are wetter than areas to the east and winter snow melts slowly in the higher elevations. June, normally the rainiest of the three summer months, often dumps additional snow on the summits. Impatient mountaineers agonize over when (or if) the big peaks might come into condition, and some years, they never really do. Late June blesses the Canadian Rockies with about 18 hours of daylight, yet sadly, the very peaks that would best benefit from this extended daylight often are choked with snow.

By July, weather patterns stabilize and snowmelt begins in earnest. Historically, the best weather typically occurs during the last week of July and the first week or two of August. After that, sporadic storms may again dust the big peaks with new snow, although it does not usually last. September and October can be fine scrambling months, but overnight temperatures drop close to or below freezing. Overnight rain leaves iced-up rock and therefore big peaks may no longer be in ideal dry condition. Summer crowds, however, have departed and many successful ascents to lower summits are enjoyed by locals and the few visitors who remain.

Access Banff, in the heart of the Canadian Rockies, is a 1.5 hour drive west of Calgary in the heart of the Canadian Rockies. Stopping in any national park requires buying a permit, available at the entrance gate. Besides the Trans-Canada Highway, the other thoroughfare is Bow Valley Parkway (Highway 1A). This quieter, scenic route begins 6 km west of Banff and runs for 30 km along the north side of the Bow River past Castle Junction to Lake Louise. To protect wildlife, the public is asked to refrain from using Highway 1A between 6 pm and 9 am during spring and until June 25 from Johnston's Canyon east to Banff. Kootenay Parkway, Highway 93, meets the Trans-Canada at Castle Junction and runs southwest toward Radium, British Columbia.

Facilities When the mountain weather doesn't cooperate, you can always brave the crowds of Banff. There is everything one could want, be it entertainment, equipment, food, knickknacks or information. Cave and Basin Hot Springs, around which Banff Park was created, is always popular. The Whyte Museum offers mountain-related exhibits, books and an interesting archive section on mountain areas of the world. Special emphasis has been placed on material relating to the Canadian Rockies. An extensive collection of excellent turn-of-the-century climbing photographs is also available for viewing, as are numerous climbing and reference books. If you cannot climb the peaks, you can browse through many excellent pictures of them and dream!

Climbing equipment and rental gear is available at better outdoor stores in town. Monod's and Mountain Magic are two of the longer-established outlets and each offers a wide selection of equipment.

West of Banff, there is a small store and a gas station at Castle Mountain Junction on Highway 1A. Located farther east at Johnston's Canyon is a restaurant. On Highway 93, meals are available at Storm Mountain Lodge when open.

Accommodation Budget-wise, the best deals are the campgrounds at Two Jack Lake, Tunnel Mountain in Banff or the co-ed YWCA, also in Banff. Most other local lodging is expensive. Farther west there are additional campgrounds along Highway 1A at Castle Mountain, Protection Mountain and Johnston's Canyon (showers), and at Marble Canyon in Kootenay Park. A youth hostel and bungalows are found at Castle Junction; rooms can be rented at Baker Creek, Storm Mountain Lodge and Johnston Canyon. The latter are not cheap and are often booked up in advance. Campgrounds fill early in the day as well. Least esthetic is the big ugly gravel pit camping area called "Lake Louise Overflow" along the main highway between Castle Junction and Lake Louise. It is most tolerable late at night.

For anyone contemplating parking at a trailhead and dozing harmlessly in a vehicle, be aware that this is allowed only during daylight hours. Personal experience has shown that come dusk, Parks Canada (especially in Banff Park) spares no effort to roust one out just when sleep comes. A misplaced park policy deems sleeping in a vehicle at night a truly heinous crime. So enthusiastically do personnel pursue illegal campers, that I once found a warning on my car left by overzealous park staff who assumed that anyone parked at a trailhead at 7:00 am could only be camping illegally. The "alpine" start concept is apparently unknown to these individuals. I suggest checking campgrounds for somebody (cyclists, for example) not using their allotted parking space and offer to sublease it. Park campgrounds simply cannot meet peak demand. Ironically, while big hotels continue to expand and new development flourishes, no thought is given to the low-impact, environmentally-friendly visitor needing only a patch of ground, a privy and a picnic table.

Information The Information Centre in Banff is on the main drag at 224 Banff Avenue. Permits, maps, trail information, bear warnings and smiles are dispensed here. Just look for a crowd of folks in a variety of attire (and with backpacks!) studying maps and brochures along the street. In Kootenay Park information is available at Vermilion crossing 31 km west of the Continental Divide.

Wardens Thinking of having an epic? Don't bother, it has already been done. To avoid an epic, the Warden Office is just east of the townsite on the north side of Banff Avenue in the Parks Compound. Specific information about particular routes and current climbing conditions on local peaks can often be obtained here. Registration is also available.

MOUNT INGLISMALDIE 2964 m

Difficulty A moderate scramble via southwest slopes
Round trip time 8-12 hours
Height gain 1450 m
Map 82 O/3 Canmore

Mount Inglismaldie rewards the victorious with a fine view of Lake Minnewanka and the Bow Corridor, but the peak doesn't see many visitors owing to the lack of a good approach trail. As you drive toward Banff from the west, this peak, along with adjacent Mount Girouard to the south, form a balanced and symmetrical backdrop on the eastern horizon. Check with Park wardens regarding access as this is now a wildlife corridor. Try from late June on.

From the Banff east overpass, follow Lake Minnewanka Road for 4.2 km and take the turn off toward Johnson Lake. Park at a pull-out marked as cross-country ski trail #1, just 0.8 km before Johnson Lake.

From the pull-out, follow the trail clockwise around behind Johnson Lake to avoid the marsh. You will intersect the dry drainage originating between Mounts Girouard and Inglismaldie in 10 minutes (cairn). Follow it. Farther up-

Southwest slopes of Inglismaldie. D alternative descent.

Near the top of Mount Inglismaldie: The forecast promised sun.

stream, you should pass remnants of two collapsed log cabins. Louis Trono, Banff writer and historian, wrote of a mysterious recluse named Billy Carver, "the hermit of Johnson Lake." Apparently this enigmatic figure holed up somewhere nearby each winter between about 1912 and 1935, but few knew where. This was likely it. Little is known about him, except that he worked summers at Brazeau Mines, and he was British. As you pass by, you may understand why he entertained few visitors: This place is right on the way to nowhere.

In early summer the creek is big enough to make crossings bothersome. Avoid climbing too high above the creek, though, as cliffs upstream will make it difficult to descend. After some three hours you reach the upper drainage forks. Go right and when possible head up left to gain the base of a long slope of good scree facing southwest. This is the easiest way up. Nearby, Mount Girouard looms silently, but unfortunately (or fortunately) is not a scramble.

Rock bands intrude near the top so traverse left over scree and slabby ledges to make a final dash up to the summit. The summit grants a fine view of lengthy Lake Minnewanka and a daunting perspective of Devil's Head to the north.

As an **alternate return** you can descend the entire face directly below the summit with little problem. When seen from the Banff east overpass, this face appears deceivingly steep, however, only a few short rock steps require detours. With good snow conditions and an ice axe this line can make for a rapid glissade to the left (north) branch of the drainage forks. Then rejoin the approach route and return the same way.

Back in 1886 or '87, when the Earl of Kintore visited, there were many unnamed peaks around, "blocking the view," as prairie folks might say. George Stewart, superintendent of the park, changed that. He quickly named the peak for Inglismaldie Castle in Kincardineshire, Scotland, the Earl of Kintore's seat. While it continued to block the view, it now at least had a name.

MOUNT AYLMER 3163 m

Difficulty Moderate scrambling via southwest slopes
Round trip time A full day even with a bike, very long without one
Height gain 1680 m
Map 82 O/6 Lake Minnewanka

Mount Aylmer is one of the more prominent points in the Front Ranges and is Banff's highest summit. Although the Palliser Range hides much of it, the lofty summit still projects enough to draw attention. Each season many parties make the as-cent despite a long approach. Some camp at Aylmer campsite, although fit parties will find this unnecessary. A bicycle approach was common in the past, but because of trail damage caused by wet-weather riding, bikes may well be banned in future. Check at the information centre in Banff. Some years the upper ridge dries off by June, but a cold rain will often deposit snow high up. These upper slopes are visible from the Banff east overpass so check before dashing off.

From the Banff east overpass, drive east on Lake Minnewanka Road for 5.5 km to the concession area. Park on the left.

From the parking lot, go past the concession area, picnic tables and washrooms. Continue along the lakeshore trail to Aylmer campsite at 7.6 km. This is a pleasant spot to rest and fill water bottles for the long, waterless grind ahead. Follow the signed Aylmer Pass/Aylmer Lookout trail that starts uphill of the campsite. Upon reaching a fork you have a choice. The right branch leads to where the fire lookout once stood and adds distance through some unnecessarily long switchbacks. From the old lookout site, you simply go north along the ridge.

The left branch of the trail to Aylmer Pass is more pleasant, gradually rising through semi-open forest. Follow this until you emerge into the open in a large avalanche gully; about one hour of fast walking. The hiking path crosses the gully and angles steeply to the left; scramblers heading for Mount Aylmer will want to leave the trail here and instead hike up this twisting gully onto the hillside near a small hump of brown scree. The two routes join on the crest of this slope.

Continue along on the ridge as it sweeps around to the right and rises east to the summit.

A close-up view. S saddle, R rock bands.
Photo: Brad White, Parks Canada.

Ahead are three short rock bands; the middle one requires downclimbing a 5 m crack. All this can be easily bypassed as follows: At the little saddle where darker brown scree meets lighter rubble, traverse diagonally to the right across the talus, then follow an easier trail along the base of the rocky face and up to the next notch on the ridge. This is just past the 5 m downclimb. Toilsome talus leads to the top. The zigzag path is more useful on descent, but ski poles do help on ascent. As you top out, stay back from the summit cornice that often partially obstructs the view to the east.

The view is pleasing but not breathtaking. The panorama includes many nameless piles of brown rubble, although green hues of Upper Ghost River and meadows beyond Aylmer Pass make a valiant effort to add colour. Front Range peaks typically dip to the southwest, and the eastern escarpments are usually most impressive. Mounts Inglismaldie, Girouard and Peechee across the lake are prime examples.

There are a few theories regarding the namesake. A popular one suggests that J. J. McArthur, a Dominion land surveyor, named the peak for his hometown in Quebec. As he made the first ascent in 1889, this explanation seems most plausible.

It seems that Aylmer was known as "Spirit Mountain" to Assiniboine Indians. Lake Minnewanka or "Water of the Spirits" was thought to be the home of a half-human, half-fish creature, and until white men arrived, Indians avoided canoeing or fishing here. Today the lake swarms with fishermen, and although stories abound of big ones that got away, nothing extraordinary has been caught yet.

Opposite: Aerial view of Lake Minnewanka and two approaches to Mount Aylmer.
Photo: Brad White, Parks Canada.

CASCADE MOUNTAIN 2998 m

Difficulty Moderate scrambling
Round trip time 8 hours
Height gain 1325 m
Map 82 O/4 Banff

Cascade and Rundle are the two classic scrambles at Banff, and since the first ascent in 1887 by Tom Wilson, thousands have probably tramped to the top. Decades ago, locals placed a mirror on top that reflected down Banff Avenue. Canmore writer Ralph Connor once wrote of finding the fossil remains of a prehistoric monster on top in an entertaining, whimsical account. The party graciously claimed to have left the remains up there for all to see. Suffice to say, it is unlikely that scramblers will discover anything so unusual, although you may see interesting rocks, if nothing else. Try this peak from July on, when the snow has cleared off the fossilized monsters(!).

From the Banff west overpass, drive up Norquay Ski Area access road. Park in lot #1, next to Cascade day lodge.

From the north end of the parking lot, walk past the day lodge and follow the signed hiking trail to Cascade Amphitheatre for 6.6 km. It descends to cross Forty Mile Creek, then rises in endless switchbacks to Cascade Amphitheatre. Be sure to take the right branch at the fork.

Upon entering Cascade Amphitheatre, you can see the gently-angled ridge sweeping skyward from right to left, straight ahead. The summit lies 800 vertical metres above, and this ridge grants the scrambler an uncomplicated route to the top.

Photo: Brad White, Parks Canada.

Photo: Brad White, Parks Canada.

Close-up showing detour around Cascade's false summit.

Turn hard right at the amphitheatre to gain this ridge crest. Owing to regular traffic, there are several trails. Nevertheless, in 1997, a death occurred here when someone explored farther into the amphitheatre and then began ascending steep, snowy slabs instead of gaining the ridge the easy way. A fatal fall then ensued.

The view from the ridge above tree line is infinitely better than the claustrophobic environs of the amphitheatre. The only obstacle you'll meet is the false summit, visible as a big bump along the summit ridge when seen from the highway. At that point you have a choice of routes. Most people don't even realize that they are on the false summit until confronted with a drop-off, then end up climbing down over the front (south) side to regain the ridge. It is easier to backtrack and skirt around it on a narrow

Opposite: Aerial view of Cascade's ascent route.
A amphitheatre, F false summit, W wrong way!

but distinct trail on the west side. Note that snow clings along the foot of this bump right into July. The terrain is slabby and becomes dangerous if snowy. You should have a good close look from the highway beforehand to be sure that this unavoidable bit is bare. Otherwise, you may have to retreat.

On your **return**, stay on the ridge crest until you can angle right and descend to the amphitheatre again. For your safety, please resist the urge to try other descents.

Cascade is Dr. James Hector's abbreviated translation of an Indian name for the peak, describing the impressive waterfall that emerges from barren rock high upon the south flanks. This learned member of the Palliser Expedition labelled many nearby landmarks, including Mounts Rundle and Bourgeau. A major peak north of Lake Louise bears his name.

MOUNT RUNDLE 2949 m

Difficulty An easy scramble via west slopes
Round trip time 6-10 hours
Height gain 1570 m
Map 82 O/4 Banff

Mount Rundle is possibly the most popular scramble around Banff, if not in all of the park. From the west its unique shape demonstrates a classic dip-slope or writing-desk geological formation. When snowfree you'll encounter few difficulties ascending the gentle, west slopes, which offer a fine view of beautiful Bow Valley and distant summits. Although straightforward, over the years this alluring mountain has contributed more than its share of call-outs for Parks rescue service. The windswept route is often clear of snow and in shape by May.

Follow Spray Avenue in Banff toward the Banff Springs Hotel and take the Bow Falls/golf course turn-off just before the hotel. Park at Bow Falls.

From the parking lot, walk across the bridge to a trail that cuts back sharply to the right immediately past the first golf course green (trail sign). Minutes later, a more detailed sign shows the Spray River and Rundle trails heading left. The signed Rundle trail diverges left again soon after this.

Rising gently through pine and fir forest, the first section is typical of eastern slope valleys in the Rockies. Before long, you grind up a series of switchbacks through the first cliff band. Thoughtless twits are causing serious erosion here by shortcutting these switchbacks on descent. This ruins the trail—please don't take shortcuts! Just past the switchbacks (1.5 hrs.), the trail splits. The left-hand path goes to the first peak; the trail to the second (main) peak continues straight ahead.

First Peak

The lower first peak is more technical and sees fewer ascents. From the junction, the trail rises steeply to tree line and a vertical cliff band. Just before the last trees, angle to the right on a narrower trail. This path traverses across well below the cliffs and crosses two gullies. You then turn left and follow the path to the right of cliffs and beside another gully. The cliff band is overcome by ascending some 50 m of downsloping, rubble-strewn slabs. This is the crux and it must be dry; scramble up carefully. For your return, be sure to look back and note the exact descent spot, as there is only one possibility.

Main Peak

This higher peak is more popular. Continue past the junction to where the trail emerges into the Central Gully, a large watercourse that reveals the upper mountain far above. DO NOT head up this gully. This is wrong. The route lies almost directly across this gully and enters forest. Conspicuous arrows clearly mark the proper route.

Continue through forest and up a feature called the Dragon's Back. This is a section bordered by the Central Gully on the left and a similar gully on the right. The last few hundred metres of scree above are tediously loose—rubble without a pause. If ever a route required ski poles, this is the one. On a hot summer day when heat waves shimmer

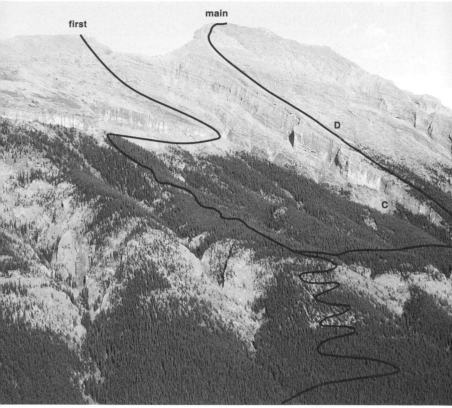

View from Sulphur Mountain of ascent routes to Rundle's first and main peaks.
C Central Gully, D Dragon's Back.

off these barren slopes, you'll truly appreciate water, a shade hat and a good pair of sunglasses.

Mount Assiniboine and Temple are two of the bigger peaks you'll see from on top, and when you've seen enough, **return** the same way. If you're contemplating a traverse over to the first peak, it is difficult, exposed and is NOT A SCRAMBLE. Climbing equipment and experience are recommended. Below the Drag-

on's Back, watch for the arrows so you don't descend too far before turning right to cross the Central Gully. Cliffs lie below and park wardens dislike rescuing inattentive novices from there.

Reverend Robert Rundle was a Wesleyan missionary and early tourist who visited Banff in the 1840s. Although he never actually attempted this peak, he apparently did try one somewhere farther east.

MOUNT NORQUAY 2522 m

Difficulty Difficult for two short sections; exposure
Round trip time 6-10 hours
Height gain 1000 m from bottom of lift; 600 m from top of lift
Map 82 0/4 Banff

Mount Norquay is an ideal place to study nearby Mounts Louis, Rundle and Cascade. The view of the Bow Valley is fine as well. If the lift is operating, you can even cheat and ride part of the way. Fatalities have occurred on this mountain owing to parties attempting it before the snow had melted off so do not rush the ascent. Try from about mid-June on.

From the Banff west overpass, drive north up the winding Norquay Ski Area access road for 6 km and park near the higher Norquay day lodge.

From the day lodge at the base of the big hill, slog up the ski run to the upper lift terminal. From there, the normal route ascends the big gully. There are two ways to gain it. Easiest is to ascend directly behind the lift station through trees, then angle to the right to get into the big gully. The other option is to follow the path from the right rear corner of the lift station to a rock wall immediately behind. Climb this short, exposed wall using solution pockets. If you find the steep wall too difficult, note that you may be turned back by another equally tricky spot before reaching even the east summit. Ascend the gully to the ridge.

Rather than ascend directly up the big gully, some parties choose a route farther to the right. Follow the path to the right, angling gradually up and crossing two gullies before heading toward the ridge more directly. The main challenge is a steep, sometimes wet wall climbed by an exposed scramble on the right side. A slip would be serious and that is why the gully route is preferable.

Once you reach the ridge, although you will have a fine view for your efforts, it is disheartening to realize that considerable distance lies between you and the higher west summit, including an apparent loss of elevation. In fact, the route travels beyond the east peak to a high col leading to the west peak, which is closer than it looks.

Continue north along the ridge to reach the crux in 10 minutes. At the crux, climb up and across a downsloping ledge that tilts to the right toward a huge drop-off. This ledge must be dry as a slip could be fatal. Scramble left up a ramp beside a steep wall and ascend this wall in a corner. The flat spot above makes a logical place from which to study the rest of the route.

Another undulating section leads to a descent on scree to the col. Where the col meets Norquay's west summit, angle to the right across a gully. At least one accident has occurred here because of a slip on snow. Depending on conditions, you may need an ice axe. Finish by angling across easy ledges up to the summit ridge.

The most impressive view lies to the northwest where rises a striking limestone fang called Mount Louis. The south face offers several technical rock routes and sharp eyes may detect climbers on it. The normal route was first ascended by the famous mountain guide Conrad Kain in 1916 along with Albert MacCarthy, the same party that made the first ascent of Mount Robson. Mount Louis is a popular climbing objective yet today and is challenging enough that even competent parties occasionally require rescuing. Parties have also been rescued off Mount Norquay, largely owing to ignorance of the proper route and too-easy cell phone access to rescue service. Unnecessary rescues together with media misinformation portray outdoor enthusiasts as an irresponsible bunch. This adversely affects all of us in the long term.

Descend the peak via the same route. Most years the lift does not operate in summer, but if it does, you can probably take the low-impact (for knees!) way down. In early summer, the gully beside (north of) the upper lift station can be glissaded if you are competent at ice axe self-arrest. An alternate descent (or ascent) from Norquay's west summit is via the south ridge to the Trans-Canada

Highway. It meets the road about 3 km west of the overpass. The main problems are scaling the roadside wire fence and hitchhiking back to your car.

Mount Norquay is named for Honourable John Norquay, a popular premier of Manitoba who climbed this peak during his term in office (1878-87). He did not use the gondola.

Route to west summit from saddle between east and west peaks.

Norquay's east side and routes. East E and West W peaks, S saddle, D optional descent.

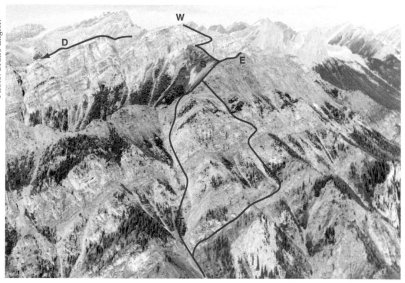

Photo: Bruno Engler.

Left to right, N North, C Centre and S South peaks from the road.

N North and C Centre peaks showing routes. Cory Pass is at lower left, South Peak is out of sight to right.

MOUNT EDITH 2554 m

Difficulty Moderate/difficult scrambling
for each peak
Round trip time 6-10 hours
Height gain 1120 m
Map 82 O/4 Banff

Mount Edith sports three separate summits offering interesting and sometimes exposed scrambling. Access is by a popular hiking trail. A dogtooth mountain like its northerly and more famous neighbour Mount Louis, Mount Edith is an uplift of Devonian age Palliser limestone—a 500 m-thick formation of sound rock prized by climbers. Palliser rock forms great grey cliffs on many mountains, fortunately it does not present a barrier to scramblers on this one. Dry conditions and a helmet are recommended. Try this outing from June on.

From the Banff west overpass drive west to Bow Valley Parkway and follow it for 0.3 km. Turn right and continue to Fireside picnic area where the trailhead for Cory/Edith Pass is found.

Wriggling down the south-facing chimney on North Peak. Photo: Don Beers.

Hike 6 km along Cory Pass trail (left at the only fork) to Cory Pass. A worn path then leads east (right) up scree to the north and highest peak 200 m above. The top is guarded by a band of cliffs, but two chimneys break through this band. They emerge close to one another. The first (steeper) is on the northwest side and may be seen from the pass. A less visible chimney, hip-width, less steep and easier starts a short way south of the first chimney and faces south, not west. At the summit, cross a notch to reach the cairn. Mount Louis is brilliantly revealed to the north.

Many people seem to find the 20-minute scramble to the slightly lower Centre Peak short but entertaining. Go along the west side of North Peak, then gain the connecting ridge. After that either traverse across horizontally left (exposure) to gain a scree gully to the summit or scramble along on top of the ridge the whole way. The ridge has two or three short tricky moves but is safer if the traverse option is not bare and dry. You can **descend** Centre Peak via a deep gully on the south side toward the South Peak (helmet advisable). Turn right and continue down a trail to Cory Pass trail as for South Peak descent.

South Peak

The South Peak is the most difficult of the three and ascends the climbers' descent route on the airy west side. The route begins just below the Centre/South Peak col in a north-facing gully (trail). This spot can also be reached from Cory Pass trail by various paths up steep open slopes.

Scramble up steepish rock in the gully for about 5-8 m toward a narrow tunnel. Alternatively, there is also an exposed ledge that detours around to the right. Unless size (your size!) is a factor, the tunnel is probably better. From the top of the tunnel, the idea is to work your way across ledges to the right (south) without gaining too much elevation. Notice trails and cairns. Scramble up a short (5-7 m) steep bit, and angle right so as to intersect the south ridge. The correct way is not too exposed, but if you're off route a slip

South Peak showing approximate route up. D descent, T tunnel.

could be deadly. Good routefinding is important. You should look back to recognize your route periodically.

Getting onto the south ridge may involve a strenuous heave up on two rocks wedged behind a big vertical flake. You can also scramble around to the right of this flake. The remaining short bit of the south ridge is exposed, so use care. Allow 40-60 minutes round trip from the col.

Return to the Centre/South col via the same route. From there, follow a beaten path beginning closer to Centre Peak, which avoids downsloping slabs in the middle of the gully below. This takes you back to Cory Pass trail.

Edith Orde accompanied Lady Agnes Macdonald, wife of Canada's first prime minister, on her 1886 journey through the Rockies upon completion of the transcontinental railway.

South Peak and col from Centre Peak. G ascent gully to tunnel. Cory Pass trail below to right.

MOUNT CORY 2802 m

Difficulty An easy/moderate scramble via south ridge
Round trip time 6-10 hours
Height gain 1370 m
Map 82 O/4 Banff

Mount Cory is a straightforward scramble in the Banff area that provides a fine view. From the Trans-Canada Highway two notable features distinguish the peak: A 300 m vertical groove in the southwest face that climbers call "Cory Crack," and a gap-

ing, dark cave to the right of Cory Crack known as "Hole in the Wall." The lower flanks offer several technically difficult rock-climbing routes on firm limestone. Located on the south side of the peak are three parallel treed ribs rising to half-height and separated by drainage gullies. The right-hand rib, identified by light-coloured, shaley cliffs visible from the road and a deep ravine to the right, is a straightforward route up. Try this ascent from mid-June on.

From the Banff west overpass drive west on the Trans-Canada Highway to Bow Valley Parkway. Follow Bow Valley Parkway for 1.9 km (1.6 km west of Fireside picnic area) to a pull-off spot on the shoulder.

The pull-off spot sits at the base of the correct rib. Find an easy way up the shaley cliffs and follow animal (and human) trails up through forest along the crest of it. Cairns appear in places and the way is obvious. Farther up, this rib eases and descends slightly to a small plateau, an ideal snack spot to enjoy a view of the Bow Corridor.

A further two hours' plod up the ridge, interrupted only by the odd little "dip," leads to the more southerly of Mount Cory's two equally-high summits. The north peak is easily reached in a further few minutes, although a cornice sometimes stops early season visits. On **return**, it is possible to descend on the east side from between the summits to gain Cory Pass trail, or from part way down the northwest ridge to reach Gargoyle Valley. Most parties simply return the same way.

Like so many mountains in the Rockies, Mount Cory, in typical bureaucratic tradition, exalts another politician. William Cory was deputy minister of the Interior during 1905-30.

The long south ridge of Mount Cory leads to a double summit.   Photo: Bruno Engler.

MOUNT BOURGEAU 2930 m

Difficulty An easy scramble via west slopes
Round trip time 7-10 hours
Height gain 1500 m
Map 82 O/4 Banff

Bourgeau Lake is a popular Banff area day hike that provides an easy, but long approach route to Mount Bourgeau. The peak was first ascended in 1890 by surveyor J. J. MacArthur and packer Tom Wilson, al-though they probably did not use this approach. The route used today visits no less than three distinctly unique mountain tarns along the way and is one of the prettier day hikes around Banff. This area records heavy snowfall, and in early summer you can often find lingering snow patches near the second lake. These slopes are ideal for practising ice axe self-arrest and make for a great glissade, too. Try from late June on.

Park at Bourgeau Lake parking lot on the southwest side of the Trans-Canada Highway, 2.9 km west of the overpass for Sunshine ski area.

From the parking area, follow the hiking trail for 7.5 km to Bourgeau Lake. Upon reaching this clear body of water, follow any of the paths down the right-hand side toward the west end and the inlet stream. The easiest way is to hike along the right side of this rushing stream to reach the high alpine basin lying west at 835655. This glacially-carved cirque is far more attractive than Bourgeau Lake itself, yet the majority never see it. Picturesque tarns and meadows invite you to relax and enjoy. Harvey Pass, the low

Photo: Gillean Daffern.

Looking back down the west ridge. Mount Ball is the snow-capped peak to right.

saddle to the south near tiny Harvey Lake (838651), reveals expansive views of alpine meadows. Beyond the scars of Sunshine ski area rises magnificent Mount Assiniboine, a prized jewel among alpinists. More importantly though for the scrambler, this pass lies next to the gentle west ridge leading to Bourgeau's top.

A pleasant walk up the ridge leads to the broad summit 400 m higher. Loose scree is practically nonexistent on this slope, and many varieties of delicate wildflowers bloom throughout much of the summer. In complete contrast to the pastoral panorama, assorted manufactured paraphernalia including a building clutters the summit. Despite these intrusions, there is still plenty of room for wandering around the expansive plateau.

Mount Ball is the hulking snowcapped peak directly to the west, and despite its challenging appearance from here, is also a scramble. To the north lies the Sawback Range. These long uplifted rock ridges have been sculpted by about 350 million years of erosion to form textbook examples of sawtooth mountains. Dr. James Hector of the Palliser Expedition named this peak for Monsieur Eugene Bourgeau, the botanist who accompanied the mission on explorations through the Rockies during 1857-60. Highly esteemed in scientific circles, Bourgeau quickly won the admiration of his fellow expedition members during their travels.

Opposite: Bourgeau's gentle west ridge ascent route starts at ice-bound Harvey Lake. Also visible is the approach route from Bourgeau Lake (bottom left).

PILOT MOUNTAIN 2935 m

Difficulty Two difficult steps via
northwest ridge
Round trip time 6-12 hours
Height gain 1535 m
Map 82 O/4 Banff

Pilot Mountain is a striking Bow Valley
landmark, highly visible from the highway.
The ascent requires a little more perseverance and routefinding than most other
Banff area scrambles. While you won't find
a nice little path to the top, it is seeing more
ascents and the route up is reasonable.
Carry an ice axe for early season trips; try
it from late June on.

Park at Redearth Creek parking lot on the
south side of the Trans-Canada Highway,
about 19.4 km west of the Banff west
overpass and 10.6 km east of Eisenhower
Junction.

From the parking area, bike or hike up
Redearth fire road. When I ascended
this peak, we went only to the first
avalanche slope (one hour on foot). Over
the years, the trees on this slope keep

growing taller and making it less obvious. Therefore, you should watch for a
small wooden bridge that crosses a drainage at the edge of more mature forest
here. Tramp up the slope near this drainage toward a northwest-facing basin
carved in Pilot Mountain's lower flanks.
To simplify routefinding, you may want
to study the approaching rock band for
the easiest line through it as there are
several possibilities.

Pilot Mountain from Copper Mountain, showing route from Redearth Creek fire road. C chimney.

Above this rock band, traverse right (south) on open rubbly hillside below the impenetrable limestone wall until you reach the northwest ridge. At the northwest ridge, erosion has reduced the wall to mere rubble—so much for impenetrable. Note: Other parties have continued farther up the road and gained the northwest ridge more directly, possibly from the second avalanche slope, but details are unclear at time of writing.

Above the rock band, scree leads to cliffs and a 10-15 m-high chimney/gully behind a huge detached flake, a logical spot to ascend. On our ascent in early June one year, this big groove was still a little snowy, although we were able to bridge across awkward spots. An ice axe and perhaps even crampons might be required in early season some years.

At the top of this chimney, move horizontally left on a ledge to easier, less exposed terrain and scramble higher. The crux is at two short, steep walls just below the top, then a walk leads to the broad summit plateau. The view of Copper Mountain's scramble route is ideal from this location.

As an alternate **descent** route, or to bag nearby Mount Brett (2984 m), you can drop down into the seldom-visited glen southwest of Pilot Mountain. Retrace your steps to the bottom of the chimney at the base of the northwest ridge. Angle down west-facing rubble slopes through short rock bands into this pristine valley. To reach Redearth fire road from here, follow the faint, bushy gully northwest to emerge near the second avalanche slope.

MOUNT BRETT 2984 m

While losing hard-won elevation down the rubbly west slopes of Pilot Mountain is tiring, continuing to Mount Brett, 700 m above, will really leave you bagged. Com-bining these two peaks makes for a very long day, but for anyone aspiring to climb Mount Brett, this saves a second trip.

Cross the glen and hike up through subalpine forest onto the broad, larch-dotted ridge above. Turn left and continue southeast toward Mount Brett. Sections of interesting scrambling lead along the ridge crest to the summit. Not surprisingly, few parties ascend this peak.

On **descent**, low-angle rubble on the west slopes of Brett allows a quick descent from the summit. Contour back around right to regain the larch-dotted ridge, cross it and descend to the glen. Head northwest down the faint, bushy drainage back to the fire road.

Pilot Mountain's familiar outline helped guide early travellers along Bow Valley. Doctor R. G. Brett once ran the Sanatorium Hotel in Banff, was active in politics and later became lieutenant governor of Alberta, 1915-25.

Lower part of the NW ridge of Mount Brett.

COPPER MOUNTAIN 2795 m

Difficulty A moderate scramble
Round trip time 6-9 hours
Height gain 1425 m
Map 82 O/4 Banff

Redearth fire road provides access to Egypt and Shadow lakes, but few parties give Copper Mountain much more than a sideways glance as they pass. It is not a major summit, but neither is it a major undertaking. In 1986 the register bore no record of any visits during the previous 14 years. It sees more ascents today, but don't expect a crowd. Try from mid-June on.

Park at Redearth Creek parking lot on the south side of the Trans-Canada Highway, 19.4 km west of the Banff west overpass and 10.6 km east of Eisenhower Junction. Mountain biking allowed; watch for horse traffic.

From the parking area, hike or bike 7.2 km up Redearth fire road to Lost Horse campsite. Hike downstream to open ava-

lanche slopes immediately to the right (north) of the huge pointy pinnacle looming above. The first avalanche slope leads to a gully left (south) of the pinnacle, but is very loose and better for descent. You should go farther downstream and up open slopes toward the gully system directly below the top. Scramble to the broad summit and a unique perspective of Castle Mountain, which explorer James Hector partially ascended and named back in 1858.

Either of two gullies south of the summit offer **descent** routes. The first is the aforementioned gully by the pinnacle and is just minutes away down the ridge; the second gully is farther south and emerges upstream of the campsite. Prospector Joe Healy once discovered copper ore in this area, hence, the name.

Copper Mountain from Pilot Mountain. Route ascends gullies above tree line.

CASTLE MOUNTAIN 2766 m

Difficulty An easy scramble via
northeast side
Round trip time 7-11 hours
Height gain 1400 m
Map 82 O/5 Castle Mountain

Castle Mountain has caught the imagination of Bow Valley visitors since man's
earliest presence. Although it looks steep
and intimidating from the road, it is easily
ascended from the back side. The approach is a pleasant and popular hike.
When James Hector saw the mountain in
1858, he noted its suggestive appearance,
named it accordingly, and the title sufficed
for nearly a century. Then, with the stroke
of a bureaucrat's pen it was changed to
Mount Eisenhower to commemorate the
post-war visit of American president
Dwight Eisenhower. In 1983, because of
public pressure, the original name was
rightfully restored. The isolated pinnacle at
the southeast end is now called Eisenhower Tower, while the cairn and register
are on a higher point slightly northwest of
the tower. The highest point actually lies
some 3 km northwest at 720863, but it is
seldom visited. Try this outing from July on.

Castle Mountain ascent route from Rockbound Lake. H Helena Ridge, S Stuart Knob, T TV Peak.

Drive to Castle Junction 31 km west of
Banff via either the Trans-Canada Highway or Bow Valley Parkway (Highway
1A). Park at the trailhead for Rockbound
Lake, located on the north side of the Bow
Valley Parkway, 300 m east of Castle Junction Service Station and across from the
youth hostel by the warden residence.

From the parking area, follow the hiking
trail for 8.4 km to Rockbound Lake,
passing Tower Lake on the way. Rockbound Lake, enclosed by steep walls of
dolomite and limestone, lies in the centre of the Castle Mountain Syncline, a
product of geologically-significant Castle Mountain Thrust. The fault line is

slightly east near Helena Ridge. This transitional feature separates the older Main Ranges of the Rockies from the younger Front Ranges.

Dipping strata of Helena Ridge provide access to the first part of the route. Hike up the lower flanks on the east side of Rockbound Lake and go through a gully in the rock band close to a large knoll at 746856. Although a beaten path winds up and over this hump, you can also skirt along the foot of it. Circle the lake counterclockwise across a broad, grassy terrace. This spacious ledge with its trickles of meltwater sits on limestone formed during the Middle Cambrian period, 530 million years ago.

Where the grassy terrace peters out, a short scramble up a gully leads to the upper bench that slopes gently toward many high points crowning the 4 km-long massif. If you plod along the crest, chasms reveal glimpses of the Bow Valley, framed by buttresses of ancient Eldon limestone. While the view is more scenic along the crest, the least tedious route is to stay low where the terrain is flatter, then angle up rubble to the right once you're close to the final slopes.

From the top there is an excellent view along the Bow Valley, with summits of the Lake Louise group dominating the skyline. If you are energetic, it is possible to traverse the entire mass of Castle Moun-

tain end-to-end in a long day. As it is difficult to descend at the northwest end, you are advised to head northeast from the highest point at 720863, hike toward Stuart Knob and descend scree slopes back to the terrace above Rockbound Lake. You could also traverse farther around to include Helena Ridge. This all-inclusive excursion is recommended for scramblers with boundless energy and enthusiasm for trudging. Expect a very long day!

The final, long trudge to Castle's summit. Least toil-some line stays low, more scenic route follows ridge.

STUART KNOB 2850 m

Stuart Knob is the pointy little peak flanked by huge talus slopes behind Castle Mountain, and is readily apparent from the Trans-Canada Highway west of Banff. Lying 1.5 km northwest of Rockbound Lake, it is easily ascended by rubble slopes beyond the grassy terrace above the lake and knoll at 746856. Allow 2-3 hours return from Rockbound Lake. Wander around left to the opposite side and scramble to the top, which is actually higher than Castle Mountain. Who would have guessed?

HELENA RIDGE 2862 m

For scramblers wanting a better view but not quite up to the lengthy tramp up Castle Mountain, there is little difficulty in attaining the highest summit of Helena Ridge. This 5 km-long ridge lies north and east of Rockbound Lake, and is a wee bit higher than Castle. Try from July on.

From Rockbound Lake a wide gully gives access to the top at 745865 via gentle southeast slopes. Only moderate challenges are involved in continuing to a neighbouring vantage point 1 km east, 75 m lower. The views includes Bonnet Peak directly north and Mount Ball to the south. From either position you get a fuller appreciation of the considerable mass of Castle Mountain, but without the drudgery of walking it.

Although scree on this ascent is the tedious ski-pole type, keep in mind this is not just any old scree—this is 530 million year-old scree. What caused it? A geologist might say that a movement known as the Castle Mountain Thrust is at fault.

The long walk to TV Peak. Route circles to right of basin and ascends ridge. D optional descent to Highway 1A.
Photo: Kris Thorsteinsson.

TELEVISION PEAK 2970 m

TV Peak is the unnamed point much farther along the Castle Mountain massif at 708893. You can reach it in about 1.5 hours from Stuart Knob. This unnamed peak lying northwest of Castle Mountain eclipses both Stuart Knob and Helena Ridge in elevation. From Stuart Knob, the ascent is merely a long and unexciting plod. Continue north to circle the intervening bowl (718895), then gain a gentle ridge extending northeast from TV Peak. The view from the top is respectable, but the walk is very long. Special note to TV repeater technicians who helicopter up: Please don't sign the summit register unless you've earned it!

Confident scramblers wishing an alternate return can **descend** the southwest side of TV Peak below the repeater building to gain the road. Downclimbing a short, steep wall right near the top is the crux. Note the rock's resemblance to precariously-piled stacks of shingles: use care. Continue west down easy terrain to tree line and eventually the Bow Valley Parkway. Yet another plod follows as you head for your vehicle 9 km down the road near Castle Junction. By this time the whole affair of peak-bagging will have begun to take on an air of pointlessness. Curious stares by tourists speeding by adds to the lark.

MOUNT WHYMPER 2845 m

Difficulty Moderate scrambling via
southeast slopes
Round trip time 6-8 hours
Height gain 1250 m
Map 82 N/1 Mount Goodsir

Mount Whymper is an excellent viewpoint for the icy north face of neighbouring Mount Stanley and despite being close to a main highway, the summit is visited infrequently. When dry, gullies on the southeast side are a direct way up and offer good scrambling. Try from about June on.

From Castle Junction on the Trans-Canada Highway, follow Kootenay Parkway (Highway 93) to Stanley Glacier parking lot, 3.4 km south of the Continental Divide.

Lodgepole pine is steadily overgrowing the south slopes route of Mount Whymper and hides much deadfall as well. The preferred route now ascends the major gully on the southeast side. Start at the avalanche slope 0.5 km up the road from the parking lot. The first rock band is perhaps steepest where you scramble up waterworn bedrock. More scrambling and slogging takes you through larger cliff bands, but shouldn't pose problems for those with experience. As it is a huge avalanche chute, conditions must be snowfree. When the rubble gets tedious near the top, angle left to the ridge.

For more exercise you can easily continue to an unnamed point just 40 minutes away to the west. While tempting to descend to the larch-filled cirque below, it's a thrash back down to the highway. Either **return** the same way you came up or use the south slopes

route, perhaps angling left onto more open avalanche slopes above tree line.

For internationally-renowned climber Edward Whymper, a first ascent of this little peak in 1901 must have seemed trivial compared to his climb of the renowned Swiss Matterhorn some 30 years earlier. Blame it on liquor and age: Despite employing four top-notch Swiss guides, his mountaineering triumphs in the Rockies were minor. Although he was expected to recommend ways to boost tourism, he spent much time criticizing his host, Canadian Pacific Railway.

The southeast slopes, seen from Stanley Glacier trail.

Approach route and west slopes of Storm Mountain from Mount Whymper.

STORM MOUNTAIN 3161 m

Difficulty A moderate scramble via west slopes
Round trip time 6-11 hours
Height gain 1500 m
Map 82 N/1 Mount Goodsir

Storm Mountain is a large, brooding summit overlooking Castle Mountain Junction and Twin Lakes. Rock climbers ascend the sweeping northeast ridge, but use the west side only for descent. Early in the summer, though, when firm snow covers some of the tedious scree and vegetation in the old Vermilion burn hasn't had too long to flourish, this climbers' descent route makes an acceptable nontechnical way up. Don't expect a crowd; you may even have the peak all to yourself. Try from June on.

From Castle Junction on the Trans-Canada Highway, drive 10 km southwest on the Kootenay Parkway (Highway 93). Park at Continental Divide/Fireweed parking lot. Scramble route starts 0.7 km south.

From the parking lot walk 0.7 km south, cross the stream and head straight through burnt forest aiming for the small valley on the west side of the peak (675738). Expect rugged going for the first distance, but travel becomes easier once you reach the valley. As you cross the boulder field, you may marvel at one house-sized mass of quartzite. Apart from the sheer size of it, its ability to have withstood what must have been a substantial fall from adjacent cliffs says much for the quality of the rock. Limestone would have undoubtedly shattered to bits, but this quartzite remained intact.

Continue east toward labourious scree slopes at the end of the valley. Foreshortening makes these much longer than they appear, which is a good reason to go during June when snow patches and an ice axe lessen the toil. As you gain elevation, a quiet cirque to the north becomes visible, complete with two alpine tarns characteristically rimmed by Lyall's larch. Higher up on the route, short cliffs can be avoided by detouring left, and once past these the angle relents for the finish. As you trudge to the top, avoid the overhanging cornice by keeping to the right.

From the top, the view is stupendous. The north face of nearby Mount Ball, resplendent under its icy cap, rivets the gaze and reveals nothing of the easier south side that scramblers occasionally ascend. To the west stand some of the Rockies' more dominant and sought-after summits: Mounts Deltaform, Hungabee and the two Goodsir peaks, all more than 3353 m. On **descent** you may decide to detour over to the nearby tarns to while away any extra time, otherwise return the same way.

Storm Mountain was an accepted qualifying climb for new members at the Alpine Club of Canada's Vermilion Pass Camp in 1912. These were formative years for the club, and anyone with a yearning to climb and who had time and money were welcomed. Many came from flatter parts of the continent and not surprisingly, found these ascents a tough way to spend a vacation. As one participant noted, "Those yielding slopes of splintered rock were a tiresome treadmill, but the climb seemed more worth the effort when the summit was reached … and the scenery at last began to present elements of beauty." The name Storm Mountain is, of course, weather-related.

MOUNT BALL 3311 m

Difficulty A remote but moderate scramble involving bushwhacking
Round trip time 1-2 days
Height gain 1820 m
Map 82 N/1 Mount Goodsir

Mount Ball's domed cap of snow and ice is visible from countless other peaks. This route is a long tedious trip with a feeling of remoteness throughout and as a result, is still tackled infrequently. Nonetheless, it is a major summit and this approach offers a fairly non-technical way up. The summit view is superb, but few who have undertaken the trek would repeat it. A massive forest fire here in 2003 has created many challenges with charred logs as well as bush. After several hours you escape Haffner Creek bush and enjoy open travel in the upper valley. A few hardy souls give it a try most years—or at least think about it! Wait until about mid-July to try the ascent; ice axe recommended.

From Castle Junction on the Trans-Canada Highway, follow the Kootenay Parkway (Highway 93) to Marble Canyon Campground, 7 km south of the Continental Divide.

Start along the creek from near the southeast corner (by loop J) of the campground. A gravel road leads down to the campground water supply by the creek.

Fifty metres past this, the proper trail, crisscrossed by deadfall, diverges left and rises above the canyon. For the first half hour this path on the north (left) side above the canyon is easily followed, but farther on deteriorates or disappears periodically into thickets of bush and stints of hillside bashing. Continue along, always within earshot of the creek, for some 2-3 hours. Now you should be near

Approaching Mount Ball from Haffner Creek. Route enters cirque to left.
B Beatrice Peak, S summit of Mount Ball.

Photo: Kris Thorsteinsson.

From Beatrice Peak route to Mount Ball follows intervening ridge, then heads up snow slopes.

the upper valley (665665). Bypass the cliff band easily by its right-hand side, whereupon open larch meadows offer a respite and a chance to study Mount Ball. The worst is now over, and the view of the finale is inspiring.

Although guarded by horizontal cliffs, the squat, snowy dome definitely appears conquerable. Long moraines and a shrunken cascade of ice speaks of a large glacier having once filled this cirque, and in fact is shown on earlier map editions. The ascent route leaves the moraine, crosses karst pavement and enters the scree-filled basin on the left between Mounts Beatrice and Ball (675678). You must gain the ridge connecting the two via a suitable gully, such as the one right below Mount Beatrice. Plod along the

undulating ridge to Mount Ball, pass the rocky buttress on the left and walk up snow patches to the rounded summit.

Not surprisingly, the view is fantastic on a clear day. Parties doing one-day ascents will probably have little time to linger on top, though. Round-trip time may exceed 14 hours so a headlamp, a steady pace and a good early start are advisable. Dawdlers need not apply.

Irish-born John Ball was a famed British alpinist and public servant who aided the Palliser Expedition in his position as Under-Secretary of State for the Colonies. As her graduating climb in order to join the Alpine Club of Canada, Beatrice Schultz climbed the peak now bearing her name. Graduating climbs have since been replaced by membership fees.

217

STANLEY PEAK 3155 m

Difficulty A difficult, exposed scramble requiring much routefinding
Height gain 1655 m
Round trip time 12+ hours; a full day
Map 82 N/1 Mount Goodsir

As seen from Kootenay Parkway, Mount Stanley's glaciated north face is impressive. This face presents a superb alpine climb and most parties summit by this elegant route. A far less esthetic line is to thrash up Haffner Creek, ascend avalanche gullies on the backside and routefind your way up rubble, ledges and steep rock bands. This approach to Stanley Peak shares part of the same tedious approach as for Mount Ball and it is not a trek that one would rush to repeat. Although

Stanley is closer, more routefinding is required on the actual peak, so like Mount Ball, it, too, will be a full day. Purists will undoubtedly label a "slog" route up this beautiful peak sacrilegious, potentially opening the floodgates to the hordes. Realistically, though, the tedious approach combined with intricate routefinding and a short ascent season will ensure that only a few parties will ever actually get up it. If you are serious about scrambling up Stanley, it is worthwhile first going up nearby Vermilion Peak for a view of the approach and possible routes up the south side. As conditions for Stanley must be snowfree, the feasible ascent window will probably be limited to August and part of September. Start early and carry an ice axe.

From Castle Junction on the Trans-Canada Highway, follow Kootenay Parkway (Highway 93) to Marble Canyon Campground, 7 km south of the Continental Divide.

Start along the creek from near the southeast corner (by loop J) of the campground. A gravel road leads down to the campground water supply by the creek. About 50 m past culverts, the proper trail, crisscrossed by deadfall, diverges left and rises above the canyon. Follow this. For the first half hour this path on the north (left) side above the canyon is easy to follow, but farther on deteriorates or disappears periodically into thickets of bush and stints of hillside bashing. Continue along, always within earshot of the creek, for about 1.5 (brisk pace) to 2 hours. Now you should reach the bottom of a wide, open avalanche slope on the left that comes to within about 100 m of the creek. Even if you're crashing about

in the bush by the creek here, the open slope should still be evident. By way of further orientation, from the edge of this slope there is a view of an ice-clad hump far up valley. I was tired of Haffner Creek here and welcomed the opportunity to ascend an open slope, especially one headed toward Stanley Peak. Note that the view from Vermilion Peak suggests that either the avalanche slope before this or others farther upstream would likely suffice, too. I, however, will not be going back to find out.

Tramp easily up this gully, then stay right when it splits. It is not necessary nor advisable to continue up onto the ridge as towers along it require detours and downclimbing. It is better to angle right over much broken rock toward the main mass of the objective. While in some places you can scramble along the ridge, often you will find gullies and ledges to the right preferable. A cairn here and there will help you identify your route for return. If on the ridge crest, a tower followed by a notch (at 652688) right where the ridge meets the main summit requires backtracking and traversing lower down between towers. From here on things get interesting and will test your routefinding skills. It is worth carefully studying the remaining steep terrain ahead, and as you might expect, it is not a feasible scramble if snowy.

I next found it necessary to make an ugly descent down a steep, dirty gully so I could cross the top of the major gully below the notch to reach the main summit mass. A traverse to the right at the same level as the notch and below a rock band led to a promising gully, and I began to work my way up from there. Frequent detours were necessary. Rather than attempt to give specifics (which will be subject to misinterpretation anyway), I'll mention that perseverance paid off despite trying moments. Expect several steep parts, loose gullies and considerable searching about. Remember, you have to find your way back down this beast, too. From Vermilion Peak it appeared that traversing much farther around to the right (toward the skyline) would have led to easier terrain. Again, I will not be going back to find out.

The route to the spacious summit finishes over brown shale and snow patches to a small cairn and register. An incredible view includes familiar big Lake Louise peaks like Mounts Temple and Deltaform, also Assiniboine, Hector, Goodsir Peaks, the Bugaboos and nearby Mount Ball. In spite of the panorama, your mind may be preoccupied with worries about the descent. **Return** cautiously the same way. Any cairns made on ascent will be pleasantly reassuring on the way down!

Edward Whymper, who made the first ascent, named the mountain for Frederick Arthur Stanley, Canada's 6th governor general. Hockey fans might also recognize the name in relation to a well-known trophy.

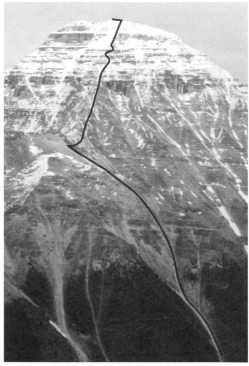

Telephoto shot of Stanley from Vermilion Peak. Route shown is approximate.

VERMILION PEAK 2622 m

Difficulty Moderate scrambling on loose shale at the top
Round trip time 5-7 hours
Height gain 1260 m
Map 82 N/1 Mount Goodsir

Most scramblers are oblivious to this fine little peak in Kootenay National Park, prob-ably because it is out of sight of the busy Trans-Canada Highway. Starting mere minutes from Highway 93, this steep but satisfying ascent requires no routefinding and offers a view almost immediately. Apart from the final shaley ridge, the outing is little more than a strenuous hike. Try from mid-June on.

From Castle Junction on the Trans-Canada Highway, follow the Kootenay Parkway (Highway 93) 11 km south of the Continental Divide, or 3.8 km south of Marble Canyon. Park on the shoulder near a clearing on the north side of the road.

Vermilion Peak sits on the northeast side of the road, and on its southwest side is an obvious open avalanche gully that does not quite extend to the present highway. This gully does, however, just barely reach what was the original roadbed, 40 m uphill. Hike up through a clearing to this old road, now becoming overgrown. If

Roadside view of ascent gully up Vermilion Peak. Route follows right skyline ridge at top.

A perfect autumn day. The Rockwall and Mount Goodsir from Vermilion Peak.

you walk south for perhaps 100 m (possible cairn), you can then head up through brief forest to easily reach the terminus of this open, grassy avalanche gully.

As you ascend, remember, bears often feed on avalanche slopes like this. Once, while scouting out this route from the car, I did see a grizzly here. To avoid surprise encounters you should holler periodically. Human voices have proven more effective than bells or whistles. For scramblers who prefer to go quietly and trust luck, it is but a short crawl to the road anyway.

Two minor rock bands interrupt the gully, but these pose no challenge. A glance over your shoulder reveals Tumbling Glacier, and Mounts Gray and Drysdale in the Vermilion Range. To the northwest, the mighty Goodsir Peaks preside over lesser summits. Lyall's larches appear just before tree line and here the gully splits. Either will suffice,

although the bushier right branch reduces some traversing. Avoid the steep loose shale slopes right below the summit and instead contour right and gain the right-hand end of the skyline ridge.

Follow the ridge to the top, detouring right at narrow or rotten sections. The summit is a perfect viewpoint for the Haffner Creek approach to Mount Ball while also revealing the tamer backside of Mount Stanley. Pyramidal Mount Deltaform is visible, while to the southwest is the Howser Towers in the Purcell Range, three shadowy granite spires ruggedly framed between Vermilion Range peaks. When your senses have been satisfactorily sated, **return** the same way.

Vermilion describes the colour of the iron-rich Paintpots found just off the highway a couple of kilometres north. Indian tribes coveted and traded this resource, which they used in making body paint.

ISABELLE PEAK 2938 m

Difficulty Moderate/difficult scramble; brief exposure
Round trip time 8-11 hours
Height gain 1535 m
Map 82 N/1 Mount Goodsir

Isabelle Peak is a good scramble with a well-graded approach trail. Because it is not clearly visible from any highway and is greatly overshadowed by neighbouring Mount Ball, the mountain has seen very few ascents in the past. For an interesting scramble and an excellent vantage point that lacks a crowd, it is a fine objective. Try from about early July on. Ice axe recommended.

Drive to Floe Lake/Hawk Creek trailhead on the west side of the highway in Kootenay National Park, 22.2 km south of the Continental Divide and 8.4 km north of Vermilion Crossing. Hawk Creek trail starts on the east side of the road; If you look carefully, Isabelle Peak is barely visible to the northeast through tall roadside trees.

Cross the road and hike alongside it northwest for 200 m to Hawk Creek. A good trail then follows the left (west) streambank. In about an hour cross a bridged tributary stream (682621), con-

tinue across rocky open slopes below steep cliffs, go past a major waterfall on Hawk Creek whereupon the trail suddenly gains elevation through a series of four or five switchbacks. The grade eases off; the forest (now replete with larches) opens and the path crosses the bottom of an avalanche slope [704631 (by GPS)] on the left (possible cairn). You have an unobstructed view of rubbly slopes leading to a broad gully on Isabelle Peak's south slopes. Allow 2-2.5 hours to here (700 m elevation gain).

A trailside view of Isabelle Peak.

Eye-balling the summit mass. S summit.

Head up the hillside, scrambling easily up the gray rock band near the bottom. A watercourse in the middle of the slope offers firm rock steps rather than scree for much of the way. You'll progress rapidly here, but will undoubtedly find yourself pausing to admire the Rockwall to the southwest and Mount Assiniboine to the east. Scramble up firm ledges in the gully but be careful of loose debris. The gully tops out on a broken ridge where a more complete panorama unfolds around you. Isabelle's summit is off to your left, but you should familiarize yourself with exactly where you came up—it may well look different and more intimidating on return.

Continue farther up the ridge, and when it looks simplest, begin traversing left across rubbly gullies below the undulating crest that curves left. To reach the highest point, scramble up a 50-75 m-high gully that is steep at the bottom, but

solid. This is likely the crux and you should note it for return. Now you emerge on a plateau with the summit close by and some 10-15 m higher. The easiest way up this last bit is around to the left.

The near horizon is dominated by snowcapped Mount Ball and Ball Glacier. To the right are Copper and Pilot mountains and Mount Brett. Major peaks of the panorama include Goodsirs, Sir Douglas and Assiniboine, as well as Farnham Tower and the Bugaboos in the Purcell Range. On a clear summer day, one could literally spend hours on this peak, which we did.

The **return** is via the same way and you may find scrambling more difficult going down. C. S. Thompson visited, explored and climbed in the Rockies at the turn of the century and named the peak for his sister.

LAKE LOUISE AREA

Mount Bell	2910 m	moderate	p. 227
Mount Niblock	2976 m	moderate	p. 229
Mount Whyte	2983 m	difficult	p. 230
Sheol Mountain	2779 m	moderate	p. 232
Mount Temple	3543 m	moderate	p. 235
Mount St. Piran	2649 m	easy	p. 237
Mount Fairview	2744 m	easy	p. 239
Panorama Ridge	2800 m	easy	p. 240
Tower of Babel	2360 m	easy	p. 242
Eiffel Peak	3084 m	moderate	p. 244

Lake Louise is without question the gem of the Canadian Rockies. Few places in the entire chain can match the grandeur of this area. Before the turn of the century, Canadian Pacific Railway recognized Lake Louise's unparalleled beauty and used it unabashedly to entice wealthy visitors from afar. The lure? A stunning picture of glaciated Mount Victoria soaring high above emerald green waters of Lake Louise. "Fifty Switzerlands in One!" boasted one poster. The ploy worked. Hordes soon began arriving and have not let up since. Even today, to miss Lake Louise is to miss the Canadian Rockies. Because of its popularity, one cannot expect solitude here. It is heavily used, to say the least, but spectacular nonetheless.

Lake Louise straddles the Continental Divide and the summit ridge of Mount Victoria, in fact, diverts water into both Alberta and British Columbia. This is an area of high precipitation that hosts not only big mountains but also large glaciers. While many summits are alpine climbs requiring glacier travel and tech-

nical climbing, you can find good scrambles, too. The highest peak in the area is Mount Temple (3543 m), and on a sunny summer day a few dozen or more parties may be scrambling up the south slopes toward the top. Although this number pales when compared with masses of 100-200 seen daily on popular summits in Europe and the United States, for the Canadian Rockies, it is an army.

In the past, the peaks in the Skoki region just north of Lake Louise were much less visited, but these too are becoming more popular. Together with the numbers of horse riders and backpackers, visitor impact has been significant enough to warrant a quota system, which may be implemented by the time this goes to press.

Scrambles around Lake Louise are distinctly different than those found in the Front Ranges. While the rock is still of sedimentary origin, many mountains are layer cake formations that have been horizontally-uplifted instead of dip-slope type. Weathering often forms alternating bands of short steep cliffs sepa-

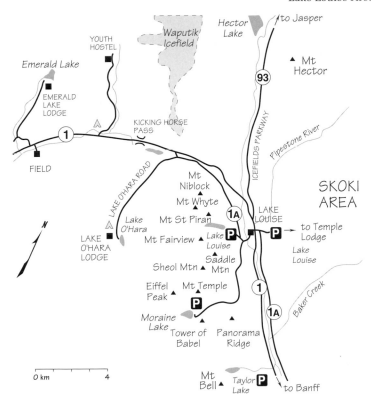

rated by flat rubble-strewn ledges. You may find this a pleasant change from tilted, downsloping strata of Kananaskis, Canmore and other Front Range areas. The scree is as tedious as anywhere, though. Quartzite is found in the lower layers of peaks surrounding Lake Louise, and cragging is well established. Most popular are steep and overhanging walls along the back of the lake in an area cleverly known as "The Back of the Lake." Note that quartzite on the peaks is often clad with lichens and when wet it is much more slippery than limestone.

Snow persists for much of the summer at higher elevations of Lake Louise, especially on north-facing aspects. Many fine alpine ice routes exist nearby. Even for scrambles, an ice axe is standard equipment just about anytime and never looks out of place here on a pack. Until July, some scrambles may in fact be more mountaineering in nature because of remaining snow. The Continental Divide bears the brunt of major Pacific storms and peaks here can sock in for days. A cold overnight rain will often dump snow at higher elevations even in midsummer and a couple of days' precipitation may spoil conditions on big peaks for days or longer. Valuable vacation time can be wasted here waiting for improvement, whereas conditions may be much better just a short drive east to Banff, Canmore or Kananaskis. Statistically, you can expect good weather about one day out of three around Lake Louise. Historically, late July and the first half of August have stable periods of good weather.

Access Lake Louise is on the Trans-Canada Highway, two hours west of Calgary. To the east, Banff is the nearest town while the next town to the west is Golden. Brewster's runs a daily shuttle from Calgary International Airport to Lake Louise and Greyhound buses stop here as well. Like anywhere in these mountains, though, a car is really what you need. Within the village, a well-marked road runs 5.5 km to Chateau Lake Louise. Moraine Lake Road branches left at 4 km and travels 12 km to the Valley of the Ten Peaks. Highway 1A from Lake Louise to Kicking Horse Pass is now closed to vehicles.

Facilities Lake Louise has grown considerably in the past decade and visitor facilities are now more complete. Samson Mall offers a grocery store, liquor outlet, laundromat, showers, sporting goods, a great little bookstore, photo shop and Laggan's. Laggan's Bakery gives probably the best dollar value of any eatery you're likely to find anywhere around and most locals' itinerary includes the requisite stop (or start!) here. Wilson Mountain Sports both sells and rents equipment including ice axes and bikes. Of the two gas stations in town, neither is open 24 hours, nor are any restaurants. The Canadian Alpine Centre/Hostel has excellent, affordable cafeteria-style meals, but, not surprisingly, becomes crowded at peak times.

Accommodation A large Parks Canada campground is found in Lake Louise as is the Canadian Alpine Centre, jointly run by the Alpine Club of Canada and the Southern Alberta Hostelling Association. This facility has a cafeteria, meeting rooms, a cooking area, sleeping and family rooms plus a lounge. Reservations are usually required owing to popularity. Expect to pay big bucks anywhere else, if you can even get in: hotels here are expensive.

Located in the adjacent backcountry are two teahouses. The Lake Agnes Teahouse is found on the approach to Mounts Niblock and Whyte, while the Plain of Six Glaciers Teahouse is below Mount Victoria and up-valley from a descent route on Mount Whyte. Both teahouses are popular hiking destinations, but remember to take cash for your goodies at these two places. Neither credit card nor singing for your supper will suffice.

Information The multimillion dollar Parks Canada Information Centre is next to Samson Mall. Information on weather forecasts, backcountry permits, trail conditions and bear closures is available here. Routes near Moraine Lake may require groups of 6 due to grizzlies.

Wardens maintain an office in the government building at the west end of Village Road, open from 0800-1600 hours. It is sometimes possible to speak with a climbing warden about current mountain conditions for specific routes and peaks. If the information centre is unable to provide the necessary information, wardens will be happy to help you stay out of trouble.

MOUNT BELL 2910 m

Difficulty A moderate scramble via southwest slopes
Round trip time 7-10 hours
Height gain 1500 m
Map 82 N/8 Lake Louise

Mount Bell is an outstanding viewpoint overlooking Taylor, Boom and O'Brien lakes. The approach is long but pleasant, circling around to easier slopes on the backside. En route you visit four separate alpine tarns. The view includes the seldom-glimpsed Boom Glacier, the Rockwall in Kootenay Park and farther west, the Bugaboo Peaks of the Purcell Range. Depending on snow conditions, part of the descent may provide an exhilarating glissade. An ice axe is recommended for this route; try it from about mid-June on.

Drive to Taylor Lake trailhead at a gravel pull-off area on the south side of the Trans-Canada Highway 8.1 km west of Castle Junction.

From the parking lot, cross the creek and follow the well-graded hiking trail 6.3 km to Taylor Lake. Lakeside picnic tables offer a convenient rest stop. From Taylor Lake, the north side of Mount Bell looms threateningly above and reveals no easy line of ascent. Continue across the bridged outlet stream and hike southeast for about 30 minutes (2 km) to O'Brien Lake. Follow the right-hand shore through stands of feathery Lyall's larch and across carpets of wildflowers to the waterfall at the west end of the lake.

Mount Bell's rubble slopes from Boom Mountain. Routes join at col.

Almost there: the summit ridge.

in this firm rock just for fun. Easier terrain is followed by pinnacles that are bypassed on the left-hand side. The last bit before the summit requires a detour to the right, going below a large block that appears to be straddling the route. Once you've had enough spectacular scenery, **return** the same way.

Mount Bell is named for Dr. Frederick Bell, founding member of the Alpine Club of Canada, and his sister, Nora Bell, also a club member, who accompanied the first ascent party in 1959.

Don't expect a marked trail; just grovel up the hillside to a beautiful valley replete with two small meltwater ponds.

From here your goal is a col at the far end of the valley past the ponds and the intervening rock debris. This col, or moreover, this notch in the ridge, gives access to easy-angled south slopes of Mount Bell. Since the wide, 150 m-high gully leading up to the col faces north, the snow may well be frozen in the morning. This is especially true after a crisp, clear night. Early in the season (June) such conditions would require use of an ice axe and possibly crampons, too. However, by the time you return, this snowslope should have softened and the potential glissade may be the best part of the trip.

Ascend this slope to the col. Looking west from there, successive ranges rise in an infinite array of shapes, forming the backdrop to surrealistic deep blues of Boom Lake. Turn right to gain Mount Bell's south and southwest slopes of scree and eroded sandstone. Continue toward huge lichen-covered quartzite blocks. You may also opt to scramble up the short chimneys

Boom Lake Approach

Boom Lake hiking trail provides an optional approach. The total distance of this route is shorter and although it should not require an ice axe or crampons, at least part of it is bushy. It has not been as popular as the Taylor Lake approach.

Begin 7 km west of Castle Junction on the Kootenay Parkway (Highway 93) at Boom Lake trailhead and picnic area. Hike to the lake, then continue along the right-hand shore to the avalanche slope above a heaped-up boulder field a few minutes farther. The slope's right side is generally open, but expect a short stint of bushwhacking lower down. It is not necessary to go completely to the ridge crest so angle left above tree line and traverse to the col, a pronounced dip in the blocky ridge. The two approach routes join here. Ascend the south side of Mount Bell as described for the O'Brien Lake approach. **Return** the same way, noting that your descent slope is above where the shoreline has been pushed well out into Boom Lake.

MOUNT NIBLOCK 2976 m

Difficulty Moderate scrambling from Lake Agnes
Round trip time 6-9 hours
Height gain 1260 m
Map 82 N/8 Lake Louise

Mount Niblock is one of the most popular Lake Louise scrambles and is reached by an even more popular hike. Neighbouring Mount Whyte is a significantly harder, more exposed scramble but capable parties can include it, too. Its inclusion allows a different, albeit longer, descent route via south slopes toward the Plain of Six Glaciers Teahouse. While not as grandiose as surrounding giants Lefroy, Victoria and Temple, both Niblock and Whyte are well worth the effort and a beaten path takes you most of the way. Do not attempt either peak too early in the summer, particularly Mount Whyte or the optional south slope descent. It might be snowy and prone to avalanche. Snowfree conditions are ideal, and July through September is generally the best time. Regardless, I recommend an ice axe and knowledge of its use. Crampons could also be considered but are not usually necessary—during summer any snow on these routes normally softens considerably by midday. If you do carry this equipment, it is sure to spark conversation among the curious hordes. Be prepared to pose for pictures and answer questions in peak season.

From the Lake Louise townsite, follow the access road 5 km to Lake Louise. Turn left 100 m before the Chateau and park in the huge paved lot.

Elbow your way along the paved lakeshore path (crux, sort of) past the Chateau to the signed Lake Agnes trail that immediately forks right. Follow it for 3.4 km to Lake Agnes. The Lake Agnes Teahouse will still be closed if you've got off to a real alpine start, so continue along the right-hand shore. At the far end of the lake, you'll find an obvious trail heading for big scree slopes and short cliffs under the high col connecting Mounts Niblock and Whyte. If you stay far to the right side, you'll find a good trail leads right toward the top of the scree cone. Tiny, furry rock-rabbits called pika occasionally dart among the rocks here. Nearby boulders are prime spots for drying carefully harvested leaves and grasses for their winter hay pile.

Go through the first cliff band from near the top of the scree-cone (beaten trail). Above that, the easiest line up to the Niblock/Whyte col angles more to the right toward Niblock avoiding steep cliff bands. Although these steeper rock bands are generally sound, the masses of rubble perched precariously on ledges dampens the charm. Depending on conditions, you may encounter firm snow patches in places. With an ice axe, step-kicking up snow is infinitely more efficient—especially for those simply following the steps! When dry, expect obvious trail(s).

On an early June ascent one year, an experienced party descended via a narrow snow gully that hid a meltwater stream beneath soft snow. A weak snowbridge collapsed, dropping the victim into a moat between a short cliff and surrounding snow. Her partner was unable to extricate her in time. Scramblers should heed this tragedy and select the route and time of ascent carefully.

View from Lake Agnes of Mounts Niblock (right) and Whyte (left), with Niblock/Whyte col at centre.

Once you reach the col and catch your breath, turn right and walk toward the buttress of Mount Niblock. Notice the weird rock here—black, blobby stuff that almost appears to have been molten once. It wasn't though. The only known occurrence of igneous rock anywhere in Banff Park occurs just south of Bow Lake, and the rounded shape here is owing to weathering.

You can ascend either side of the brown buttress. Most popular is a gully around the shadier left side. You might encounter lingering snow, but it otherwise offers no difficulties. Continue along the ridge to reach the top in an easy 20 minutes. Mount Niblock is one of the more favoured scrambles in the vicinity, and during three recent summers some 60 parties had signed the register. Its popularity continues to grow, too. Nude sunbathers be warned!

MOUNT WHYTE 2983 m

The ascent of Mount Whyte is more technical than Mount Niblock, requiring better scrambling and routefinding abilities. It is also more exposed. Judging by numerous trails leading the wrong way, it seems that many folks are still honing those routefinding skills. There is no quick, easy way down and this ascent is definitely NOT recommended for beginners. Allow about 35 minutes to ascend Mount Whyte and about the same to return to the Niblock/Whyte col. The return to the col will prove more difficult than the ascent.

Walk toward Mount Whyte from the Niblock/Whyte col and find an easy spot (probably to the right) to gain the crest of the ridge. Scramble along and when the ridge narrows you may have to make a brief detour right before it steepens. Higher up, traverse left on a prominent scree ledge (exposure) toward a right-slanting gully. Do NOT climb the gully. It could be icy, wet and it is dangerously exposed. Scramble up the easiest place to the right of the gully. Use caution as a fall would be fatal. Above this, traverse on a ledge to the right of a steep rock wall to the first broad gully (easiest). Scramble up on firm ledges of limestone to the ridge above, then continue along the ridge to the cairn a few minutes away.

The summit immerses you in some of the finest scenery the Canadian Rockies offer. Upper Victoria Glacier is complemented by Mount Lefroy and the ancient receding tongue of ice snaking from Abbott Pass to the Death Trap below. Abbott Pass Hut is barely visible—a minuscule dot straddling the pass between Lefroy and Victoria. With its rooftop diverting drizzle into both Alberta and British Columbia since 1922, the shelter stands in simple, silent testimony to the unwavering persistence and foresight of the Swiss guides who built it.

On **return**, either retrace your steps or descend south slopes toward the Plain of Six Glaciers Teahouse. Note that the south slope descent is no cakewalk either, but here's the route: Scramble down a short distance on the south side of Mount Whyte toward the gully between it and the next peak south (avalanche danger if much snow remains). It is steep initially, but eases to scree/snow slopes and occasional short rock bands. When feasible, work your way right over a hump to gain the next major gully. If you continue straight down instead, cliffs will require major routefinding or even rappels. Unless visiting the red-roofed teahouse for goodies, turn left upon hitting Plain of Six Glaciers trail and tramp 5 km to your car. This descent may be longer than returning to Lake Agnes, but does add variety. Expect a long day.

In 1886 two Canadian Pacific Railway officials visited Lake Louise. Today Mounts Niblock and Whyte commemorate these none-too-modest dignitaries.

A cloudy view of Mount Whyte from Mount Niblock. C col, W Mount Whyte, O southwest outlier.

SHEOL MOUNTAIN 2779 m

Difficulty Mostly moderate scrambling
Round trip time 5-9 hours
Height gain 1060 m
Map 82 N/8 Lake Louise

Though an unlikely choice for a first scramble at Lake Louise, Sheol Mountain does give impressive views of Paradise Valley area, especially Mount Temple's forbidding north face. Sheol is not a prominent peak, but merely the end of Haddo Peak's north ridge. It shouldn't be called a separate summit, but it is. The approach trail is excellent, so if you've done other nearby peaks, or want solitude while watching the usual crowd on Mount Fairview, give it a go. Try from July on.

Park at Paradise Valley trailhead, about 2.3 km along Moraine Lake Road.

Trailside view of Sheol's ascent gullies. Summit is to right.

Follow Paradise Valley trail reaching the Lake Annette junction in about an hour. Take the right branch (Giant Steps) for 10 minutes, upon which you'll emerge from deep forest into a wide avalanche run-out zone. The obvious gully above leads to Sheol's summit ridge; the actual summit is to the right. Stay out of this gully if there is still snow as it could be an avalanche trap. You can avoid those scrubby firs on the first part of the avalanche slope by keeping left where there is a clear corridor. Lake Annette, huddled in shadow below Temple's threatening north face, gradually appears as you trudge toward rock bands above. Silhouetted outlines of adjacent Pinnacle and Eiffel peaks add to the eerie effect.

Higher up the gully splits, and although either branch will do, the right-hand one presents less rubble and perhaps better scrambling. A view of Mount Hector greets you to the northwest once you gain the ridge. Before the highest point to the northeast a drop-off interrupts the ridge crest and requires descending a series of loose, shaley ledges on the right side. Choose your hand and footholds carefully here as even big blocks may be loose. This bit is the crux.

From the summit, Paradise Valley lies at your feet, guarded at the south end by Mount Hungabee. At the foot of

Pinnacle and Eiffel peaks from Sheol Mountain.

Hungabee lies a monstrous mud puddle, a natural settling pond for murky meltwaters of Horseshoe Glacier. This feeds Paradise Creek only to be gulped by thirsty scramblers savouring the fresh mountain water.

Return the same way. It looks tempting, but there is no easy way down the back side toward Mount Fairview. Samuel Allen, early explorer of Lake Louise, thought the adjacent valley a gloomy place and named it "Sheol," a Hebrew word for the Underworld. The peak isn't that bad, though.

Photo: Tony Daffern.

Mount Temple's ever-popular "tourist" route from Larch Valley. S Sentinel Pass.

MOUNT TEMPLE 3543 m

Difficulty A moderate scramble via southwest scree/snow slopes
Round trip time 7-12 hours
Height gain 1690 m
Map 82 N/8 Lake Louise

Mount Temple is the ultimate scramble. Towering majestically over Lake Louise, this hulking giant, third highest in the southern Rockies, presents a dauntingly impregnable wall of vertical rock capped by perpetual snow and ice. This impression is a facade. Hidden away on the southwest side lies the heavily-used "tourist" route. Temple is the most accessible 3353 m (11,000 ft.) peak in the entire Canadian Rockies and probably the most often climbed. With an apparent blessing by Mother Nature one summer's day in 1996, the sun shone while a small wedding ceremony was performed on the top. It is believed the wedding night was spent elsewhere.

Since 1894, when three intrepid members of the Yale-Lake Louise Club clambered up this face, hundreds of adventurers have uneventfully wheezed their way to the snowy summit. However, in 1955 seven teen-aged American boys, poorly equipped and inexperienced, perished here in Canada's worst-ever mountaineering accident. Ironically, adults supervising the group attempted to hold Parks Canada liable in the aftermath. They stated their own ignorance was owing to inadequate information from Parks Canada. Sadly, such irresponsible behaviour is even more prevalent today. Therefore, anyone doubting the conditions (either their own or that of the mountain!), should consult the Lake Louise Warden Office before heading out. In a typical year, the route is in condition by mid-July. Carry an ice axe. **Note:** Owing to grizzly activity, this trail may be closed or restricted to large groups. Check at the Warden Office or Information Centre regarding closures and required permits first.

From the Lake Louise townsite, drive 15 km to Moraine Lake parking lot.

Hike along the right shore of Moraine Lake to gain the Larch Valley trail, just past the lodge. Relentless switchbacks rise past a junction (keep right) and continue to open meadows at Larch Valley. Above tree line is a foreshortened view of the route as you hike past the two Minnestimma Lakes. More switchbacks lead to Sentinel Pass where you should have no trouble finding a path beaten into the scree of the southwest ridge, just right of the pass.

Churn your way up the scree. Below the first towering wall, traverse horizontally right on a path dotted with cairns and ascend the third gully to the right to overcome the black rock band. The first two gullies are much more demanding. Continue up more gravel-strewn black ledges, angling right to reach an easy spot to scramble up the next rock band, grey in colour. Cairns are abundant and seem to multiply yearly. Although the rock is generally firm, rubble on ledges and slabs requires caution. Well-trodden paths coax you up the slope to the ridge to a final band of firm, cream-coloured

Another sunny day in Paradise. L-R Mounts Deltaform, Goodsir and Hungabee.

Scrambling up a rockband.

rock. Handholds are plentiful and ascending this short band is pleasant.

The rest of the way up the ridge is straightforward, but the terrain is still steep and rubble is precarious. Even without snow, an ice axe helps im-

mensely. As you heave upward through the ever-thinning air, myriads of deep channels worn in the scree testify to the popularity of the peak. The angle finally relents for the final plod to the summit cairn. Stay well left of cornices on your right that project over the steep east face.

On a clear day you can see the stark, granitic spires of the Bugaboos, 80 km away. During late September golden larches, a dusting of snow and the characteristic smoke-free fall horizon make this panorama particularly beautiful. Although the ascent is a simple undertaking in dry conditions, it is a major peak and should be treated seriously. Sufficient warm clothing and an ice axe are strongly advised. Runners, of course, are useless. On the first ascent in 1894, scholar-come-mountaineer Walter Wilcox surmised that given the temperature at Lake Louise and that which he recorded on top, he felt it would never exceed 40°F (4°C) on the summit. It actually does occasionally, but prepare for cool temperatures anyway. Sir Richard Temple was president of the Economic Science and Statistics Section, British Association, 1884.

MOUNT ST. PIRAN 2649 m

Difficulty Easy, no difficulties
Round trip time 4-7 hours
Height gain 900 m
Map 82 N/8 Lake Louise

Like nearby Mount Fairview, Mount St. Piran is just a hike, but for an easy day out with a fine view it is worth doing. The view of surrounding peaks is outstanding, and whether you decide to traverse it or not, the return ties in well with a visit to Lake Agnes Teahouse for eats and treats. An ascent of Mount Niblock (described elsewhere) could easily be tagged on for a very full day. To traverse it in early summer usually requires an ice axe. Try from mid-June on.

Mount St. Piran from Mount Fairview. S summit, D optional traverse descent.

From the Lake Louise townsite, follow the access road to Lake Louise. Turn left 100 m before the Chateau and park in the paved parking lot.

Thread your way through crowds along the lakeshore trail past the Chateau to the signed Lake Agnes trail that branches right. Hike past Mirror Lake, watching for the marked trail to Little Beehive. This trail cuts back sharply to the right at 3.3 km, moments before the stairs leading up to Lake Agnes Teahouse. Crowds disappear once you branch off onto this less-travelled path. Within a few minutes and before Little Beehive, the signed Mount St. Piran trail, much narrower, heads left into the trees. After winding through delicate larch forest you emerge onto open alpine terrain where stunted patches of evergreen known as "krummholz" hug the ground. As they methodically zigzag to the top, the final rising switchbacks grant a beautiful view of a rugged landscape of peaks and glaciers.

Mount Daly and Bath Glacier from the top.

The broad summit is where ardent cairn-builders practise their craft. Depending on recent wind velocity, spectacular cairns may be standing, including a rock windbreak for overnight bivouacs. To the northwest, Hector Lake and Bath Glacier are evident while closer by, snowcapped Mounts Lefroy and Temple rule the heights. Other scramblers are often seen trudging up adjacent talus slopes of Mount Niblock.

If you fancy a traverse, continue west toward Mount Niblock and down rubble to the Niblock-St. Piran col. Although the curvature of the slope below this col suggests there could be cliffs, there are only minor rock outcrops. Angling down to the right toward Mount Niblock works

well. As the angle is steep, snow cover would render this part significantly more technical, while also creating a potential avalanche slope. Dry conditions are preferred.

If, upon reaching the teahouse, you are without money for goodies, you may as well forget begging, too: Many small but learned creatures will have been working the crowd long before you arrive. They have been begging for generations and competing will be fruitless.

According to *Place Names of the Canadian Alps* (Boles/Laurilla/Putnam), the town of Piran in Cornwall, England was the birthplace of Willoughby Astley, first manager of Lake Louise Chalet.

MOUNT FAIRVIEW 2744 m

Difficulty Largely a hike via Saddleback
Round trip time 4.5-6 hours
Height gain 1000 m
Map 82 N/8 Lake Louise

Mount Fairview provides a terrific view of Mount Victoria, Victoria Glacier and Bow Valley. The ascent has been a popular addition to a favourite Lake Louise hike for decades. Adjacent Saddle Mountain (2434 m) can be ascended with minimal extra effort. If, while in Lake Louise, your time and energy are limited, this trip probably makes the best use of those precious resources. Try from mid-June on.

From the Lake Louise townsite, follow the access road 5 km to Chateau Lake Louise. Turn left 100 m before the Chateau and park in the paved parking lot.

Saddleback trail starts near the boathouse along the lakeshore and leads to Saddleback in 3.7 km. Charred remains of the resthouse that once catered to turn-of-the-century trekkers are still here, more than 50 years after cancellation of its lease in 1937. The southeast slopes of Mount Fairview are straightforward and a beaten trail zigzags upwards from among scattered Lyall's larches. Although not as lofty as nearby Mounts Niblock or Whyte, Mount Fairview is aptly named, and if the weather cooperates, I'm sure you'll agree—the view is fabulous! **Return** by the same route. DO NOT attempt to descend gullies toward Lake Louise.

Fairview's gentle slopes, seen from Sheol Mountain. S saddleback.

PANORAMA RIDGE 2800 m

Difficulty Easy
Round trip time 4-6 hours
Height gain 1000 m
Map 82 N/8 Lake Louise

Although Panorama Ridge is not a singularly impressive summit, by proximity it offers a terrific view of the north face of Mount Quadra, east face of Temple and an unrestricted panorama of the Bow Valley. It is an easy ascent and the only crux is crossing Babel Creek without wetting your feet. Try from mid-June on.

From the Lake Louise townsite, drive the Moraine Lake access road 15 km to the Moraine Lake parking lot.

Follow Consolation Lakes hiking trail beginning near the parking lot washrooms and the bridge over Moraine Creek. You will reach Lower Consolation Lake in a half hour. Panorama Ridge, mostly a big scree slope, lies along the opposite side and you can hike up most any open avalanche path to the top.

Cross the outlet of the lower lake, either by logs, rocks or simply by wading (calf deep). A short bit of forest intervenes before an open avalanche slope leads to the top. Travel is easy and the scenery breathtaking almost immediately. Naturally, if there should happen to be enough snow to avalanche, then you should not be walking up this slope. Firmer snow, however, would alleviate the plod and could grant a glissade descent if you have an ice axe.

Panorama Ridge and the easy gully from Consolation Lake.

Looking back along the ridge toward Mount Temple.

You can continue along the ridge crest as far as you like, but even if you don't, you can still claim the summit. Continuing along involves much clambering over big quartzite boulders as you approach obvious pinnacles farther along. These pinnacles require routefinding, steep scrambling and a few detours. You're on your own there. From where you first gained Panorama Ridge you should allow two or three hours to reach the higher point beyond. It is actually less than 60 m higher but a full 2 km away.

Steep, icy north faces of Mounts Quadra and Bident dominate the view, rivalled by mighty Mount Temple's hulk-ing east side. The east ridge of Mount Temple is clearly visible, too, the site of periodic climbing rescues. These spectacular peaks contrast with the gentler landscape of the Bow Valley and the serrated Sawback Range to the east. Once you reach the top of Panorama Ridge the name seems entirely logical.

To **descend**, almost any spot will take you back to Consolation Lakes. Ski poles lessen the toil, as the terrain is mostly coarse, bone-jarring rubble rather than fine, pleasant scree. Above the upper lake, watch for a trail on the crest of the adjacent moraine that joins the east shoreline trail.

TOWER OF BABEL 2360 m

Difficulty An easy scramble, mostly grovelling up a gully
Round trip time 2.5-4 hours
Height gain 450 m
Map 82 N/8 Lake Louise

The Tower of Babel is a quartzite monolith that has long been popular with rock climbers. It is a lesser outlier of Mount Babel, one of the Ten Peaks towering above world-famous Moraine Lake. Although consider-

ably overshadowed by its larger neighbours, the top gives a wonderful perspective of the lake and more grandiose nearby peaks. The route described is actually the climbers' descent route, but if you can spare a few hours, the view justifies the trudge. You could even do it as an alternative to a rest day. Try from late June on, or whenever the gully is snowfree. The ascent gully is very confined; a helmet is recommended.

From the Lake Louise townsite, drive 15 km to Moraine Lake. The Tower of Babel and the described route are visible from the road just before you reach the lake.

From the Moraine Lake parking lot, find the hiking trail beginning near the washrooms and picnic area by Moraine Lake's outlet stream. Follow it toward Consolation Lakes for five minutes. Now you should be at the base of a rubble slope that leads directly up to the Tower of Babel. Trails are found in places but you can slog up anywhere. The ascent (climber's descent) gully lies to the immediate right of the Tower, hugging the flank.

Before you enter this gully, be aware that this is a confined chute that narrows and steepens as it rises. Owing to much loose talus, bouncing rockfall generated by parties above poses a very real hazard, especially if they are

Tower of Babel from Moraine Lake Road. Route circles left above gully.

242

Tower of Babel: big cairns, bigger scenery.

descending. Wear a helmet and be alert. For protection, the left side of the gully offers overhanging rock walls to duck behind, while on the right side you can scramble up rock ledges above the gully for at least part of the way. The middle of the gully is the WORST place to be. Parties are more likely to be descending in afternoon, making morning ascents safer.

From the top of the gully, a clear view of Mount Bident rising above Consolation Lakes unfolds. Here you turn left and follow the path to the broad summit plateau, just moments away. The summit consists of huge, lichen-covered plates of quartzite. Almost as impressive as the Ten Peaks is the number of large cairns perched along the edge of the plateau, possibly the handiwork of wishful or unemployed stonemasons.

Once you've frittered away enough time admiring the scene, **return** the same way. Keep in mind that others may be ascending, and knock down only as many rocks as you would enjoy dodging if you were below.

EIFFEL PEAK 3084 m

Difficulty Moderate scrambling via southeast slopes
Round trip time 4.5-9 hours
Height gain 1230 m
Map 82 N/8 Lake Louise

Eiffel Peak overlooks the Valley of Ten Peaks, a scene once pictured on Canadian $20 bills. The entire landscape is dazzling.

If the weather is unsettled, this scramble is a practical alternative to more demanding Mount Temple and gives a good view of Mount Temple's normal route. With Eiffel's spectacular location amid the Rockies' grandeur, it should be on any scrambler's list. Although there may be bigger peaks nearby, the summit view here ranks with the best. Try this from July on.

Eiffel's southeast slopes from Tower of Babel. L Larch Valley.

From the Lake Louise townsite, drive 15 km to the Moraine Lake parking lot.

Hike along the shore of Moraine Lake to Larch Valley trail, beginning just past the lodge. Relentless switchbacks lead to the flat, open meadows of Larch Valley where three peaks command the scene. Mounts Temple and Pinnacle form the stalwart buttresses of Sentinel Pass, while to the left a sweeping ridge rises to the uppermost heights of Eiffel Peak.

Wander south across a small stream and gain the broad shoulder arcing gracefully skyward toward Eiffel's summit,

850 m above. Many trails in the scree suggest the popularity of the objective. To put difficulties into perspective, a past summit register entry recorded a successful canine ascent. Near the top, wide gullies lead through the rock band upon which short, rubbly slabs give way to the summit and cairn.

On the northwest side stands an imposing 70 m-high pillar called Eiffel Tower, and the peak is named for this feature. Although details of the 1951 first ascent are lacking, the 1952 ascent required nine hours from the notch. It has been largely ignored since then.

Soaking up the scenery on Eiffel Peak. E Eiffel Tower, A Aberdeen, Y yours truly.

SKOKI AREA

Ptarmigan Peak	3059 m	moderate	p. 249
Mount Richardson	3086 m	moderate	p. 250
Pika Peak	3033 m	difficult	p. 251
Skoki Mountain	2697 m	easy	p. 252
Fossil Mountain	2946 m	easy	p. 253
Oyster Peak	2777 m	moderate	p. 254
Mount Redoubt	2902 m	difficult	p. 255
Brachiopod Mountain	2650 m	easy	p. 256
Anthozoan Mountain	2695 m	easy	p. 256

As a backcountry base for scrambling, few locations can match Skoki. It is truly paradise. Ascents are many and the surroundings are nothing short of spectacular. Starting elevations are high, so you need not worry about bushwhacking, while an established network of trails makes for easy approaches. You could spend an entire week here and bag a new peak each day! By Rockies' standards, rock quality in the area is acceptable and few ascents involve any steep or difficult scrambling. In the past, the only deterrent was an unavoidable 4 km trudge up Temple Road to the trailhead. Now, since adopting recommendations of the Bow Valley Study in 1997, Parks Canada has a quota system in place that restricts the number of visitors to the area. Check with the information centre in Lake Louise. **Note**: Bikes are not allowed on Temple Fire road.

Although the access road may be an unesthetic start to your visit, it is not without merit. Almost 100 years ago one perceptive visitor noted, "Looking back the view of Mount Temple, Paradise Valley and the Ten Peaks is a wonder, and you realize that in order to see these mountains you must really cross the Bow Valley and climb up on the other side." This "other side" just happens to be the route into Skoki.

Skoki Valley has long been popular with backcountry skiers, horse riders and fisher folks. Hikers, backpackers and peak-baggers are a relatively recent phenomena, especially the latter. The area retains a distinctly wild nature, despite its long-standing popularity. Lodge staff have witnessed wolves passing through and fishermen have glimpsed wolverine, a small vicious creature known for its ferocity. The high meadows and open slopes of nearby Lake Louise ski area attract grizzlies. Our group once experienced the unforgettable sight of a sow grizzly gambolling with four tiny cubs across the meadows at Baker Lake. The previous evening, an inquisitive young grizzly wandered into camp at dinnertime, convincing us to scurry over to a nearby shack, Halfway Hut, rather than sleep in our flimsy tent. Park officials were quick to close the area until the bears moved on, a situation that has since been repeated. Take all bear precautions when in this area. These are mentioned in the "Hazards" section at the start of this book.

Skoki Lodge's location was chosen because it promised the reliable, deep snow needed for a backcountry ski lodge. Consequently, scrambles do not get into condition until the snow melts about July or later and the season usually winds down about late September.

Backcountry camping permits and a backcountry pass must be obtained from the Parks Canada Information Centre in Lake Louise by Samson Mall. Expect a quota on visits in future, also.

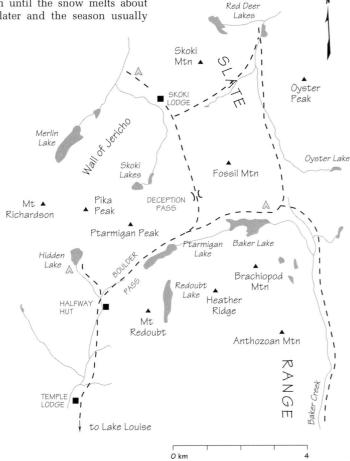

Left to right: Mount Richardson, Pika Peak and Ptarmigan Peak from Mount Redoubt.

Access From the overpass at the Lake Louise townsite on the Trans-Canada Highway, drive 1.6 km toward Lake Louise ski area. Turn right onto Temple Lodge access road and continue for 1 km to Fish Creek parking lot on the right side of the road before the gate. Park here.

Hike or bike the gravel access road 4 km toward Temple Lodge, which is located 100 m downhill of the road. The road ends at the edge of the ski run above the lodge, near a wooden building that formerly housed the Parks Canada avalanche research station. Ascend the ski run 200 m to the start of the well-used and signed trail. Hidden Lake campsite is located a few minutes' walk north of Halfway Hut (closed to overnight visitors) about 4 km from Temple Lodge. To reach Baker Lake campground, continue over Boulder Pass and along the left (north) shore of Ptarmigan Lake to the east end of Baker Lake. For Skoki Lodge and the backcountry campsite, turn left from the east end of Ptarmigan Lake and hike the trail over Deception Pass and down into Skoki Valley.

Accommodation If you're planning on spending time in the area, Hidden Lake campsite is ideal for ascents of Richardson, Pika, Ptarmigan Fossil, Redoubt and Heather Ridge. Baker Lake is closer for ascending Oyster, Anthozoan or Brachiopod peaks. Skoki Lodge is a rustic backcountry chalet beside Skoki Mountain. It caters mainly to horse-riding groups in summer but will usually sell snacks to non-guests. The backcountry campsite is 1 km north of the lodge.

PTARMIGAN PEAK 3059 m

Difficulty A moderate scramble via south scree slopes
Round trip time 4-7 hours from Hidden Lake
Height gain 780 m
Map 82 N/8 Lake Louise

Ptarmigan Peak is a straightforward ascent that is often feasible earlier than its neighbours and is sometimes climbed in winter, also. Near the top, a short, mildly exposed dip in the ridge adds variety.

From Hidden Lake, gain the broad south slopes slightly west of Boulder Pass. If you stay more to the left of the wide rubble slope, you'll have more scrambling and less scree plodding. Just before the highest point at the east end, the ridge dips and narrows for 5 m directly above a long narrow gully cleaving the south side. To this point the way is easy and the problems few. This brief section is only of moderate challenge but does interrupt the simplicity of the ascent momentarily. Crossing this arête exposes you to a terrific drop on the north side.

Occasionally, when avalanche conditions are favourable, ski parties ascend this peak, but judging by entries in the register, lads of the British Army mountain training units seem to make up a larger number of visitors.

Once on top, Mount Hector commands the northerly vista. When viewed from easterly and southerly directions such as when you drive west toward Lake Louise, many people have noticed an apparent resemblance between Mount Hector's outline and the popular cartoon dog "Snoopy" in a familiar prone position atop his dog house. **Return** the same way.

R Mount Richardson, P Pika and Pt Ptarmigan Peak from Mount Redoubt. H Hidden Lake.

MOUNT RICHARDSON 3086 m

Difficulty Easy/moderate scramble via scree on south aspect
Round trip time 3.5-6 hours from Hidden Lake
Height gain 800 m
Map 82 N/8 Lake Louise

Mount Richardson is the highest peak in the Skoki area, and is an enjoyable scramble with an option to traverse and descend by a different route. If camping at Hidden Lake, the mountain is right out your tent door. Map editions as late as 1980 crroneously indicate massive glaciation covering most of the peak and extending east to Pika and Ptarmigan Peak, but this is simply not so. An ice axe is recommended for the traverse toward Pika Peak. Try from July on.

On the summit of Mount Richardson with the Lake Louise group behind.

The south ridge above Hidden Lake is the easiest way to this expansive summit. Although the summit ridge isn't particularly narrow, be aware of cornices and a steep glacier on the north side. You can also reach the top after scrambling to the col between Richardson and Pika, although the slope above the col is often snowy and may require step-kicking and an ice axe. This route also serves well for descending and can be used to complete a traverse. The summit gives a terrific view of Mount Hector, the big peak to the

north, and all the giants surrounding Moraine Lake and Lake Louise. Sir John Richardson was surgeon and naturalist on the Franklin Arctic Expeditions.

If you're really keen, a traverse of Mount Richardson can be extended to an ascent of Pika Peak via the west ridge. This is a worthwhile and recommended day trip from the campsite. Note that the ascent of Pika is a difficult scramble compared to the easy trudge up Mount Richardson.

PIKA PEAK 3033 m

Difficulty Difficult scrambling via Richardson/Pika col and west ridge
Round trip time 3.5-6 hours from Hidden Lake
Height gain 750 m
Map 82 N/8 Lake Louise

Although it is a grade or two more difficult than nearby Richardson, Pika is a delightful scramble once the snow has gone and the rock is dry. As noted by mountaineers Delafield and Earle in 1911, "this (westerly) arête, which at a distance looks difficult, and which, in fact, is steep, is composed of rocks so broken as to render the ascent quite easy."

Gain the Richardson/Pika col via either the Pika's lower rubbly flanks above Hidden Lake or by traversing from nearby Richardson. The ridge to the summit consists of several short steep steps, sometimes cleft by short chimneys that make the ascent easier. The rock is excellent—firm and rough in texture. Stick close to the crest and avoid straying around to the exposed north side as it drops abruptly to a pocket glacier below.

Protruding like a stony fin just north of Pika Peak is an impressive freestanding wall of rock known as the Wall of Jericho. It has apparently been ascended!

Although I don't recall seeing it, Pika Peak is apparently named for a rock formation near the top resembling a mountain pika or "rock rabbit."

The freestanding Wall of Jericho from Pika Peak. Drummond Glacier in the distance.

SKOKI MOUNTAIN 2697 m

Difficulty An easy ascent via north scree slopes
Round trip time 2-4 hours from Skoki Lodge
Day trip from Hidden Lake
Height gain 530 m from Skoki Lodge; 735 m from Hidden Lake
Map 82 N/9 Hector Lake

Skoki Mountain is a quick little ascent right behind Skoki Lodge. This diminutive mountain has been ascended by some nine different routes by Edwin Knox, a former employee of historic Skoki Lodge. It is not a complex peak. The most common way follows an old logging road, now a wide swath, hacked into dense forest. Try from July on.

From Skoki Lodge, easy slopes lead up Skoki Mountain. Route goes around to north side near summit.

The most sensible starting point for this outing is the backcountry campsite 1 km north of Skoki Lodge. If you are camping at Hidden Lake, the approach hike will be much longer. During the 8 km approach, you must gain some 200 m elevation to cross Deception Pass, then promptly lose all of it and more before reaching Skoki Lodge and the base of the peak. This modest summit hardly justifies such a long-winded march, despite fine scenery en route.

Begin immediately back of the lodge near the present site of the outhouse. After rising through forest, the path leads to open meadows at tree line on the north side, and then a scree plod up open slopes takes you to the top. Expect confusion if the outhouse is moved.

An early visitor to the region hailed from Skokie, Illinois; also, Skoki is purported to be an Indian word meaning "marsh" or "swamp," some of which lies in areas to the east.

FOSSIL MOUNTAIN 2946 m

Difficulty An easy ascent from
Deception Pass
Round trip time 4-6 hours from Hidden
Lake
Height gain 670 m
Map 82 N/8 Lake Louise

This ascent is nothing more than a walk up a scree slope, and because it is so easy, backcountry skiers occasionally ascend this peak in winter, too. The view of the surroundings is spectacular.

From Deception Pass, tramp up the windblown west slope, usually bare even in the deep of winter. Coral fossils litter the route and add interest to an otherwise mundane march. The trek is far from boring, though: Picture-perfect Skoki Lakes, cerulean jewels snugly nestled between Ptarmigan Peak and the Wall of Jericho, is in itself reward enough. When seen by a group of American mountaineers in 1911, they named the lower of the two lakes Myosotis, "not only on account of its colour, but also on account of its forget-me-not qualities."

To the south, beyond the ski area, are the dazzling big peaks like Victoria and Temple that lure so many visitors to Lake Louise and Moraine Lake.

On **descent** you may be able to glissade the broad southwest gully toward Deception Pass if you have an ice axe. Steer clear of this slope in winter—wind-loading creates soft slab avalanche conditions, which resulted in two fatalities in the winter of 1988. A memorial plaque on top recalls this tragedy. Unfortunately, thoughtless morons have scarred it with graffiti.

Fossil Mountain and Ptarmigan Lake from Boulder Pass. D Deception Pass.

OYSTER PEAK 2777 m

Difficulty A moderate scramble via west-facing slopes
Round trip time 3-5 hours (south summit only) from Baker Lake
Height gain 600 m
Map 82 N/9 Hector Lake

Oyster Peak affords good scrambling to the south summit and along the ridge to the north end. The view of the Pipestone and Red Deer valleys is excellent, and you probably won't find other parties on top. Try from July on.

From Baker Lake campsite, stroll across Baker Creek valley and ascend straightforward rubble slopes at the south end. Continue easily along the broad crest for an hour to the true summit at the north end, which is about 40 m higher. You can speed the return by descending westward down scree and perhaps occasional slabby bits to Baker Creek valley. The nature of the terrain allows much scope for variation on both ascent and descent.

The tiny lake below the north end was at one time known as "Hatchet Lake," a name that has since been lost to time. Don't axe me why. The discovery of large quantities of fossils similar to common oysters induced geologist G. M. Dawson to title this peak accordingly. It is likely they were brachiopods, which you may also notice on your ascent.

Is it a ridge? No, it's Oyster Peak. N north, S south.

MOUNT REDOUBT 2902 m

Difficulty Moderate/difficult scrambling via northwest ridge
Round trip time 5-8 hours from Hidden Lake
Height gain 475 m (approximately) with loss and regain
Map 82 N/8 Lake Louise

The northwest ridge of Mount Redoubt grants good scrambling in grand surroundings. As usual, though, a certain amount of scree-bashing is involved. The view toward Mount Temple is stunning. Try from mid-July on.

The north side of Mount Redoubt and route from Redoubt Lake.

From Hidden Lake, head up over Boulder Pass and along the south shore of Ptarmigan Lake. Hike south up to Redoubt Lake, then gain height easily up over the north ridge of the objective. You then must lose elevation and cross a small rubble-strewn (not glaciated as some maps show) basin en route to the northwest ridge. This roundabout route is not problematic, but sounds more confusing than it actually is. Once on the northwest ridge the scrambling is delightful, with many horizontal ledges and big firm handholds. The backdrop is

a signature of Lake Louise, revealing giants like Victoria, Lefroy and Temple, three of the 53 Rockies peaks exceeding 3353 m (11,000 ft.). Overcome the final short cliff below the summit plateau by surmounting it on the right. **Return** the same way.

A. O. Wheeler, founding member and president of the Alpine Club of Canada, fancied the mountain resembled a military formation known as a redoubt. In this formation, forces are drawn up in a tight cluster, and this is often a last stand attempt with no flanking defenses.

BRACHIOPOD MOUNTAIN 2650 m
ANTHOZOAN MOUNTAIN 2695 m

Difficulty Easy scrambles via the west slopes
Round trip time 3-6 hours from Baker Lake
Height gain 410 m
Map 82 N/8 Lake Louise

Neither of these objectives poses any difficulty, and each is readily ascended by west-facing scree slopes. With a camp at Baker Lake, both can be done in one day and you'll be back in time for dinner. Each of these summits is a good argument for use of ski poles because of the looseness of the terrain. Try from July on.

From Baker Lake campsite, ford the outlet stream to approach these peaks. If you're starting from Hidden Lake, either cross the meadows between Ptarmigan and Baker lakes, or follow around the south shore of Ptarmigan Lake from Boulder Pass. Clamber up talus on the west slope of whichever one you have chosen. As a final respite from rubble, Brachiopod proffers a brief change of pace at a short slab near the top, whereas Anthozoan—more or less a continuation of the same ridge but farther south—is entirely a slog. If you're interested, nearby Heather Ridge to the west is an equally simple outing via the west slopes.

Brachiopod is a common fossil found hereabouts; anthozoan is a particular class of fossil. The Mount Brachiopod first ascent party in 1911 found "five species of coral, three varieties of Brachiopods, a sponge and several other fossils such as Crinoids, Bryozoa, etc." This proliferation of fossils is an intriguing aspect of the Southesk Formation— 370 million year-old rock that comprises most of the west face.

Easy slopes of B Brachiopod and A Anthozoan from Deception Pass.

FIELD AND LITTLE YOHO VALLEY

Mount Burgess	2599 m	easy	p. 260
Wapta Mountain	2778 m	difficult	p. 262
Mount Field	2635 m	easy	p. 264
Mount Bosworth	2771 m	difficult	p. 265
Paget Peak	2560 m	easy	p. 266
Narao Peak	2974 m	moderate	p. 268
Mount Yukness	2847 m	moderate	p. 270
Mount Stephen	3199 m	difficult	p. 272
Mount Niles	2972 m	moderate	p. 274
Mount Daly	3152 m	difficult	p. 276
Isolated Peak	2845 m	moderate	p. 278
Mount Kerr	2863 m	easy	p. 280
Kiwetinok Peak	2902 m	difficult	p. 281
Mount Pollinger	2816 m	easy	p. 282
Mount McArthur	3015 m	difficult	p. 282
Mount Carnarvon	3040 m	difficult	p. 284

Field, British Columbia is the quieter neighbour of dazzling Lake Louise, lying 25 km west on Trans-Canada Highway and some 300 m lower in elevation. Field is the administrative centre for 1300 sq. km Yoho National Park. This park encompasses a section of the western slopes of the Rockies, where rushing streams begin their headlong journey to the Pacific Ocean. Many rare fossils have been discovered here and renowned Burgess fossil beds have been recognized as a world heritage site.

"Yoho" is said to be an exclamation of wonder in the Stoney Indian tongue. Field huddles at the foot of massive Mount Stephen, the highest peak in the vicinity, which towers more than a mile above. The ascent presents a daunting gain of elevation but the view is worth every tedious step. Like Lake Louise, Field experiences heavy snow accumulation. Summer can be short, effectively reducing the scrambling season to as little as two months or less for the bigger peaks. In winter and spring, Pacific storms from British Columbia get caught up along the Continental Divide, the air rushes down the east side warming as it descends, resulting in very strong, warm winds through the foothills. These are called chinooks, and are much appreciated along the eastern slopes of the mountains. While Kananaskis, Calgary

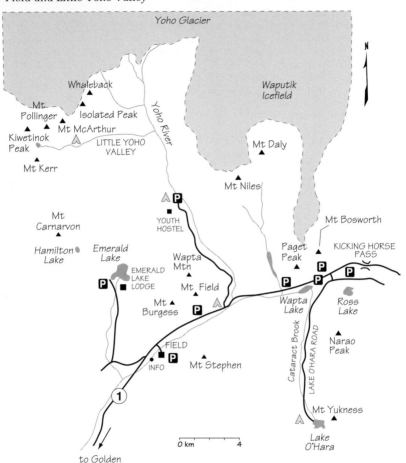

Yoho Glacier

Waputik
Icefield

N

Whaleback

Mt
Pollinger
Isolated Peak

Kiwetinok
Peak
Mt McArthur
LITTLE YOHO
VALLEY

Mt Kerr

Yoho River

Mt Daly

Mt Niles

Mt
Carnarvon

YOUTH
HOSTEL

Mt Bosworth

Hamilton
Lake
Emerald
Lake

Wapta
Mtn

Paget
Peak
KICKING HORSE
PASS

EMERALD
LAKE
LODGE

Mt Field

Mt
Burgess

Wapta
Lake
Ross
Lake

FIELD

INFO

Mt Stephen

Cataract Brook

LAKE O'HARA ROAD

Narao
Peak

1

Mt Yukness

Lake
O'Hara

0 km   4

to Golden

and Canmore bask in warmth and wind, Field and Lake Louise may well be enduring a blizzard.

A variety of rock is encountered in this area, and peaks vary considerably in formation. Some have undergone tremendous upheaval, with evidence of severe folding. Others have been uplifted and are of layer cake formation. Loose shale exists in great quantity at lower elevations here but higher peaks often have firmer rock above this crud. Care is imperative owing to loose rock, and an ice axe is often useful. Rentals are available in Lake Louise at Wilson's Sports.

Access Field lies 35 minutes east of Golden and 20 minutes west of Lake Louise on the Trans-Canada Highway. Greyhound buses stop daily.

Facilities and Accommodation Field has several bed and breakfasts, hostels, chalets and bungalows. Amiskwi Hostel is in the hamlet, while Whiskey Jack Hostel is near the end of Yoho Valley Road. This road branches off the Trans-Canada Highway at the bottom of Field Hill, east of town. Monarch and Kicking Horse campgrounds, Cathedral Mountain chalets and a small store are found within the first 2 km of this road. Walk-in campsites are near thundering 300 m-high Takakkaw Falls at road's end. Situated west of Field are additional campgrounds at Hoodoo Creek and Chancellor Peak. Emerald Lake Lodge is definitely not for the budget traveller but does offer pleasant little extras like a sauna and hot tub. Weather not cooperating? Head for the exercise room. For shopping, "The Siding" in Field has groceries, meals and liquor.

If visiting Lake O'Hara, you need a reservation on the bus and a strict quota system is in place. Call 250-343-6433. For overnight visits, a backcountry pass is required and can be purchased beforehand or upon boarding the bus. Located at Lake O'Hara is a campground, Lake O'Hara Lodge and Elizabeth Parker Hut. The hut is booked by calling the Alpine Club of Canada at 403-678-3200 and is normally locked when no custodian is present. The lodge is pricey and has its own faithful clientele, many of whom book months or years ahead and return annually. Only a few of the 30 campground sites are first-come first-served. Contact Parks Canada in Field at 250-343-6433 for reservations.

Le Relais is a small day facility at Lake O'Hara that sells snacks, soft drinks and tea. This non-profit service is fulfilling its main purpose: At teatime, day-trippers no longer block the lodge's front steps.

Information is happily dispensed at the Parks Canada Information Centre at the entrance to Field. Whether your questions concern trails, permits, reservations, route conditions or lodging, they will be pleased to assist. Owing to the proximity of fossil beds, you'll need to obtain a special permit here to climb Mount Stephen.

Wardens Yoho Park Warden Office is located at Boulder Creek Compound a few kilometres west of Field on the right (north) side of the highway.

MOUNT BURGESS 2599 m

Difficulty An easy scree ascent from Burgess Pass trail
Round trip time 5-8 hours
Height gain 1330 m
Maps 82 N/8 Lake Louise, 82 N/7 Golden

Mount Burgess is a quick and easy scramble with an excellent approach trail. It overlooks braided Kicking Horse River and the hamlet of Field to the south. To the north is beautiful Emerald Lake ringed by Mount Carnarvon, the President and the Vice-President. This area is world-renowned for the Burgess shale beds, where many unique and previously unknown fossils of invertebrate life forms have been found. The route described takes you to the north, or lower summit. Reaching the marginally higher south peak is more challenging and requires routefinding skills, but is feasible. Try this ascent from late July on.

Park at Burgess Pass trailhead on the north side of the Trans-Canada Highway, 0.4 km east of Field.

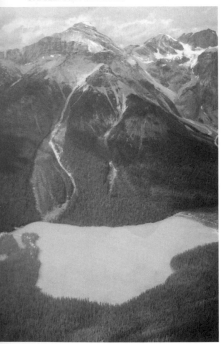

Mount Carnarvon and Emerald Lake from summit.

Follow the steep Burgess Pass trail, passing the only source of water in 20 minutes. Continue through cool, sombre forest and massive firs, crossing a short section of washed-out trail rebuilt since heavy spring rains of 1990. Shortly before reaching Burgess Pass, you emerge onto a huge avalanche slope a couple of hundred metres wide, and are treated to an unobstructed view of Mount Stephen across the valley. Of more concern, however, are steep walls of Mount Burgess, above you. Allow one hour of fast walking to here.

The open slopes up to the base of the mountain are mostly bare with only limited scrub and stunted evergreens surviving. A wide gully immediately to the right of a large treed island hugging the base of this face is the route of ascent. This prominent gully is visible from the highway below, but suffers foreshortening as you stand immediately below and gaze up at it. Farther to the right the lower mountain flanks are also quite heavily treed, but there is no indication of any reasonable way up. Once you plod up the rubble toward the face it will become clear where to go. The correct gully is comparatively low-angled and not difficult. Keep to the right once you're in it until you reach open scree below the top.

Mount Burgess ascent route showing N north and S south summits. P Burgess Pass.

South Peak Option

The intervening ridge to the main (south) peak is more difficult. Dropping down into the rocky basin between the north and south summits is preferable. Ascend a narrow gully toward the north end of the ridge that trends south to the main peak, then detour left (east) and descend slightly. This avoids the narrowest part of the final bit along the ridge. To bypass these exposed portions, you may have to traverse across ledgy slabs toward little gullies that lead more directly to the main peak. Sound confusing? The lower north peak provides the perfect location to assess and perhaps justify the excursion. Most parties are content to stay on the north peak.

Return to Burgess Pass by descending the same gully you ascended; it is easily reached from the rocky basin between the north and south summits by contouring east (left). Any other gullies are steep and are not feasible descent routes. Alexander Burgess was commissioner of Public Lands for Canada, 1897.

WAPTA MOUNTAIN 2778 m

Difficulty Difficult, exposed section at top
Round trip time 6-9 hours
Height gain 1330 m
Map 82 N/8 Lake Louise

Wapta Mountain forms part of the backdrop of beautiful Emerald Lake. The logical way up is not obvious, so in spite of popular hiking trails nearby, in the past, few parties have attempted the summit. A good view and no crowds should be incentive enough, though. Try from July on, and carry an ice axe.

Of three possible approaches, the most direct way is from Yoho Valley, just east of Field, British Columbia. Follow Yoho Valley Road 12.6 km to Whisky Jack Hostel, about 0.6 km before Takakkaw Falls. Yoho Pass trail begins here. You can also reach Yoho Pass by two other trails. From Emerald Lake, a signed trail to the pass diverges east from the popular lakeshore circuit. This adds about 200 m elevation gain, or, you could take Burgess Pass trail beginning 0.4 km east of Field adjacent to the highway. This approach

not only adds almost 300 m elevation, but extra distance, too. The preferred Yoho Valley start is described below.

From Whisky Jack Hostel, follow the Yoho Pass trail to reach Yoho Lake in about an hour. DO NOT follow the Iceline trail. Continue past Yoho Lake toward Emerald Lake and within 10 minutes reach a fork in the trail. Take the left fork toward Burgess Pass. Shortly after the trailside cliffs end, you emerge onto a wide avalanche slope with open views,

The north end of Wapta Mountain from near Emerald Peak.
P Yoho Pass, C cliffs, A avalanche slope, B Burgess Pass.

Wapta Mountain from Burgess Pass. Route emerges from north-facing basin shortly before the summit S.

20 minutes past Yoho Lake. An obvious watercourse coming right down to the trail here gives access to the northwest side of the mountain.

Keep to the right side of the watercourse ascending the steep hillside. It will become clear that the impressive cliffs above are much lower to the right of this drainage. Aim for that general area. Climb the first rock band near the midpoint where a right leaning gully slices into it— possibly a cairn here. A spectacular view down to Emerald Lake gives reason to pause once you reach slabs above.

Continue up scree toward the peak's north end, past buff-coloured cliffs and traverse along the right (west) side of the final summit uplift. Any rocks dislodged here could potentially land near Burgess Pass hiking trail below, so move with caution. The easiest place to scramble up onto the summit ridge is some 50-75 m before the far south end. Here the cliffs are less steep and slightly stepped. There may be cairns. Check it out thoroughly and remember, you must also descend this terrain, which will undoubtedly prove more difficult. The crumbly, exposed south ridge now leads quickly to the summit. Use care, much of it is loose and the east side drop is terrific. A fall would be fatal.

From the top, a view of the Waputik Icefield, Mounts Balfour and Stephen is superb. "Wapta" is the Stoney Indian word for river, and makes no sense at all as a summit name. The **return** route is the same as you came up.

MOUNT FIELD 2635 m

Difficulty An easy ascent from Burgess Pass
Round trip time 5-8 hours
Height gain 1365 m
Map 82 N/8 Lake Louise

Mount Field is a very non-committing ascent offering a unique viewpoint for Mount Stephen's north glacier and distant Takakkaw Falls. One wonders why this bump at the southeast end of Wapta Mountain has been designated a separate peak. The ascent of Mount Field is one of the simplest in the vicinity, since all but the final 400 vertical metre slog uses well-graded Burgess Pass hiking trail. The view is worthwhile, but your accomplishment may not totally amaze your friends. Try from mid-June on.

Park at Burgess Pass trailhead on the north side of the Trans-Canada Highway, 0.4 km east of Field.

Follow Burgess Pass hiking trail, crossing the only source of water within 20 minutes. Continue for about two hours to a signed junction at the top of the pass. Take the YOHO PASS/ YOHO LAKE option only to where it curves left (north) toward Mount Wapta, leave the trail here and trudge up open shale and scree slopes. Trend right, aiming to intercept a dry gully that drains south and over the south side of the pass. The simplest place to breach the short rock band is above this gully at the southernmost end.

W Wapta Mountain, B Burgess Pass and Mount Field ascent route.

From the top you can see Mount Stephen's north glacier in a much-expanded and more engaging view than the normal foreshortened glimpse from Field Hill. The distant pointy snow-peak left of Mount Wapta is Mount Des Poilus; farther right is Yoho Glacier, Mount Balfour and Takakkaw Falls. Slightly north of you along the ridge toward Mount Wapta sits Walcott Quarry of the world-famous Burgess fossil beds. This site is a restricted access area and unescorted visitors are FORBIDDEN. Spot checks for would-be fossil hunters are ongoing, and thieves are prosecuted. Take solace in knowing that you would find little of interest anyway—authorized "digs" occur periodically through summer months and these meticulous groups generally leave no stone unturned.

Cyrus West Field, promoter of the first trans-Atlantic cable, visited this area at the insistence of CPR bigwig Cornelius Van Horne, who then patronizingly named it after his guest—the sole reason being to secure investment for continued railway construction. Mr. Field was amused, though, but that was about all.

MOUNT BOSWORTH 2771 m

Difficulty Difficult scrambling for 30 m at top
Round trip time 5-7 hours
Height gain 1160 m
Map 82 N/8 Lake Louise

Mount Bosworth is a small, unpretentious roadside peak rising directly on the Continental Divide that provides a fabulous view of much larger, more famous peaks nearby. A steep rock band just below the top is the crux. If you are near Field or Lake Louise, this is a good little trip that still does not see that many visitors. For a better view of the mountain, look from Highway 1A. The intersection is 0.6 km west. Try this route about late June or early July.

Start at the huge avalanche slope on the Trans-Canada Highway 0.6 km east of the Highway 1A (Lake O'Hara) intersection and 2.3 km west of the Yoho National Park east boundary east of Field, British Columbia.

Assuming there is no longer any snow on the avalanche slope, tramp up the left edge of it where brush is thin. A minor cliff band partway up the avalanche slope is surmounted via a gully that may have a trickle of water flowing in it. Above tree line, cross over into the next gully, and continue working up and left crossing yet another gully. Aim to top out on the main ridge immediately east of the summit block. It is a steepish face with a horizontal band of black rock just below the top. This band is the crux—30 m of more difficult scrambling on ledges and up corners to overcome this black band. There are many possibilities, depending on your expertise. The cairn and register are 10 minutes farther.

On a clear day, you will be treated to a panorama that includes the icy north face of Mount Victoria to the south with the stark, brooding Goodsirs just to the right. Ski tourers may recognize landmarks on the Wapta Icefields to the north such as the snowy face of Mount Collie. An alternate descent suggested in previous editions has not proven popular, so you may as well **return** the same way. If you decide to descend the main gully right under the summit, all goes well until the black band lower down. You must then hillside traverse two gullies east to reach the original line of ascent. This option avoids the 30 m crux but has little else to recommend.

G. M. Bosworth was fourth vice-president of the Canadian Pacific Railway.

A avalanche gully, C crux on east ridge.

PAGET PEAK 2560 m

Difficulty An easy ascent via Paget
Lookout trail
Round trip time 4-5 hours
Height gain 1000 m
Map 82 N/8 Lake Louise

Paget Peak, near the Continental Divide, is
the end of a long ridge that rises high above
Kicking Horse River and Field. This nonde-
script nubbin provides a view and a feeling
of accomplishment that far surpass the
actual effort involved in the ascent. Overlooking Sherbrooke and Wapta lakes, it is
easily reached via a popular hiking trail to
an abandoned fire lookout. You gain almost three-quarters of the elevation on the
hiking trail, so you could sleep in and still
make the top. The glaciated north face of
Mount Victoria, snowy Mount Balfour and
distant Selkirk Range peaks are just a
fraction of the panorama. Try from late
June on.

Drive to Wapta Lake picnic area at the
west end of Wapta Lake, British Columbia, 5.1 km west of the Continental Divide.

From the parking area, follow the
Sherbrooke Lake/Paget Lookout trail that
starts near the picnic shelter. Almost immediately it splits: The right branch descends to West Louise Lodge, Paget and
Sherbrooke are to the left. At the next and
only other junction take the right fork for
Paget Lookout. As of 1996, the small
square lookout building still perched on
the lower slopes of the peak. It is no longer
used as satellite technology has now su-
perseded human observation as the preferred method of spotting forest fires.

Well-worn paths behind (north of) the
lookout take you through the last belt of
trees and onto shale and talus slopes that

Aerial view of Paget Peak. L site of old lookout. Photo: courtesy of Parks Canada.

From Paget Peak, Mount Ogden rises above Sherbrooke Lake.

lead to the summit some 425 m above. The ascent has always been straightforward, and now time and popularity have further simplified things with beaten paths and many superfluous cairns. The view is unobstructed the whole way up.

Having reached Paget Peak with so little trouble, it is possible to continue north along the ridge for an additional half hour or so to a slightly higher viewpoint. It offers a correspondingly fuller panorama. From either perspective, the imposing relief of Mount Stephen's north side glowering 2000 m above the Kicking Horse flats is a particularly striking feature of the landscape. Equally close are Mounts Niles and Daly, just north of Sherbrooke Lake. These two scrambles are also described in this volume.

Paget Peak is a part of what geologists identify as the Main Ranges. Geology and topography here are quite different and more interesting than what you find in the younger Front Ranges to the east. Staring groundward on Main Range ascents often reveals a much wider diversity of rock types and colours including Gog quartzite, the hardest rock in the

Rockies. This delightfully solid rock makes up the lower sections of peaks at Lake Louise and Moraine Lake including the popular climbing crags at the back of Lake Louise.

Another difference between Front and Main Range topography is the number of glaciers and icefields in the Main Ranges. This is the backbone of the Rockies and a major barrier to Pacific storm systems. These big peaks literally wring out the moisture, resulting in a localized climate that is both cooler and wetter. As proof, we still see significant glaciation on mountains like Victoria, Temple and Lefroy, all of which are over 3353 m (11,000 ft.). While on the subject of glaciers, some editions of the topo map show glaciation on the south- and east-facing slopes of Paget and nearby Mount Bosworth. You can plainly see bare scree slopes everywhere, and glaciers probably haven't existed here for centuries.

Paget Peak was first ascended by Reverend Dean Paget of Calgary along with A. O. Wheeler, a founding member of the Alpine Club of Canada.

NARAO PEAK 2974 m

Difficulty Moderate scrambling along north ridge
Round trip time 6-10 hours
Height gain 1225 m
Map 82 N/8 Lake Louise

An ascent of Narao Peak rewards you with a fine panorama of major summits along the Continental Divide. The north ridge is a long, enjoyable scramble, largely walking highlighted by short, horizontally-bedded rock steps. Because much of the west side is a boring scree slope flanked by forest, scramblers ascend the peak infrequently. Two steep, parallel ice couloirs on the north side are the most striking features and these couloirs attract keen alpinists who perhaps make just as many ascents. Although the ice couloirs are more challenging, the view along the scrambler's route is far more scenic. Try from July on.

Drive to Lake O'Hara parking lot at the west junction of Highway 1A and the Trans-Canada Highway, 3.1 km west of the Continental Divide and 1.5 km east of Wapta Lake service centre. Cross the railway tracks and turn right.

The initial challenge is to find the path of least resistance through forest on the west slopes. You can readily study this side from the Trans-Canada Highway, and you may want to take time to do this. Wander along the Lake O'Hara access road for about 2 km (markers on trees), then head left and make your way through bush to tree line and the north ridge. Small, crumbling cliffs along the crest are all surmounted either head-on or by moving around to your right; none is very high. Shortly before the summit

A foreshortened telephoto view of Narao's north ridge. Lake O'Hara Road to right, Narao cirque, left. S Summit.

you reach the exit of Narao's 300 m-long north ice gully, a wide, gaping maw. The summit cairn lies a few minutes past this chasm.

Nearby, Mount Victoria's brooding icy north face rears up; beyond, the tranquil, mysterious Goodsir Peaks loom over rarely-visited Ice River and Ottertail valleys. The emerald waters of Sherbrooke Lake are flanked by a backdrop of Mounts Niles, Daly and Balfour on Waputik Icefield.

If you choose to **descend** the north ridge all the way, just above tree line is a 10 m-high cliff. Go around it slightly right of the end of the ridge. Below this, you have two options.

You can contour around into meadows of Popes/Narao cirque (481975) and by heading north, you'll emerge onto a broad scree ledge hugging northeast flanks of Narao Peak, several hundred metres above Ross Lake. A goat path on this well-trodden ramp leads north and you can then descend bush (steep!) to the south end of Ross Lake below. Follow the hiking trail back to Lake O'Hara Road. Otherwise, simply tramp back down the west slope where you ascended to regain Lake O'Hara Road.

Narao is reputed to mean "hit in the stomach" in the Stoney Indian language. In 1858, a spooked horse that had fallen in the nearby river—Kicking Horse River, kicked James Hector of the Palliser Expedition in the chest, and that may explain the funny name. Pure speculation, though.

Descending Narao's north ridge.

MOUNT YUKNESS 2847 m

Difficulty From Opabin Lake, easy scramble to col and northwest summit; moderate scrambling to southwest (true) summit
Round trip time 6-9 hours
Height gain 810 m
Map 82 N/8 Lake Louise

Mount Yukness is a strategic viewpoint in surroundings unmatched almost any-where in the Rockies. The biggest challenge, though, is getting to Lake O'Hara, the starting point. It is a lovely but fragile area and Yoho Park places a quota on visitor numbers. Because a bus reservation is required, you can seldom visit on short notice. Although you can ascend the peak and ride the bus out in a day, it is far more enjoyable to camp overnight and enjoy the fabulous scenery instead.

Access to Lake O'Hara, the starting point, is via a 12-km bus ride. (Call Parks Canada for bus/campground/backcountry permit information at 250-343-6433.) Lake O'Hara parking lot is at the west junction of Highway 1A and the Trans-Canada Highway, 3.1 km west of the Continental Divide and 1.5 km east of West Louise Lodge. Cross the railway tracks and turn right. The bus runs daily, June through September. Cycling in is not allowed.

Mount Yukness from west Opabin Plateau. N north summit, S south (higher) summit.

Photo: Kris Thorsteinsson.

A spectacular, steep diversion en route to the south summit.

From Lake O'Hara Lodge, hike along the south (right) shore and up the Opabin East trail to Opabin Lake at the southeast end of the plateau (1 hour). From Opabin Lake it is a straightforward scramble up the south side of Mount Yukness to a col between the two summits. Begin on a path along the left shore of Opabin Lake signed "Opabin Alpine Route," that goes up to the right side of a wet rock wall. An unmaintained but well-cairned trail then heads up to the left near the base of the cliffs. Go through the cliff via ledges on the right side of the leftmost of the visible gullies. If the lower northwest summit is your destination, do not go to the col, but angle left across talus from here.

To reach the true (southeast) summit, continue up the trail to the col. The least-problematic, least-exposed route from there does not follow the ridge, despite a path. Instead, traverse at about the same level as the col, staying well below both the spectacular pinnacles and the steep walls around them. Routes closer to the pinnacles are exposed and difficult. Cross a couple of scree gullies before scrambling back up toward the top.

Upon topping out, you will undoubtedly be inspired by the grand surroundings. For a little alpine flavour, you might try a yodel or two: This summit is an especially good place to hear echoes. If you face Lake Oesa and Abbott Pass, reverberations bounce back at you from a natural amphitheatre amid quartzite walls of Mounts Yukness, Lefroy and Victoria. If you can't yodel, a simple, "S-o-o-o-e-e-e!" or two will do. Once the novelty has worn off or your voice has gone hoarse, **return** the same way.

Yukness is the Stoney Indian word for "sharpened," such as a knife. Oesa means "ice" and that is exactly what covers the lake for most of the year. So much for a cool dip.

MOUNT STEPHEN 3199 m

Difficulty Difficult for final 125 vertical
metres via southwest slopes
Round trip time 8-12 hours
Height gain 1920 m
Map 82 N/8 Lake Louise

Mount Stephen is a demanding ascent that
requires more routefinding and stamina
than do most other scrambles. It is the first
Rockies peak above 3050 m of which there
is irrefutable evidence of ascent. While
employed by the government to chart the
railway's mountain section, in September
of 1887, McArthur and Riley struggled up,
lugging heavy surveying impedimenta.
Tom Wilson's claim of a prior ascent was
never substantiated.

The vertical relief between this brooding
behemoth and Field is imposing, rising as
a largely uninterrupted face towering 1900
m above. No doubt this loftiness accounts
for most of the attention Mount Stephen
receives today. The mountain consists
mainly of dolomites and shales from the
Cambrian period some 550 million years
ago, a period that produced the first abundant fossils. Examples litter lower flanks.
Incidentally, removal of fossils is a punish-
able offense and park wardens rigidly en-
force it by periodic surprise checks. In dry
years you can try this ascent from about
mid-July on. A summit cornice turns back
too-early attempts, so if in doubt, wait till
August. An ice axe is recommended.

Park at Stephen Fossil Beds trailhead
near the creek at the end of First Street
east in Field. Because of past thefts of
fossils, climbers now require a park permit and trail use is carefully monitored.
Permits are available at Yoho Park Information Centre at the highway turn-off.

From the trailhead, an unrelenting grind
takes you to the first part of the fossil beds
in an hour. Not surprisingly, the path
dwindles soon after. Only parties ascending the peak are given Parks permission to pass freely through this area, and
they MUST NOT stop and search for
souvenirs. Contravention of this regula-
tion will prevent access entirely, so for
the sake of future parties, please don't
abuse the privilege and ruin it for all!

Above the fossil beds, continue up
broken rock to a wide shoulder where
again a path appears, wending its way

*Farther than it looks: Mount Stephen from Mount
Dennis. S shoulder.*

Photo: Kris Thorsteinsson.

Easy does it! Descending steep terrain on Mount Stephen.

of the rock bands encountered. Innumerable cairns clutter ledges, and you could conceivably spend the day merely traipsing back and forth visiting these. Finally, after gaining the nearly horizontal summit ridge, an exposed ridge traverse completes the ascent. This crest is NOT for anyone prone to vertigo. If the tedious trudge up didn't leave you breathless, one quick glance down the front may do it—Field lies nearly 2 airy km below. Because a stubborn cornice often clings to this crest, you would be well advised to save this endeavour for later in summer. During one "dry" year, early July was too soon, and disappointed parties were rebuffed just minutes short of success. **Note:** Parties have apparently traversed around more to the south (right) and continued to the top on ledges, thereby avoiding the ridge entirely. Feasibility of this route is also dependent on remaining snow.

over shale and scree toward a short rock band. A gully cleaves this to your right. Continue up more scree. Behind you, a panorama of peaks unfolds. The distant, snowcapped Selkirks rise to the west, and to the north the President and Vice-President emerge.

The last 125 m of elevation gain requires routefinding through numerous short cliffs. Detour right to surmount most

Scotsman George Stephen, later Lord Stephen, was a stalwart supporter and president of the Canadian Pacific Railway during its difficult formative years. Upon realizing that the peak was to bear his name, he reciprocated by adopting the title "Mount," thereby becoming Lord Mount Stephen, in what will surely stand throughout history as a unique case of name-swapping.

MOUNT NILES 2972 m

Difficulty Moderate scrambling via west slopes
Round trip time 8-12 hours
Height gain 1350 m
Maps 82 N/9 Hector Lake,
82 N/8 Lake Louise

Mount Niles is Mount Daly's nearby partner. Both are in a true wilderness setting of rock, ice and meadow. Despite a good approach trail and a lack of difficulties, it has not been ascended frequently in the past, probably because it is not clearly seen from the highway. As it borders the expansive Wapta Icefield system, the resultant heavy snowfalls shorten the scrambling season. Expect a unique view of Yoho Valley, local peaks and adjacent glaciers together with plenty of Yoho rubble. You should carry an ice axe. Try from about mid-July on.

Drive to Wapta Lake picnic area at the west end of Wapta Lake, British Columbia, 5.1 km west of the Continental Divide at Kicking Horse Pass.

Reaching Niles Meadow

The first step is to reach Niles Meadows. From the parking area, hike to Sherbrooke Lake via the signed trail near the picnic shelter and continue down the east shore. Two peaks rise north of the lake: Leaning Mount Niles on the left and Daly, looking more like a ridge, is on the right. The trail continues past the lake gaining height to a meadow, re-enters mature forest and curves left up Sherbrooke Creek. In 1996, all stream crossings had bridges or a log and the path was well defined. About two hours from the parking lot, the path crosses to the left (west) side of Sherbrooke Creek. Hop a side stream and cross the main channel on a large log. Within 10 minutes

Keeping the young'uns in line.

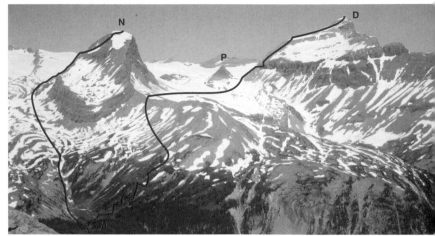

*From Mount Ogden, M Niles Meadow, N Niles,
P pyramid, D Daly.*

you cross back again, then hike near a 20 m-high waterfall above an avalanche slope. After switchbacking over a hump, the path descends to emerald green Niles Meadow, right below Mount Niles. Mount Daly lies to the east beyond the ridge bordering the meadow. Both peaks could be done from a nearby bivouac.

From Niles Meadow, a switchbacking trail rises on the hillside to the right and leads toward the south end of Niles. Look for a stand of about 15 firs at the right edge of the meadow by a shaley watercourse (cairn). A good path leads up open slopes or you can simply hike up alongside the gully directly toward the peak. Head for the west (left) skyline ridge where stands a big pinnacle, crossing a boulderfield en route. Lingering snow patches at the col will require step-kicking. Upon reaching the col, glistening Waputik Icefield and glaciated Mount Balfour appear to the north, both of which drain into a silty gray-green collecting basin. This milky pond, in turn, feeds thundering Takakkaw Falls below in Yoho Valley.

From the col, follow a hint of a trail up the slope on the back side of the pinnacle. Angle right when the terrain steepens and easily work your way up shaley rubble to the snowcapped summit, an hour or less from the col. Be wary of cornices on top.

Despite cloud, I could briefly savour a glimpse of Mount Stephen and its north glacier to the southwest and familiar peaks encircling Little Yoho Valley. With luck, you will see much more. Whatever the conditions are, **return** by the same route.

A horrific grizzly bear attack occurred near Sherbrooke Lake in 1939, involving Canadian Pacific Railway photographer Nick Morant and Swiss guide Christian Haesler. Haesler was badly mauled. Although he survived, despite having been in excellent health beforehand, he never fully recovered and died within two years. Mount Niles honours W. H. Niles, an early climber in the area.

MOUNT DALY 3152 m

Difficulty A difficult scramble via southwest slopes
Round trip time 10-14 hours
Height gain 1530
Maps 82 N/9 Hector Lake,
82 N/8 Lake Louise

Mounts Daly and Niles form the portal through which ski tourers pass when completing the famous Wapta Icefield ski traverse. Looking west from the highway at Lake Louise, Daly appears as a long ridge on the horizon; Niles is a rounded peak

behind. Mount Daly rates as a fairly serious trip as it is in a less-travelled area. The ascent involves avoiding a glacier, a bit of steep scrambling, traversing a loose ridge and perhaps ascending a steep snow slope. Therefore, it is recommended for experienced parties. The mountain is readily approached via Sherbrooke Lake hiking trail. This region receives heavy snowfall so the ascent is recommended for late July or August when conditions should be drier. An ice axe is recommended.

Drive to Wapta Lake picnic area at the west end of Wapta Lake, British Columbia, 5.1 km west of the Continental Divide at Kicking Horse Pass.

Reaching Niles Meadow

The first step is to reach Niles Meadows. From the parking area, hike to Sherbrooke Lake via the signed trail near the picnic shelter and continue down the east shore. Two peaks rise north of the lake: Leaning Mount Niles on the left and Daly, looking more like a ridge, is on the right. The trail continues past the lake gaining height to a meadow, re-enters mature forest and curves left up Sherbrooke Creek. In 1996, all stream crossings had bridges or a log and the path was obvious. About two hours from the parking lot, the path crosses to the left (west) side of Sherbrooke Creek. Hop a side stream and cross the main channel on a large log. Within 10 minutes cross back to the right side again, then hike near a 20 m-high waterfall above an avalanche slope. After switchbacking over a hump, the path descends to emerald green Niles Meadow,

right below Mount Niles. Mount Daly lies to the east beyond the ridge bordering the meadow. Both peaks could be done from a nearby bivouac.

A good trail rises on the hillside to the right of Niles Meadow and leads toward the south end of Niles. To reach Mount Daly you must hike up over the long ridge extending south of Niles. From a stand of about 15 fir trees at the right edge of the meadow, find a trail by a shaley watercourse (cairn). This path switchbacks high up onto the ridge crest, which is then easily crossed and grants a clear view of Daly's ascent route.

As seen from this ridge crest, the line of ascent begins on a west-facing cone of tedious rubble close to and facing a small rocky pyramid. The topo map shows the snout of Niles glacier extending between Niles Ridge and this pyramid. Unless properly equipped, do not contour high to avoid elevation loss as you will be crossing glacier and there just might be crevasses. To be safe, you should descend into the basin and go around below. Cross the outflow stream, then ascend steep snow or scree slopes to the col

Close-up of Daly from the ridge. C cliffs, P pyramid.

between Daly and the little pyramid. Trudge up steep, loose rubble on Daly (snow toward the northwest side of the rubble cone may be preferable) to a cliff band. From just below the high point of this slope, traverse right (south) on a good-sized ledge and scramble through the loose cliffs where it's least steep. This is the crux. Rubble or short rock steps above lead to shale slopes, snow patches and the summit ridge. Beware of cornices! On my ascent a 6 m-high overhanging snowcap covered the summit.

Farther north beyond this snowcap waits an apparently higher summit and a register. The 20-minute traverse to this gray summit is not as difficult as it appears. However, from there, the southern summit of brown rock looks higher. Both, however, are typical crumbly Yoho rubble.

On a clear day the view includes the Dawson Group, a line of four glaciated peaks thrusting up in the distant Selkirk Range to the west. Closer by, peaks near Lake Louise are every bit as entrancing. Anyone who has skied the area will find this lofty perspective ideal to scout out crevasses on Waputik Icefield. Few are evident. Once you're all scouted out, **return** the same way.

According to *Place Names in the Canadian Alps* (Boles/Laurilla/Putnam), J. F. Daly served as president of the American Geographical Society, although Reginald Daly, a famous Canadian geologist, may have also bolstered official acceptance of this name.

ISOLATED PEAK 2845 m

Difficulty Moderate scrambling on loose rock if dry, possible steep snow-climbing
Round trip time 8-10 hours from Takakkaw Falls parking lot, 5+ hours from Little Yoho Valley
Height gain 1400 m from Takakkaw Falls, 700 m from Little Yoho Valley
Map 82 N/10 Blaeberry River

Isolated Peak adjoins a large glacier and is close to both the hut and campground. The peak can be comfortably done as a loop day trip from Takakkaw parking lot to include a traverse of Whaleback Mountain, or as a shorter day trip from a base in Little Yoho. Both objectives are visible as you look northwest from Spiral Tunnel viewpoint on Field Hill east of Field. "Fabulous" best describes the location and the approach trails are excellent, too. The rock, unfortunately, is trashy Yoho shale. It may be fine for fossils, but it's crud for climbers. Unless competent at climbing steep snow slopes, wait until late July when the west slopes will be steep, loose shale instead. Folks seeking an esthetic experience will be disappointed on this ascent unless roped up and ascending the adjacent glacier.

Park at Takakkaw Falls parking lot at the far end of Yoho Valley Road east of Field, British Columbia. Little Yoho Valley trail starts at the north end of the parking lot.

Takakkaw Falls Approach

Hike the Yoho Valley trail to Laughing Falls Campground, then follow the left branch signed Little Yoho/ACC Hut. In 1.5-2 hours from the trailhead, branch off to the right up a steeply switchbacking trail to the Whaleback. Whaleback Mountain is the long southeast ridge of Isolated Peak and the open south end where the Parks trail crests it is called the Whaleback. Allow at least two hours to here. The hiking trail then descends toward Twin Falls, but DO NOT continue on past here.

Upon reaching the Whaleback, leave the Whaleback trail and hike left up a faint path (cairns initially) leading toward the ridge above you. This is just left of the rock face on the skyline, part of Whaleback Mountain. Vast glistening icefields and towering peaks are now your companions for the rest of the trek.

Due south are north faces of the President and Vice-President, each dominating its respective glacier below, while your objective, though less impressive, is clearly visible straight ahead.

As you approach Isolated Peak it is tempting to continue onto the south slopes to avoid losing unnecessary elevation. The fact is, though, the ledges on that aspect are awash in heaps of precariously perched shale and are very exposed. Do yourself a favour and simply follow the trail down from the col and regain this height as you slog around to the west side. Avoid the adjacent glacier. On the west side, a lengthy shale or snow slope narrows to a gully above, at which point it is possible to work left on big ledges (not clearly seen from below) onto easier ground. Continue up toward the summit. Unless you are competent at climbing steep snow, you should stick to the shale. By August there will probably be nothing but shale anyway. The final slope rises above a small plateau jutting out into Des Poilus Glacier on the northwest side and is a mere walk.

Approaching Isolated Peak from the Whaleback. Route circles to west side.

Little Yoho Valley Approach

A surprisingly good approach trail leads to the hanging valley between Stanley Mitchell Hut and Isolated Peak. It begins at the outhouse at the east (right) end of the hut, rising quickly through mature forest to heathery alpine meadows, complete with a bubbling stream and waterfalls. Cairns direct you north across glacial outwash below steep rock walls and alongside cascades toward Isolated Peak. The two approach routes coincide below the col (note the pinnacles). Trudge left around the base and continue to the summit as described previously.

The summit view is adequate compensation for the thrash you've endured and includes the distant Howser Towers in the Bugaboos of British Columbia and more recognizable giants surrounding Lake Louise. You should also be able to pick out the **return trail** to the right of the stream as it wanders south through meadows to the hut below. These mead-ows are an idyllic and special place. Carpeted in heather, fed by a clear stream and far removed from the human traffic of Little Yoho, they beg you to have a snooze before descending. Try it, you'll like it. Once you reach the hut, turn left and hike east back to Takakkaw Falls in two or three hours.

Isolated Peak was first ascended in 1901 by four Swiss guides and two very notable climbers. Reverend James Outram, who a month later bagged "the Matterhorn of the Rockies" (Assiniboine), and Edward Whymper, who had already conquered "the Assini boine of the Alps," the Matterhorn. According to *Place Names of the Canadian Rockies*, by Boles, Laurilla and Putnam, Isolated Peak is so-named because it is neither a part of the Balfour group, east, nor the Rockies, lying west. Outram found it "extremely valuable for a survey of the glaciers surrounding the head of Yoho, and of the various tributary valleys." You probably will too.

MOUNT KERR 2863 m

Difficulty An easy scramble from Kiwetinok Pass
Round trip time 3+ hours from Little Yoho Campground
Height gain 790 m from campground
Map 82 N/10 Blaeberry River

The most straightforward ascent in Little Yoho Valley, Mount Kerr is readily approached by a well-trodden hiking trail to Kiwetinok Pass. The summit view is vastly better than what you glimpse from the pass, and includes glaciated peaks in the Purcell and Selkirk ranges far to the west. An ice axe could be needed if snow patches linger; try from mid-July on.

The hiking trail to Kiwetinok Pass lies on the south side of Little Yoho River. From Stanley Mitchell Hut, cross the meadow and the bridge, turn right and hike to the pass in about an hour. Mount Kerr, the south buttress of the pass, is visible on the skyline and most of the ridge you see as you approach is the line of ascent.

Once you reach the pass, simply follow the adjacent ridge south toward the peak. Work around to the right onto more westerly slopes at steeper rock bands, scrambling over blocks and large plates of loose shale. If you're a photographer, morning light will emphasize the distant view west toward the Selkirks while afternoon light is more favourable for seeing Waputik and Wapta icefields. From

this side Mount Carnarvon, just south, presents a pyramidal shape even more striking than that seen from the Trans-Canada Highway. One wouldn't think it would be a scramble.

Although the pointy peak lying immediately south is slightly higher, this lower summit is called Mount Kerr, so you need not go farther. Robert Kerr of the Canadian Pacific Railway did much arranging for Edward Whymper, conqueror of Switzerland's Matterhorn, to visit and publicize the Rockies. Yoho Valley itself played host to Whymper and his entourage of four Swiss guides in 1901, with all completing the first ascent of this mountain. It is unlikely their skills were taxed on this route.

KIWETINOK PEAK 2902 m

Difficulty A difficult, loose and exposed scramble by east slope
Round trip time 4-5 hours from Little Yoho Campground
Height gain 825 m from campground
Map 82 N/10 Blaeberry River

Kiwetinok Peak forms the north buttress of the pass of the same name, but is probably ascended less frequently than its companion, Mount Kerr. Care is needed because of loose rock and although the route is short, it is exposed. You can readily combine this ascent with Mounts Pollinger and McArthur for a three-peak day. A fine view of big Rockies and Selkirk peaks almost makes you forget the miserably loose rock. Almost. Try from late July on.

From Kiwetinok Pass, hike around the lake's west shore and trudge up rubbly slopes to the ridge connecting Kiwetinok Peak with Mount Pollinger, 1 km northeast. This ridge is broad but scramblers should avoid the large, permanent ice patch on the face above the ridge.

Stay left of the ice patch, angling across rubble and slabs to reach short, rotten bands of shale. The farther left you go, the more eroded and easier it is. Where steep, this shale can be dangerously loose, so look for gentler slopes. The horizontal summit ridge leads quickly to a crumbling cairn.

The view is similar to what you see from Mount Kerr, and includes Mount Forbes, the Goodsir Peaks, as well as Mount Sir Donald in the distant Selkirk Range to the west. Below, wide Amiskwi Valley lies scarred by both logging and burning. As for the name, Kiwetinok is apparently an Indian word for "on the north side."

The summit "hump" of Kiwetinok Peak from Pollinger. Lake is to left.

Opposite: Mount Kerr from the Whaleback. P Kiwetinok Pass.

*From Mount Kerr, K Kiwetinok, M McArthur,
L lake, P Pollinger.*

MOUNT POLLINGER 2816 m
MOUNT McARTHUR 3015 m

Difficulty Easy hiking to Pollinger, one
short, steep downclimb to reach
McArthur
Ascent time 1.5 hours from either
Kiwetinok Lake or Kiwetinok Peak

If you've climbed Kiwetinok Peak, it is
worth the extra effort to traverse Mount
Pollinger—a mere bump along the
ridge—and continue over to Mount
McArthur. Follow the ridge northeast
from Kiwetinok Peak. The only difficulty
en route is a short but steep downclimb
(5-7 m) right after Mount Pollinger. The
rock is solid, but when snowy, parties
rappel this part. It is possible that a ledge
on the east side would be an alternative.

There is a large permanent snow patch
before you reach McArthur's summit,

Kiwetinok Peak and connecting ridge from McArthur.

but no actual glacier on the south side, despite what maps show. Note that Des Poilus Glacier does abut the summit ridge on the north and east sides, though. After a few hundred years of global warming, this vast glacier and its accompanying crevasses will be gone. Lucky scramblers will then continue unimpeded over bare, scoured rock to Isolated Peak and the Whaleback. That's the complete reverse of Outram's traverse done in 1901, and probably no worse. (Note the rhyme!)

Mountain ranges between Mount McArthur and the Selkirks are comparatively low, and this allows an unrestricted view of heavily glaciated peaks in British Columbia's Interior ranges. The Bugaboos and Mount Sir Donald Range are particularly dominant and on a clear day, time will quickly pass if you've brought maps and binoculars along.

The **return** can be shortened if you don't mind slogging across a boulder-strewn valley. Several places between Pollinger and McArthur allow you to drop down to the hanging valley on the southeast side. They are evident from near Pollinger. You may encounter short rock bands initially, but a carefully chosen line will simply be knee-jarring rubble. Tramp back toward Little Yoho Valley, descend open talus slopes and meet Kiwetinok Pass trail just upstream of the campground.

J. J. McArthur was a topographic surveyor involved with both the railway survey and the 49th parallel. His work yielded several first ascents including Mount Stephen. Joseph Pollinger was one of Whymper's Swiss guides in the Rockies in 1901.

Summit view of (L-R) Waputik Icefield, Mounts Daly, Niles, Vice-President and the President.

MOUNT CARNARVON 3040 m

Difficulty Difficult scrambling via south ridge for final 100 vertical metres
Round trip time 7-10 hours
Height gain 1735 m
Map 82 N/7 Golden

When travelling the Trans-Canada Highway, glancing north at a point some 12 km west of Field, you can see Mount Carnarvon rising like a great pyramid to eclipse snow-capped President and Vice-President peaks to the right. Its striking shape and challenging scrambling on good rock makes Mount Carnarvon worth a visit. This route requires dry, snow-free conditions. An ice axe is recommended; Try from late July or August on.

Mount Carnarvon is possibly the best scramble near Field. It boasts a well-maintained approach trail, fine surroundings and unlike many Yoho peaks, offers good, solid rock. Elevation gain is significant.

From Field drive west 2.6 km to Emerald Lake Road and follow it for 9 km to Emerald Lake parking lot.

Find the trailhead for Hamilton Lake on the west side of the parking lot near the entrance. Hike the steep 5.5 km-long trail to scenic Hamilton Lake. After the unforgiving approach hike, this is a perfect place to rest and fortify yourself for the tough 900 m of elevation gain ahead. Cross the lake's outlet stream and ascend

the meadowy hillside that leads to brown shale and the south ridge. You can stay on the ridge most of the way to the summit with few detours necessary. Steeper rock steps are typically quite solid (by Rockies standards!) and are great fun when tackled head-on. Detour left onto easier terrain if needed. The strata are horizontal or dip inward and

From Hamilton Lake, route ascends scree to follow challenging south ridge.

A head-on view of Carnarvon's south ridge (route approximate).

the abundance of good handholds makes for an enjoyable ascent.

One hundred vertical metres below the top the route becomes more serious. Walls rear up steeply. Here you must traverse left 75 to 100 m and ascend gullies to overcome this last section. It is likely you will encounter snow in these gullies and it will require an ice axe and perhaps crampons, too. Cairns and a bit of trail have magically appeared in the last few years, but you should note your ascent gully carefully, anyway. They may all look alike on descent.

A short walk leads to the cairn and the often snow-clad summit. To the north-west is the large glaciated Mummery Group, while closer by are Mount Balfour and Wapta Icefield. When you have frittered away enough of the afternoon, **return** the same way. Mount Carnarvon is named for Henry Howard Molyneux Herbert, Fourth Earl of Carnarvon, and parliamentary author of the British North America Act.

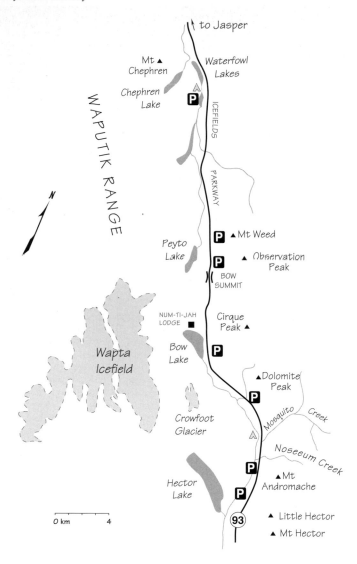

ICEFIELDS PARKWAY

Little Hector	3125 m	moderate	p. 290
Mount Andromache	2996 m	moderate	p. 292
Dolomite Peak	2998 m	difficult	p. 294
Cirque Peak	2993 m	easy	p. 297
Observation Peak	3174 m	easy	p. 298
Mount Weed	3080 m	moderate	p. 299
Mount Chephren	3307 m	difficult	p. 300
Mount Sarbach	3155 m	difficult	p. 303
Mount Coleman	3135 m	difficult	p. 305
Nigel Peak	3211 m	moderate	p. 307
Mount Wilcox	2884 m	moderate	p. 309
Tangle Ridge	3000 m	easy	p. 311
Sunwapta Peak	3315 m	easy	p. 312

Peaks in this chapter border the Icefields Parkway (Highway 93) joining Banff National Park to neighbouring but larger Jasper National Park. The Icefields Parkway has rightly been called the most scenic drive in the world. Visitors gasp, awestruck, at craggy, towering peaks cloaked in glaciers soaring far above the highway, and each bend in the road unveils new wonders. This is particularly true of the southern half of the 245 km-long highway. For many, the biggest thrill lies at the Columbia Icefield.

The Columbia Icefield is a 380 sq. km sea of glaciers and icefalls straddling the Continental Divide. Many of the Rockies highest peaks are found here including Snowdome (3518 m). This peak is truly unique as it is the hydrographic apex of North America. Its snowmelt flows in three different compass directions and eventually empties into the Pacific, the Atlantic and the Arctic oceans. The icefields are local mountaineers' favourite playground and the area is often used as a pre-expedition primer for world-class alpinists. Less adventurous (more sensible, some would say) folks can ride snocoaches out onto Athabasca Glacier for a firsthand inspection. Fools sometimes wander up from the toe of the glacier parking lot, ignore posted warnings and occasionally, somebody falls in a hidden crevasse and dies. Remember, this icefield is a spectacular, but dangerous, marvel.

Although many peaks along the Icefields Parkway are technical ascents, easier ascents exist too. The highest scramble in this chapter is Mount Chephren at 3307 m. Because of its height and location, snow lingers and the mountain has a very short scrambling season. Mount Wilcox, behind the Icefields Centre, is highly recom-

Morning light on Howse Peak from the ascent slopes on Mount Chephren.

mended. On a clear day, the view over the icefields is outstanding. As the Icefields Parkway lies close to the Continental Divide, precipitation is high. The highest amount occurs at Columbia Icefield, which records more than 900 mm of precipitation annually—twice that of Banff or Jasper and half as much again as Lake Louise. Statistically, odds of a clear day at the icefields are about one in four. Count yourself lucky if you visit it in sunshine. With a mean annual temperature of -2°C (yes, minus two. Told you it was mean!), small wonder so much ice prevails.

Access The region is reached by Highway 93, the Icefields Parkway, which intersects the Trans-Canada Highway 2 km west of Lake Louise, then travels northwest for 245 km to Jasper. Meeting it at Saskatchewan Crossing is Highway 11, the David Thompson Highway, which runs east to Red Deer. Highway 16, the Yellowhead Highway, joins Edmonton and Prince George, B.C. via Jasper. As for transportation, Brewster operates a daily shuttle from Calgary to Jasper; Via Rail trains stop in Jasper from Edmonton and Prince George, as do Greyhound bus lines. This is all extremely fascinating, to say the least, but to really do much, you need your own set of wheels—preferably four with a motor attached.

Facilities Few businesses are found along the Icefields Parkway and most cater to the sightseeing tourist with a fat wallet. Supplies are generally limited. Buy whatever you need in either Jasper or Lake Louise, including gas. Gas is available at Saskatchewan Crossing and Sunwapta, but costs much more. Cafeteria and restaurant meals are available in the newly-constructed Icefields Centre. If nothing else, the interpretive displays at the centre are worth seeing. Saskatchewan Crossing caters mainly to the tour bus crowd. Grocery selection is both poor and high priced so unless you really need postcards, the place has little else for hikers and climbers. I may rethink this, though, if they decide to support local guidebook authors like myself.

Accommodation Lodges, cabins and chalets along the parkway are typically expensive and booked up. For the budget traveller, however, many campgrounds and hostels can be found along the way and in Jasper. All are popular during summer and fill up fast. Two campgrounds are close to the Icefields Centre: Icefields Campground, the smaller of the two, is where climbers and cyclists often share a picnic shelter on a wet evening or may even sublease space on a tent pad! Motorhomes are not allowed here. Located 2 km south is the larger Wilcox Campground. Additional campsites are found along the parkway at Mosquito Creek, Waterfowl Lakes, Rampart Creek, Jonas Creek, Honeymoon Lake, Mount Kerkeslin, Wabasso, Wapiti and Whistlers.

Information Icefields Centre is an impressive new (in 1997) information centre built in conjunction with Brewster, who operates the sno-coaches. This is the one and only information centre along this road. Park staff are helpful regarding local conditions on both climbs and scrambles and also provide weather forecasts.

Warden Offices are just south of Saskatchewan Crossing, at Sunwapta Falls, east of Jasper toward Maligne Lake and in Lake Louise Village. Wardens can also provide information to help keep you out of trouble.

LITTLE HECTOR 3125 m

Difficulty Moderate scrambling
Round trip time 6-9 hours
Height gain 1260 m
Map 82 N/9 Hector Lake
(unmarked at 502155)

Little Hector is an unofficial name for a peak 2 km northwest of, but attached to, Mount Hector. Mount Hector, at 3394 m, requires glacier travel; this adjacent summit offers a similar view but avoids the glacier. When viewed from farther north at Mosquito Creek bridge, the peak has a striking pyramidal shape and the route up is clearly visible. The approach is short and you can descend by a slightly different route for variety. Try from about mid-July on.

Park in a small roadside pullout on the west side of the Icefields Parkway at Hector Creek, 20 km north of the Trans-Canada Highway.

Cross the road and follow an obvious trail on the right (south) side of Hector Creek through forest, going left when it meets a wider trail. The trail soon emerges into the open below a waterfall and crosses to the left side of the stream. Scramble up easy ledges to the left of the next waterfalls. Move right, then cross a small stream upon which you enter a pleasant, open basin between Little Hector (502155) on the right and Mount Andromache above on the left.

From here you have a fine view toward the objective, although the perspective is very foreshortened. The idea is to continue up-valley along the right side for a short way and pick a good spot to ascend steepish slopes on the right. This is the north end of Little Hector. If you continue east too far the rock below Little Hector becomes too steep to ascend. We chose to ascend the slope just before a cliff band of overlapping rock layers de-

Roadside telephoto shot of Little Hector. Mount Hector behind; Andromache would be to left.

What a day! Hector Lake and Wapta Icefield from Little Hector.

scends from Little Hector and forms a headwall across the valley. This slope mentioned above may be less steep. Depending on where you choose to head up, expect masses of rubble with possible sections of waterworn, downsloping slabs—slick when wet!

As you gain height, the view becomes more breathtaking with every step, with Hector Lake and Mount Balfour competing for camera time. The final slope to the top is gentler-angled but still loose and rubbly. A few thousand feet tramping up and down might help stabilize it a little! Once you reach the top, it becomes obvious why this peak is not noticeable from the south. A long, almost horizontal ridge connects to higher Mount Hector (3394 m) and were it not for the glacier farther up, Mount Hector, too, would be a scramble. Unless you are equipped for glacier travel, though, you should not continue. There are crevasses and a bergschrund. You should also be aware of the possibility of a cornice on the east side of Little Hector.

This summit is strategically-placed and many major peaks are visible. Giants of the Lake Louise group like Lefroy, Temple, Victoria and Hungabee cluster together, with the Goodsirs and Mount Stephen close by. Other features that contribute to sensory overload are the Wapta Icefields and pointy Mount Chephren, farther up the Icefields Parkway.

On **descent**, perhaps the quickest way is via a wide gully of rubble facing northwest below the summit. Head back down the slope you tramped up and continue descending into this broad gully. The well-defined ridge alongside it on the left aims for the road and may seem tempting to descend, but it is not just a simple walk: this gully is. Trudge down it almost to tree line, then contour left going around the end of a ridge (animal trails in places). Gradually lose elevation as you work your way around left and down toward the highway below. Bushwhacking is no problem and the descent may take only a couple of hours in total.

MOUNT ANDROMACHE 2996 m

Difficulty Moderate scrambling
Round trip time 8-10 hours to traverse
Height gain 1140 m
Map 82 N/9 Hector Lake
(unmarked 492182)

Mount Andromache (An-DROM-a-kee) is an easily approached peak alongside the Icefields Parkway that gives a fine view of nearby Hector Glacier. As the title is unofficial, it is unnamed on the map. In the past it has not been a well-known objective, but that should not stop real peak-baggers. The approach distance is short and the view is magnificent. A traverse allows you to cross a higher unnamed point along the way. Try from July on.

Park in a small roadside pullout on the west side of the Icefields Parkway at Hector Creek, 20 km north of the Trans-Canada Highway. The traverse finishes about 2 km north at Noseeum Creek.

In previous editions I suggested that this peak might be better climbed from Hector Pass and descended via the north ridge. Subsequent parties have confirmed this, so following are these directions.

Cross the road and follow an obvious trail on the right (south) side of Hector Creek through forest, going left when it meets a wider trail. The trail soon emerges into the open below a waterfall and crosses to the left side of the stream. Scramble up easy ledges to the left of the next waterfalls. Move right, then cross a small stream upon which you enter a pleasant, open basin between Little Hector (502155) on the right and Andromache

A Andromache, U Unnamed, H Hector, L Little Hector. Routes start near P Hector Pass.

H Hector Pass and U Unnamed from Little Hector. Andromache is to the left.

above on the left. Hector Pass (510168) is due east. Stay left and traverse hillside on scree below Andromache and the Unnamed peak adjacent. The terrain flattens out toward Hector Pass. Scramblers need only go until the rock bands above on the left peter out. Turn left and trudge up the slope to gain the unnamed peak straight above. A view of Hector Glacier is spectacular, while double-peaked Molar Mountain rises majestically across the valley to the east.

To reach Mount Andromache (492182), you can readily continue in a northwest direction along an open ridge. Despite what some maps show, ice does not cover the connecting ridge. The small Molar Glacier does abut the north side of the peak, though, so scramblers should avoid it and stay on the scree. Allow 30 minutes from the unnamed peak. The panorama from the top is magnificent, with Hector and Bow lakes adding much colour to the landscape of craggy peaks and glaciers to the west.

On the **return**, you have the option of either retracing your steps or completing a traverse by descending the mountain's broad, rubbly northwest ridge. This descent is without problems and leads down scree to the highway by Noseeum Creek, 2 km north of Hector Creek.

In Greek mythology, Andromache was the wife of the noble hero Hector; in Canadian mountain lore, however, Mount Hector commemorates Dr. James Hector of the Palliser Expedition. His wife was not Andromache, which perhaps explains the absence of official endorsement for the name.

DOLOMITE PEAK 2998 m

Difficulty Difficult scrambling, some
routefinding necessary
Round trip time 5-7 hours
Height gain 1100 m
Map 82 N/9 Hector Lake

Dolomite Peak is a recommended scramble close to the road with the best part at the top. Despite much rubble on the lower slopes, rock on the upper section is generally firm and the summit view is spectacular. Dolomite is an altered (and improved) form of limestone, appreciated by climbers because of its solid nature. Here it occurs

in the top 300 or so metres of the mountain. Steep towers give exhilarating scrambling, but all are not as difficult as glances suggest. As the strata are bedded almost horizontally, so, too, are ledges, and despite the ever-present Rockies debris, the last few hundred metres are a fine finish. This area has been closed because of grizzly bear activity in the past, so don't be surprised if you arrive to find a closure sign. If in doubt, check with Banff Park wardens at Lake Louise and have an alternative objective just in case. Try the ascent from July on.

Dolomite Peak, showing routes to towers 3 and 4 (highest).

Approach via the normal winter ski trail to Dolomite Pass (unsigned), beginning at Helen Creek, 28.5 km north of the Trans-Canada Highway on the Icefields Parkway. Park at a small gravel parking area at the north end of the bridge.

From the parking area, the trail heads steeply up over a ridge, then angles down and crosses the stream. As you hike along you should note the exact outline of the tower that you are aiming for as there are many. The highest point is the fourth tower from the north. You may even want to drive farther north to positively identify its specific shape. After about 25 minutes you'll come to the second avalanche slope, about five minutes beyond the stream crossing.

There are many ways up the open shale slopes of the lower flanks, and you'll probably choose a fairly direct line to your objective. Some of the terrain is tediously loose in places. Crumbling cliffs break the monotony of this section but pose no real problems. Upon reaching the base of the actual summit mass, you must traverse north (left) toward the gully between towers three and four. This chute provides access to tower four, the highest point. Most people continue along the base of steep walls all the way to the gully between towers 3 and 4, rather than gain the big ledge system and traverse left. Watch for a cairn at the base of the gully.

Once you're directly beneath these towers, foreshortening makes it hard to decide which is which. The fourth tower is wider than either the third one or the fifth, and the right-hand side of the second tower shows an impossibly steep and smooth buttress rearing skyward. This is perhaps the most recognizable feature of any tower from this shortened perspective.

The proper gully should be the widest one you come to. Ascend this gully to just past the spot where a 3 m-high wall of rock briefly divides the channel of debris like a shark's fin out of water. This is about 12-15 m below the top of the gully. Gain rubbly ledges on the right-hand side and work your way around to the right on these ledges in a rising traverse into another smaller gully (cairns). Go straight up rubbly ledges and a bit of steep but enjoyable scrambling, which leads to the double summit of the

tower. There is room for route variation and the rock is sound, but several years of increased visitation by scramblers has loosened much more rubble. You should consider wearing a helmet, especially if you are with a group.

Tower three can also be reached from near the "shark's fin" in the gully. It is easiest to traverse north (left) on a wide scree ledge below the top and then scramble a short distance up rock steps to the summit.

The view from Dolomite Peak encompasses the complete spectrum of mountain landscape, from drab, crumbling peaks to the east, to shining glacier-clad summits piercing the Wapta Icefield in

In the gully between towers 3 and 4.

Telephoto picture of person on tower 3. Chephren, Cirque and Observation peaks behind.

the west. In between lie the emerald greens and azure blues of alpine meadows and lakes. Dominant mountains include Mounts Willingdon, Hector, Temple, Balfour, Chephren and Cline. Even distant Mount Assiniboine is visible on a clear day. A camera is essential.

The quickest **descent** is straight down the middle of the 3-4 gully to Helen Creek. Two short rock bands lower down require brief downclimbing, probably toward the right (north). Fine shale in places gives the knees a respite and you can expect the return trip to take less than half the ascent time.

In 1899 Dolomite Peak was named for its resemblance to the European Dolomites by Ralph Edwards, a well-schooled English transplant who was periodically employed by Banff packer Tom Wilson. On this occasion, he was accompanying "dudes" on a climbing and exploration trip up Pipestone River toward Siffleur River and Bow Lake. Today, adjacent Mounts Thompson, Noyes and Weed commemorate members of the excursion. Lakes Helen and Katherine near Dolomite Pass were named after daughters of a fourth party member, Harry Nicholls.

CIRQUE PEAK 2993 m

Difficulty An easy ascent, largely hiking
Round trip time 5-8 hours
Height gain 1050 m
Map 82 N/9 Hector Lake

Cirque Peak is a virtually foolproof ascent reached by a popular trail to classic alpine surroundings. There are no difficulties, and in fact, the ascent is sometimes done in winter. The views includes major nearby icefields and distant ranges, including Mount Assiniboine, almost 70 km away. Try from July on.

Drive to Helen Lake-Dolomite Pass trailhead on the Icefields Parkway, 33.2 km north of the Trans-Canada Highway and 7.8 km south of Bow Summit. The parking lot is on the east side of the road.

Hike the well-graded trail for 6 km to Helen Lake. While it is tempting to merely fritter away the day lounging in these lovely alpine meadows by Helen Lake, the view is much better from the easily-attained summit of nearby Cirque Peak. Continue along the trail toward Dolomite Pass until you see an easy place to head up onto the shaley shoul-

der. Then follow your nose. With every metre gained, a wider and better panorama of glaciated Wapta Icefields unfolds to the west. To the southeast lies Mount Hector draped under a blanket of ice. A ski ascent of this glacier is a popular undertaking for winter mountaineers bent on bagging the Rockies peaks over 3353 m (11,000 ft.).

The east peak of Cirque is marginally higher and often has a register. Allow 1.5 hours from Helen Lake for your ascent, and less than half that for the rapid descent. The name "Cirque" describes the amphitheatre formed by adjacent peaks.

Cirque Peak is an easy ascent in alpine surroundings.

Photo: Gillean Daffern.

OBSERVATION PEAK 3174 m

Difficulty Easy/moderate scrambling
Round trip time 5-9 hours
Height gain 1100 m
Map 82 N/9 Hector Lake

From Observation Peak, the view across Bow Lake to Wapta Icefield is spectacular, to say the least. The west side of the mountain by the road is largely scree, particularly south of the described ascent route, and so there are many possible ways up. Try from late June or July on.

Park on an old gravel road on the east side of the Icefields Parkway at the crest of Bow Summit, 41 km north of the Trans-Canada Highway.

Walk along the old road to just past a sharp bend to the left, then follow a major gully left of avalanche zone and bush. Halfway up the peak are short cliffs, barely noticeable from the valley. Although they look problematic as you approach, you can easily dodge these around the right side on ledges (cairns). Similarly, you could avoid them entirely by starting your ascent slightly farther south and reduce the trek to nothing but endless rubble. Above half-height the slope becomes more ridge-like. Continue to the false summit, watching for large cornices that overhang the east side.

These can prevent you continuing. Descend slightly and plod 20 minutes toward the northwest to reach the spacious summit, which is about 100 m higher.

Charles Noyes, a Boston clergyman, made several Rockies first ascents including nearby Cirque Peak and Mount Balfour. He observed that this peak was one of the best viewpoints his party had attained on their exploratory foray of 1899. You will likely see why. A careful squint will reveal several significant summits such as Sir Donald, Mount Forbes, Assiniboine and Mount Hector. To the west, surrealistic milky-blue waters of Peyto and Bow lakes lend a feeling of sublime tranquillity to the scene.

G gully, F false summit, S true summit.

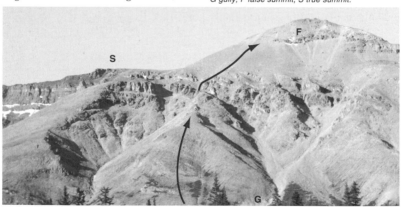

MOUNT WEED 3080 m

Difficulty Moderate scrambling via south side
Round trip time 6-9 hours
Height gain 1340 m
Map 82 N/15 Mistaya Lake

Despite its prominence along the Icefields Parkway, as of 1998 this fine viewpoint had seen only a dozen ascents in the previous 10 years. The approach, although not entirely obvious from the road, is straightforward. Considering the number of ascents, it should make a good "getaway" objective. On a clear day the view is absolutely fabulous. Try from about July on. Ice axe required if snowy.

Park at a small pull-off area on the west side of the Icefields Parkway, 7 km north of Bow Summit and 48 km north of the Trans-Canada Highway. Mount Weed rises directly east and the ascent route is readily seen as you drive north from Bow Summit.

From the parking spot walk north along the road for about five minutes (0.5 km) then head east into the forest, quickly arriving at a drainage. Follow the right-hand side of the drainage through forest. As you approach the first rock band, visible from the highway, leave the creek and ascend slopes to the right. Almost immediately the drainage splits and you can see that the left branch becomes a canyon. You should instead follow the right-hand branch, now a dry, rocky gully. By continuing straight up this gully you will avoid any further cliffs and it will lead to an open avalanche slope and the base of the final gully. If you're on the correct avalanche path, you'll notice two huge boulders side by side near tree line, one as large as a small house.

From the boulders, plod straight upslope on good scree toward a big gully. Glancing behind reveals a view of Bow, Peyto, Mistaya and Waterfowl lakes, not to mention an ever-increasing array of summits and Icefields. As you reach the summit cliffs, there are 400 vertical metres to go. With firm snow, the gully would be fine for step kicking, otherwise, expect tiring scree. Either way, rockfall is a hazard and scrambling up ledges to the right is preferable. The terrain eases at the top, but beware of cornices in early season.

A few of the peaks visible are Mounts Columbia, Cline and Forbes and the Lyell and Mummery groups. Multi-pinnacled Mount Murchison lies just north, while the Lake Louise group rises to the south. **Return** via the same way; the gully will then be faster. G. M. Weed accompanied C. S. Thompson on explorations in the area in 1899, making the first ascent of Cirque Peak along the way.

Telephoto view of route from Bow Summit area.

MOUNT CHEPHREN 3307 m

Difficulty Difficult for a short distance even if dry; ice axe suggested
Round trip time Two days or one very long day
Height gain 1630 m
Map 82 N/15 Mistaya Lake

Mount Chephren is a stunning eye-catcher situated along one of the world's most scenic drives, the Icefields Parkway. Mountains tower along both sides of this road, although most are not as accessible as this one. The summit view is unequalled, but the massive height and location of this pyramidal giant makes it a serious endeavour. Granted, Mounts Temple and Stephen require more elevation gain, but Chephren's approach is longer, and the path down the left-hand (east) shore is marginal at best. The right-hand shore is wicked bushwhacking that you should avoid entirely. To surmount the first cliff band, even the easiest spot will involve scrambling up steep, exposed terrain, but for fit, capable parties equipped with ice axes, this ascent is highly recommended. As a day trip, an alpine start by headlamp is suggested so that you can be well up the south-facing slopes before the full heat of the day hits. This is a mid to late summer ascent when, hopefully, the route will be snowfree. If it is not, both an ice axe and crampons will be required, raising it into the realm of a technical ascent, not merely a scramble. In favourable years, the steep grey-black cliffs and gullies on the south side should be free of snow and ice by late July or August. Other years it may never dry off completely and then it is best left to more technically-oriented climbers.

Start at Chephren Lake trailhead at the southwest end of Waterfowl Lakes Campground on the Icefields Parkway, 57.4 km north of the Trans-Canada Highway junction and 19.7 km south of Saskatchewan Crossing. Drive through the campground to the west end and park near the footbridge across Mistaya River.

Follow the Chephren Lake hiking trail to the lake in about an hour, and muddle along the left shore through forest and across rockslides. Barring moose or bear encounters, which stymied one group (!), you should reach the second inlet stream at the west end in another hour or so. Slower parties will choose to camp by this silty stream and make it a more leisurely two day affair. If you are fit and moving steadily, one day will suffice, but you may at least want to wet your whistle here as there will be little or no water beyond and the elevation gain has yet to start.

Either hike along the right side or gain the awkward steep crest of the lateral moraine leading toward the Chephren/White Pyramid col. Walk along this just a short distance to grassy, south-facing slopes—tasty little blueberries here—and head right to follow a watercourse up the open hillside. If water is flowing here, the ascent will probably require crampons higher up. This drainage splits farther up and the left branch leads toward an obvious scar breaking the lowest cliff band. The easiest places to get through this band are either here or some 75-100 m farther left: The greenish rock is steep but solid. As you go, remember to look back down so you will recognize the terrain on your return. It will look different from above—steeper, that is!

Photo: Bruno Engler.　　*Mighty Mount Chephren and south slopes route. W White Pyramid, C col.*

The second wall is a black band about 20 m high. Traverse left on scree below it for 100 m or so and ascend an easy gully of light brown rock. Contour farther left again over a rounded scree shoulder until the Chephren/White Pyramid col is visible. You now have a choice of routes. Either skirt northwest along the foot of a short cliff (toward the col) and plod summit-ward from that point, or you can angle up more directly to the top over snow patches and rock steps. En route a little chute cuts through a steep wall. Wearisome loose rubble leads to the summit ridge, and a short walk ends at the cairn and register. Despite myriad peaks to admire, it is likely that the **return** trip, which is the same way, will curtail your available visiting time.

Major peaks visible on a clear day include Mount Columbia—second highest mountain in the Rockies, mighty Mount Forbes, all five Lyell peaks and also the Goodsir Towers. Even the Howser Towers in the Purcell Range, 75 km away, are evident. Most awe-inspiring is the scene just left of adjacent White Pyramid—a multitude of glaciated summits awash in a sea of ice that is collectively known as the Freshfields.

Chephren (Kef-ren) was the builder of the second of the great pyramids of Egypt; the mountain was once known as Pyramid Mountain but was renamed in 1918 owing to one already so-named above Jasper.

Columbia Icefields Area

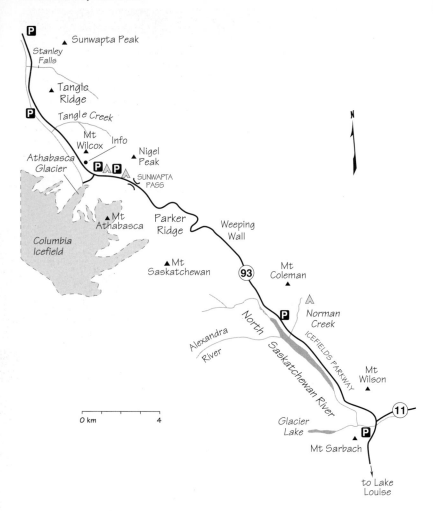

P
▲ Sunwapta Peak

Stanley
Falls

▲ Tangle
Ridge

P

Tangle Creek

Mt
Wilcox   Info
▲   •

Nigel
Peak
▲

Athabasca
Glacier

P △ P
SUNWAPTA
PASS

N

▲ Mt
Athabasca

Parker
Ridge

Weeping
Wall

Columbia
Icefield

▲ Mt
Saskatchewan

93

Mt
Coleman
▲

P

Norman
Creek
△

Alexandra

River

North Saskatchewan River

ICEFIELDS PARKWAY

Mt
Wilson
▲

11

0 km   4

Glacier
Lake

P

Mt Sarbach ▲

to Lake
Louise

MOUNT SARBACH 3155 m

Difficulty Difficult scrambling along the exposed and loose summit ridge
Round trip time 10-13 hours
Height gain 1630 m
Map 82 N/15 Mistaya Lake

Mount Sarbach, along with Kaufmann Peaks and Epaulette Mountain, forms part of a vertical escarpment rising 1600 m above the Icefields Parkway near Saskatchewan Crossing. Each supports large hanging glaciers below sheer east faces. Of the three summits, only Mount Sarbach is a scramble, and even then, only when free of snow and ice. In cool, wet summers these conditions may not occur at all. This is a high mountain with a whopping amount of elevation gain, and because of the dangerously loose nature of the final summit ridge, should only be attempted by capable, experienced parties. Its location guarantees a superb view, and a good trail alleviates the approach. As with any big peak, take an ice axe—even crampons might be needed. Try from August on.

Park at Howse Pass/Mistaya Canyon trailhead on the west side of the Icefields Parkway (Highway 93), 5.2 km south of Saskatchewan Crossing and some 73 km north of the Trans-Canada Highway.

Follow the trail as it descends to Mistaya Canyon. This deep gorge is an impressive attraction and worth a moment's pause. Cross the bridge and turn right, going uphill to a junction. Take the left fork for Sarbach. The trail rises gradually through forest and in 5 km reaches an old fire lookout site, now a flowery alpine meadow overlooking the Icefields Parkway. This is a logical snack stop as elevation gain to the summit is still 1100 m.

Follow a trail directly back into the woods and grovel upslope to tree line and the north ridge. Immediately the panorama wows you, revealing shimmering Glacier Lake and the Lyell Icefield. You might almost forget what the objective is! The first section of ridge is easy except for 2 notches, the second of which is harder. Some find it "no real problem" but one party (with big packs)

Upper ridge on Mount Sarbach.

North end of Mount Sarbach from the Icefields Parkway. C Chephren, S first summit, N notch.

gladly bypassed this via a ledge on the north side. If this proves problematic, you should forget the ascent: It gets tougher.

Climb out of the notch and trudge up much debris. The ridge curves right, leading to a football field-sized plateau, then steepens as it rises toward the false summit. Scramble up short cliff bands choosing the easiest line. Much of the rock is loose so use caution. Gullies around to the right may be useful or may be icy, while the ridge itself may be dry. I found it best to stay close to the crest. Higher up you get a glimpse of the true summit, looking rather like a knob on flat ridge off in the distance. You could probably traverse hillside on rubble and bypass the false peak, but if cairn size is any indication, most parties stop at this lower spot.

Unless you are comfortable traversing a narrow hodge-podge of loose blocks, you too may also be happier at the first summit. Even when dry, the last 15 m is a precarious line of horizontally-stacked individual blocks. With the best of intentions, I happily began to push away

the most precarious boulders, but the task seemed endless. The exposure is unforgiving and a short climbing rope would be an asset crossing here. Use extreme caution.

Thankfully, the summit is level and spacious. You can nestle in and savour one of the finest Rockies vistas you're likely to set eyes on. The scenery west of Howse River to the Freshfield Group is stunning, as are the Lyell Peaks and nearby Mounts Forbes and Wilson. On a clear day, you can see as far south as Mount Hungabee at Lake O'Hara. Be sure to take enough film along.

Return the same way. You should remember to stay near the ridge crest on descent and do not be lured into easier looking gullies angling down to your left. Near tree line at the north end of the ridge, head for the small meadow to find the hiking trail again.

Peter Sarbach was a famous Swiss guide who accompanied J. Norman Collie's expedition to the Rockies in 1897. While here, he led some notable first ascents, including Lefroy, Victoria and this mountain.

MOUNT COLEMAN 3135 m

Difficulty Difficult and exposed summit ridge
Round trip time 8-12 hours
Height gain 1700 m
Map 83 C/2 Cline River

Ascending Mount Coleman gives a definite feeling of remoteness and reveals many normally unseen big peaks. The peak sits high above the east side of the Icefields Parkway and is visible from the roadside at about 3 km and 1.6 km south of the trailhead. Elevation gain is substantial and the ascent makes a long, tiring day despite the excellent approach trail. A backcountry campsite at nearby Sunset Pass is ideal for an overnight trip. This outing is for experienced scramblers as the final narrow ridge abuts a steep ice face. Try from about mid-July on when the summit ridge should be snowfree. Carry an ice axe.

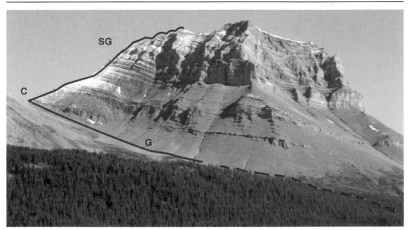

An approach view of Mount Coleman. C col, G gully, SG shallow gully.

Drive to Sunset Pass/Pinto Lake trailhead on the east side of the Icefields Parkway, 16.7 km north of Saskatchewan Crossing.

Hike up the well-graded path to Sunset Pass. Minutes before the pass you get a first glimpse of the objective to the north, including the ascent route. At Sunset Pass, the trail angles right toward the stream and campsite before continuing east toward Pinto Lake. To climb Mount Coleman, you first need to gain the big gully separating the southwest face of the peak from the rocky ridge just west of it. Then you hike to the high col between. If you walk farther along Sunset Pass trail, it should be obvious when to head north (left). Cross marshy flats and trees to reach this gully, but don't expect a real trail; use your intuition.

The wide gully leads easily to the col, with rubble underfoot occasionally revealing brachiopods and other small fossils. The col (048735) provides a respite

A picture-perfect summit view of Mounts B Bryce, S Saskatchewan and C Columbia.

and a chance to survey both the unfolding panorama and final 300 or so metres remaining. A shallow gully leads directly to the crux, the summit ridge.

Once on the ridge, the summit lies south. A steep glacier abuts this narrow ridge so be cautious as you make your way along it. After you descend a minor dip in the ridge, the less-exposed option follows the path of least resistance around to the right across slabs, then up to the cairn.

From the top, at least 20 of the Rockies peaks above 3353 m (11,000 ft.) are visible. Some, like Mount Alexandra at the head of the wide river valley lying west, are so remote that they see few ascents even today. A plethora of towering peaks, glistening glaciers and green valleys surrounds you, and, if the weather is clear, what more could you ask for? Perhaps a safe **return**, via the same route.

Professor A. P. Coleman and his brother Lucius did much exploration in the Rockies before the turn of the century. Three summers were spent in search of legendary Rockies giants Mount Hooker and Brown, reputed to be some "17,000" ft. high. Celebrations were appropriately scaled down when the long-sought after peaks measured in at 7,000 ft. below expectations.

NIGEL PEAK 3211 m

Difficulty Moderate scrambling, much scree and perhaps snow slopes via southwest side to north ridge
Round trip time 4-8 hours
Height gain 1175 m
Map 83 C/3 Columbia Icefield

Most parties overlook Nigel Peak in favour of loftier, neck-craning mountains nearby, but for a nontechnical ascent these summit views rival those granted by the glaciated, but less-easily attained, giants on Columbia Icefield. When clouds cloak Mounts Athabasca and Andromeda, climbers too can probably salvage the day with this ascent. Try from July on; ice axe suggested.

Park at the entrance to Wilcox Campground on the Icefields Parkway, 2.7 km south of the Columbia Icefield Centre. The trail to Wilcox Pass starts here.

Follow Wilcox Pass trail for about five minutes to an opening in the forest and hike up the steep hillside toward Nigel Peak. Cross undulating meadows toward scree slopes on the southwest side of a subsidiary ridge trending northwest from point 878868. Stay left of the stream

draining the summit mass that flows down through Wilcox Campground. Occasionally, waterworn slabs give you a temporary respite from the tedious scree underfoot and are particularly welcome where the terrain steepens near the ridge.

From the ridge, a rounded saddle connects to the main mass of the peak. Trudge up this—possible cornice on the right—detouring left at rotten rock steps. Some years snow lingers right into August on this shaded slope. As you must

Telephoto of Nigel Peak from sno-coach road. B northwest bowl, N north ridge.

A tantalizing view of Mount Athabasaca from Nigel Peak.

either traverse across or above it to reach the north ridge, an ice axe is invaluable. It is a considerable distance down to the tiny snowfield below.

Although there have been ascents straight up the northwest bowl, rocks are often damp while ledges hide under precarious piles of stones. Traverse farther left to the north ridge for a safer ascent. It is not necessary to tread on the minor glacier clinging to the left side of this ridge, but if the ridge is snow-covered you should avoid straying left of the crest.

This strategic viewpoint reveals at least 22 of the Rockies' 50-odd 3353 m (11,000 ft.)-high peaks from the top. Attempting to identify each should provoke discussion if not outright debate. Mount Robson qualifies as most distant, but Mount Bryce, although clearly seen from adjacent Mount Wilcox, hides behind Mount Andromeda from here.

Parties also sometimes reach the north ridge route by hiking along Wilcox Pass, then going around the north end of the rock "wing" and up the northwest slopes. This is a less steep but much more circuitous approach and, unless snow-covered, does little to eliminate the ever-present scree. **Return** the same way you came up. The shaley basin around the creek flowing to Wilcox Campground is a poor descent as the banks are steep hard dirt or gravelly slabs—unpleasant at best.

Nigel Vavasour, guide, accompanied climbers and explorers J. Norman Collie and Hugh Stutfield during their explorations of 1897. On this historic trip they ascended Athabasca, gazed west and discovered the now-famous Columbia Icefield.

MOUNT WILCOX 2884 m

Difficulty Moderate scrambling via southeast ridge, mild exposure near the top
Round trip time 3.5-6 hours depending on starting point
Height gain 900 m
Map 83 C/3 Columbia Icefield

Mount Wilcox pales in elevation compared to neighbours Athabasca, Andromeda and Kitchener, but its strategic location and straightforward route makes it far more accessible to the average hiker or scrambler. When the weather cooperates, Mount Wilcox offers possibly the best view in the entire Rockies for the energy expended. On a clear day the panorama simply can't be beat. Try from July on.

Begin either directly behind the Icefields Centre or at Wilcox Campground and Wilcox Pass trail, 2.7 km south.

The most direct approach lies immediately behind the Icefields Information Centre. Faint trails lead to a somewhat obvious gully through the rock band above, although you can also find many other places to the right to ascend. Rubbly slopes ease to rolling alpine terrain of Wilcox Pass, often the haunt of bighorn

sheep. You can also reach this point via Wilcox Pass hiking trail, although it is slightly longer. From the broad expanse of the pass, hike over to the southeast ridge and along a well-worn path that travels just below the crest. The view is magnificent. Only short sections require any hands-on scrambling, but toward the top expect a few mildly exposed spots. If, at some point, you find yourself looking clear down to the road on your left while confronted by a steep wall, you are prob-

Approaching Mount Wilcox from Wilcox Pass. Route ascends left skyline ridge.

Photo: Gillean Daffern.

A spectacular view of Mounts Athabasca (L) and Andromeda (R) and Athabasca Glacier from Mount Wilcox.

ably off route. Backtrack and go around to the right instead. In general, keep right at any narrow bits and detour around steep snow patches that linger.

From the top you could spend considerable time with map and compass attempting to identify surrounding peaks. The icy giant between Mount Andromeda and Snow Dome is Mount Bryce, a highly-prized but seldom-climbed 3353 m (11,000 ft.) peak. North Twin, Twins Tower, Mounts Woolley and Diadem are just a few other major peaks you can see. If nearby Nigel Peak is on your "To do"

list, most of the scramble route up it is visible also. Once you reach sensory overload, **return** the same way.

Walter Wilcox, Yale scholar, explored the Lake Louise area about 1893 with fellow students Samuel Allen and Lewis Frissell. His book, *Camping in the Canadian Rockies*, was an instant hit. Wilcox Peak was named by the renowned British alpinist, John Norman Collie, whose explorations in the Rockies from 1897 to 1911 added considerably to the scarce information then available about this fabulous region.

TANGLE RIDGE 3000 m

Difficulty Easy, mostly a hike
Round trip time 4-7 hours
Height gain 1100 m
Map 83 C/6 Sunwapta

Tangle Ridge is another summit ideally located for photographing awe-inspiring peaks of the Columbia Icefield region.

From the top you can see major summits not visible from either Nigel or Wilcox peaks. Tangle Ridge also offers a long easy ridge walk with a loop back on Wilcox Pass trail. Despite lack of a path partway through the intervening forest, reaching the top is straightforward. Morning light is preferable for photos. Try from late June on.

Roadside view of Tangle Peak's upper slopes.

Park at Tangle Falls, 7 km north of the Columbia Icefield Centre on the Icefields Parkway.

To the right (south) of Tangle Falls is the signed trail for Wilcox Pass. Follow this for about 30 minutes, at which point you should be close to both the creek and a streambed on the opposite side. Cross the creek and head up through forest along the side of this often dry drainage. The left side leads more directly to the summit.

Continue up through forest to tree line onto patches of meadow, then good scree to the top. Behind you, familiar outlines of Mounts Athabasca and Andromeda loom. To your left glaciated Mounts Kitchener and Stutfield are overshadowed by mighty Mount Columbia, second highest peak in the Rockies. To the southeast, Nigel Peak displays a distinc-

tive horn shape while farther beyond, the many towers of Mount Murchison stand tall. On a clear day the panorama is breathtaking—even the solar-powered repeater on top doesn't spoil the majesty of it all. One note of caution: Be wary of the glacier that abuts the ridge on the north side.

You can either **return** the same way, or for variety, hike along the ridge toward Nigel Peak, then descend scree slopes to the open environs of Wilcox Pass. The well-used hiking trail leads back to Tangle Falls and the starting point.

"Tangle" refers to difficulties encountered by an early party as they exited Wilcox Pass by this creek. Before the Icefields Parkway opened in 1940, Wilcox Pass was the normal travel route here. This was not because of the Athabasca Glacier, but because of the Sunwapta River's canyon.

SUNWAPTA PEAK 3315 m

Difficulty Easy scrambling via south-west slopes
Round trip time 7-12 hours
Height gain 1735 m
Map 83 C/6 Sunwapta Peak

Sunwapta Peak is deceiving as it is higher and takes significantly longer than what the highway view suggests. Besides an ice axe for snow lingering on the upper slopes, you'll need nothing special except perseverance. On a clear day, the view of major peaks is terrific. Try from late June on.

Drive 15.6 km north of the Columbia Icefield turn-off (2 km south of Beauty Creek Hostel) to the Stanley Falls hiking trail sign. Park at a pull-off area on the east side of the Icefields Parkway. There is a less foreshortened view of the mountain about 2 km south.

From the pull-off spot the trail curves over into the trees to a paved section of old highway. Do not follow the road south to Stanley Falls, but instead walk north (left) for a few minutes to the first stream where there is a gravel barricade. As seen from the highway, this water-course is the more southerly of two parallel drainages on Sunwapta's slopes.

Hike up the left side of the drainage. Despite some deadfall, you should find a recognizable trail to tree line, then angle right toward the ridge, trudging up long and often snowy slopes of rubble. Although appearing inconsequential from the road, this upper part now seems unending. No wonder: Just this above-tree line stretch alone entails 1000 vertical metres height gain! However, the route is largely a walk and as you toil along, you may be interested (and probably discouraged) to know

Looking northwest from the summit of Sunwapta. Mount Clemenceau is in the distance to the left. The pointed peak to the right is the eastern summit of Mount Smythe.   Photo: Gillean Daffern.

that Steve Tober made an ascent in less than 2.5 hours in 1998. Feeling even more sluggish now? A periodic glance west toward Mounts Woolley, Diadem and Alberta may help. On top, beware of a possible cornice on the east side. The **return** is via the same way.

During his exploits at the turn of the century, Professor A. P. Coleman used this Stoney Indian word meaning "turbulent water," referring to the fast-moving nearby river.

Foreshortened roadside view of Sunwapta Peak, showing routes.

JASPER AREA

Indian Ridge	2720 m	easy	p. 316
Pyramid Mountain	2763 m	easy	p. 318
Hawk Mountain	2553 m	difficult	p. 320
Cinquefoil Mountain	2260 m	easy	p. 322
Roche Miette	2316 m	moderate	p. 324
Utopia Mountain	2564 m	difficult	p. 326
Roche à Perdrix	2135 m	moderate	p. 328

This section covers the Jasper townsite and the area east of Jasper along the Yellowhead Highway (Highway 16). Most of this is dry, Front Range country, and both topography and climate are not unlike Kananaskis and Banff. Peaks are comprised of steeply dipping limestone, and slabby west faces offer technical climbing routes, while ridges and east-facing gullies often provide feasible scramble routes. During periods of bad weather along the parkway, a drive east of the Jasper townsite may save your day, rather like heading for Kananaskis when Lake Louise socks in.

Access The region is reached by Highway 93, the Icefields Parkway, which intersects the Trans-Canada Highway 2 km west of Lake Louise, then travels northwest for 245 km to Jasper. Meeting it at Saskatchewan Crossing is Highway 11, the David Thompson Highway, which runs east to Red Deer. Highway 16, the Yellowhead Highway, joins Edmonton and Prince George, B.C. via Jasper. As for transportation, Brewster operates a daily shuttle from Calgary to Jasper; Via Rail trains stop in Jasper from Edmonton and Prince George, as do Greyhound bus lines. Your own vehicle is really the only practical way to get around, though.

Facilities Jasper has almost anything you will need. Totem Men's Wear and Ski Shop both sells and rents equipment. Weather and information are available at the Parks Centre on the main street. For a more relaxed outing, a gondola whips you up to the Whistlers, where an easy scramble of Indian Ridge begins. Near the park's east entrance, you can get mellow (and clean!) in Miette Hot Springs, which is also near a few good scrambles. Gas, snacks and limited facilities are found at Pocahontas, 44 km east of Jasper on Highway 16, the turnoff for the hot springs.

Accommodation Lodges, cabins and chalets along the parkway are typically expensive and booked up. Jasper has a range of hotels and motels. For the budget traveller, campgrounds and hostels can be found along the way and around Jasper. All are popular in summer and fill up fast. A few kilometres south of Jasper, Wapiti and Whistlers campgrounds offer public (coin) showers. Located east of Jasper are Snaring River and Pocahontas campgrounds.

Information A rustic building on the north side of Connaught Drive (main street across from the train station) houses the Parks Information Centre. Finding it should be easy as it is about the only green space on the entire strip. Staff are helpful and enthusiastic about local ascents and current conditions.

Warden offices are just east of Jasper toward Maligne Lake.

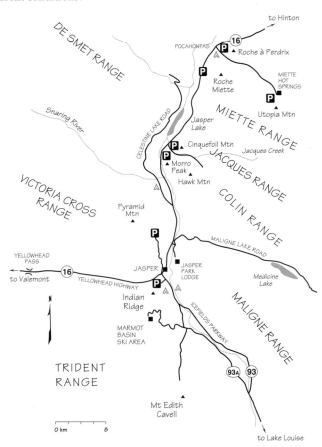

INDIAN RIDGE 2720 m

Difficulty Mostly an off-trail hike to summit; easy scrambling if traversed
Round trip time 4-6 hours from top of Whistlers Tram; 5-7 hours to traverse
Height gain 660 m; loss 180 m
Add 960 m and several hours if you do not ride the tram.
Map 83 D/16 Jasper

Close to the Jasper townsite, Indian Ridge is an easy, scenic jaunt that benefits from the popular Whistlers tram. From the upper tram station, the entire trip rambles above tree line granting an expansive view of peaks and lakes. Whether you traverse it or simply hike to the highest point, it's worth buying a lift ticket. For purists considering hiking up to the Whistlers rather than riding the tram, there are NO free rides back down. Try this trip from mid-June on.

Follow the Whistlers access road that leaves the Icefields Parkway (Highway 93), 1.7 km south of the Jasper townsite. Drive some 3 km to the lower tram station.

From the upper tram station, join the droves of puffing tourists hiking to the open plateau called Whistlers summit. As you tramp up, you'll notice the massive quartzite boulders. These "erratics" were transported from nearby mountains during the last glacial advance, but now sit far from any sign of permanent ice. Similarly, glacial erratics also rest on Mount Hawk, Roche Miette and other peaks east of Jasper. From the Whistlers, Indian Ridge sits some 2.5 km to the southwest across rolling alpine tundra. It is a pleasant hike to reach it whereon paths along the rounded shaley crest lead to the highest point. Only for the last few metres will you actually have to use a handhold or two.

Looking south to Trident Range from Indian Ridge.

Notch

Indian Ridge from the Whistlers, showing traverse loop.

Ice-clad Mount Edith Cavell is the commanding peak lying south, while the white cone shape of Mount Robson, highest peak in the Canadian Rockies, towers in the distance to the northwest. Jasper's many lakes dot the valley like puddles of ink spilt on a carpet of olive. One can enjoy much pleasant wandering here and that includes most of Indian Ridge. The far (northwest) end of this ridge has a couple of interruptions requiring brief detours and a short scramble off the ridge crest on the left (west) side. The rest is easy. Bypass the last part on the right, then walk down shale slopes to the stream between Indian Ridge and the Whistlers. Finally, regain 260 m back up to Whistlers and rejoin the masses again. Welcome back to reality.

Indian Ridge is next to Indian Pass, but whether the pass was ever used much is questionable. Whistlers, more commonly known as marmots, are true sun worshippers and often bask on warm rocks in alpine areas, oblivious to the aging effect of UV rays. Their loud, sharp whistle is not a sign of admiration—no, quite the contrary. It is a warning cry: they find you alarming.

PYRAMID MOUNTAIN 2763 m

Difficulty Easy scrambling
Round trip time A full day
Height gain 1585 m
Map 83 D/16 Jasper

Pyramid Mountain, guardian of the Jasper townsite, is one of the better scrambles

near town if you have a mountain bike. The 12 km-long access road is drudgery without one, but you can rent one locally. Clambering over big quartzite blocks and a far-reaching view makes for a pleasurable ascent with a bit of hands-on scrambling. Try from late June on.

Pine Avenue, which becomes Pyramid Lake Drive, intersects Connaught Drive (main street) near the west edge of town. Follow it 7 km passing Pyramid Lake and park at the locked access gate.

From the parking area, the gravel road rises gradually at first through montane forest, seemingly indifferent to the peak's location. Instead it meanders well east

of it. Cyclists will welcome the occasional small streams, especially on the big hill that leaves everyone puffing, and perhaps pushing too! At 8 km you

View of Pyramid Mountain from the lower part of the north ridge. For variety, the left skyline ridge can be D descended.

pass by the rougher road branching right to the Palisades. Finally, the road flattens somewhat and crosses a final stream, and you now see the east side of the peak rising skyward ahead of you. Despite the road, it is a lovely subalpine setting and makes an aesthetic start to the ascent.

The normal route up is via the north ridge, the one on your right. It is straightforward to simply tramp up open slopes nearby to reach it. Once you gain the crest, Snaring River valley is your companion to the north, while the mighty Athabasca River meanders its way east.

The ridge rises in steps, and you scramble up, over and around big, lichen-clad quartzite blocks. The way is obvious. Mount Robson, draped in white, dwarfs every other peak in sight, which isn't exactly a revelation. It is, after all, the Canadian Rockies' highest summit. To the south, Tonquin Valley Ramparts vie for attention, too. After you've admired the scenery long enough, you can decide on your descent route.

On **return**, either descend the same way or go down the southeast slope, circling back toward a small tarn below, then continue back to the approach road. On descent, this convex slope suggests cliffs below, but if you aim for the point where the ridge meets the slope, it should all work out. Contour right at any nasty

Big quartzite blocks on the north ridge.   Photo: Gillean Daffern.

gullies or the short rock band at the bottom and hike back to your bike. If cycling, the ride down is a good adrenaline rush and requires much braking. Be sure the brakes work well and stop to let the rims cool when they get too hot to touch.

Apparently a strenuous multi-day trip is possible toward Elysium Pass from Pyramid Mountain, visiting peaks like Mount Kinross, Cairngorm and Mount Henry. Park wardens may have information about this long trek.

HAWK MOUNTAIN 2553 m

Difficulty Moderate via west face and northwest ridge except for 5 m of difficult slab scrambling. Some routefinding required.
Round trip time 5-8 hours
Height gain 1500 m
Map 83 E/1 Snaring River

Hawk Mountain is a deservedly popular scramble in the Colin Range northeast of Jasper. The Colin Range, named for Colin Fraser of the Hudson's Bay Company, is typical Front Range topography. Steeply-tilted, slabby limestone faces are the norm; ridges are often long, undulating and sometimes quite exposed. Hawk Mountain is one of the more accessible peaks in this range, and provides a fine view of the surroundings. Try from about mid-June on.

From Jasper, follow the Yellowhead Highway (Highway 16) northeast toward Edmonton for 20 km. Park at a pull-off spot at the east end of the bridge over the Athabasca River.

From the parking spot by the end of the bridge, go up the dirt bank on a beaten path frequently used by rock climbers doing short practise climbs on Morro Peak. This trail, interestingly enough, is part of the historic Overlanders Route of 1862. The Overlanders were an adventurous group of 150 hardy souls who journeyed through here from Ontario to

the B.C. Interior, long before moving out west became so commonplace.

Follow the trail for about 40 minutes as it contours south above the valley floor to intersect Morro Creek drainage, the first one you reach. Hike up the right side of this often-dry stream through a burnt area to where you can gaze down into a canyon complete with a splashing waterfall. From there, follow a well-trodden animal/human trail rising gently off to the right, keeping roughly midway between brown slabs above and blackened timber below. This trail wanes on a shaley hillside overlooking a more southerly drainage at 281750.

From here, hike straight up toward the slabby face, going through a short belt of trees and clamber up a big rubble slope to the first band of grey slabs. It is important to find the 3 m-high chimney that cleaves these slabs. There may be flagging, and as well, a dead stump sits at its left side. The chimney is more awkward than are the slabs to the right. Above the chimney an eroded trail climbs directly upward. Grovel up the

Hawk Mountain's ascent route viewed from Highway 16. C crux chimney.

dirt to the base of more slabs. The path angles up to the right and within minutes easily overcomes this band of slabs also.

Continue up steep terrain on an obvious path and enter forest. This is a critical place to recognize on your return, and there are usually several cairns here. Evidently, everyone wants to construct his own landmark, and you may want to as well if you can find room. Otherwise, you should at least familiarize yourself with this spot so you can identify it on descent. The section from the chimney to here is the crux, and now that you are on the very backbone of the mountain, it would be difficult to go wrong.

Hike through timber along the ridge and, in 20 minutes, emerge onto slabs, rough and waterworn through eons of wind-driven rain. The summit is now visible but still distant. When the ridge peters out, descend slightly and gain the next one over. There is some nice scrambling here. Now you are on the main spine leading to the summit. Curiously,

Opposite: Looking along the summit ridge. Here the route crosses over to slabs and follows the crest.

there are many quartzite boulders perched willy-nilly along this mass of limestone. They look entirely out of place and they are. These "erratics" were transported from farther west (Mount Edith Cavell is quartzitic) by ancient glaciers, then deposited in unlikely spots such as this one. As the curious tourist once asked: "Where has the glacier gone now?" Back for more rocks!

In the past, parties saw the remains of a moose skeleton lying on the north ridge of Hawk Mountain facing Mount Colin. Whatever drove a great gangly swamp-lover far from the valley and up onto technical rock will always be a mystery. Perhaps, simply, "because it was there."

Most parties **return** the same way, watching carefully for the specific point to descend the west face slabs. It is also feasible to traverse partway toward the Hawk/Colin col, then descend south to 320730 and follow a treed ridge north-west back to the burned area and the second drainage to the south at 284750. It is, however, of no particular advantage.

CINQUEFOIL MOUNTAIN 2260 m

Difficulty An easy scramble
Round trip time 4-7 hours
Height gain 1230 m
Maps 83 E/1 Snaring River
83 F/4 Miette

Cinquefoil Mountain is the first high point of a long, lazy ridge in the Jacques Range east of the Jasper townsite. Readily accessible, it involves little actual scrambling and offers a straightforward way to get up high enough for an expansive view. All told, it is a pleasant outing and not likely to be crowded. Try from May on.

Drive to Merlin Pass trailhead on the south side of the Yellowhead Highway (Highway 16), 24 km east of Jasper and 20 km west of Pocahontas.

Follow Merlin Pass trail, reaching a small lake within minutes. Shortly past here the brush and forest open up, and you should head left, making a beeline for green, open lower slopes of Cinquefoil Mountain, immediately east. Once on the open slopes, the objective is clear: go up. Use whatever trails you encounter to link one clearing to the next. At a forested dip in the ridge you can angle left uphill into trees to avoid losing height. While paths through the woods are helpful, you can't help but notice how much better suited they are to bodies under a metre tall. Note to the

Irish: They are, however, unlikely to be the work of "The Little People." Not unless they leave hoofprints, anyway.

A rocky outcrop higher up provides an opportunity to admire the unfolding panorama of Jasper and Talbot Lakes below with square-ended Roche Miette rising behind. As well, you can study the last section to the summit, although it will be in shadow in early morning. Clumps of small firs huddled on isolated ledges give way to limestone ribs, which avoid some of the adjacent rubble. Soon after, you realize that the summit is not one specific high point but rather a series of points along a broad, undulating ridge.

Hiking along this ridge is delightful. Underfoot, patches of moss campion anchor small plant communities, and there is much evidence of bighorn sheep—

The long, lazy ridge of ascent, seen from Celestine Lakes Road. S summit.

Bighorn sheep posing on Cinquefoil Mountain.
Pyramid Mountain behind, just right of centre.

watch where you sit! When they aren't serving as roadside attractions on the highway below, this mountain is a favourite getaway for the sure-footed creatures. Many have a high tolerance for cameras and will pose willingly.

Most parties will be happy to lounge around on Cinquefoil Mountain and then **return** the same way. Continuing south immediately involves steep rockclimbing followed by ever-increasing amounts of loose rubble. The farther you go, the less enjoyable it becomes. As you look northwest, it appears that Mount Greenock and Cinquefoil once formed a continuous upthrust ridge, now worn through by the Athabasca River. Cinquefoil (Sank-fwa) or five-finger is an alpine plant with five bright yellow petals that grows here and on many other mountains.

ROCHE MIETTE 2316 m

Difficulty A moderate to difficult scramble via northeast face
Round trip time 3.5-7 hours
Height gain 1425 m
Map 83 F/4 Miette

Roche Miette's vertical walls have stirred emotions since bygone days when voyageurs plied the waters of nearby Athabasca River. While the west face is towering and dramatic, the back side is tame, offering a much easier ascent. This scramble is one of the more frequented outings in the region, and as a result there is a beaten path that also serves as the climbers' descent route. Try from about June on.

Follow the Yellowhead Highway (Highway 16) northeast from the Jasper townsite toward Edmonton for 40 km, or 3.5 km southwest of Pocahontas, to a gravel access road on the south side of the highway. Park at the locked gate alongside the highway.

Walk through the clearing, angling right toward an opening in the trees, then head sharply left at a 2 m-high gravel dike (which hopefully is still there!). This now points you onto a track heading northeast, or a bit left of the peak. Within 10 minutes, a beaten trail diverges right (cairn here), and aims more directly for the mountain. Soon you cross the more easterly of two drainages originating below the north end of Roche Miette. The path ascends hastily; take the right fork at the first intersection and left at the next one. In about one hour you emerge on open slopes revealing the mighty Athabasca winding east beyond Disaster Point toward rolling woodlands.

The high point of this ridge offers a delightful panorama and a good place to eyeball the rest of the route. A faint trail angles left from the connecting saddle to a gully cleaving the first cliff band. Successive bands are similarly short. Most are easily overcome by traversing left to convenient gullies that allow you to ascend these obstacles with minimal fuss and only moderate scrambling. A more exciting, but exposed, option is to angle left onto clean slabs for the finish.

The top of Roche Miette is a broad, undulating plateau sprouting tiny mosses, hardy alpine flowers and scattered patches of grass that nourish local bighorn sheep. The summit awaits 15 minutes southeast past a small hump. For those with time and energy to waste, you can also ascend two slightly higher points lying south from the separating col. These involve only a bit of steep scrambling but are not really worth it. The west one is especially rotten and may have collapsed in a strong breeze by now.

The summit block of Roche Miette is made entirely of a particularly erosion-resistant limestone called the Palliser Formation, a rock type that forms the steepest cliffs of many peaks throughout the Canadian Rockies. You may also notice the odd lichen-clad quartzite boulder resting innocuously here and there. As on Mount Hawk, which is closer to the Jasper townsite, these glacially-transported specimens originated farther west in the Main Ranges, close to quartzite peaks like Edith Cavell and the Ramparts. When the glaciers retreated, these erratics were left high and dry, sometimes on limestone summits like this one.

The easy side. R ridge, S saddle, F first cliff band.

Roche is a French word meaning "rock." Miette was a legendary French Canadian voyaguer who apparently had enviable qualities for tolerating the hardships of travel. It is said he could play the fiddle and tell yarns with the best of them, too. When taunted by comrades about climbing this mountain, he responded to the dare by doing just that, dangling his legs over the precipice while contentedly puffing his pipe—or so the story goes.

The usual view of Roche Miette from Highway 16.
Photo: Tony Daffern.

UTOPIA MOUNTAIN 2564 m

Difficulty Difficult for short section; exposure
Round trip time 7-10 hours
Height gain 1180 m
Map 83 F/4 Miette

Utopia Mountain may not be complete paradise, but it is an interesting scramble. It has seen comparatively few ascents in the past. Located in the dry Front Ranges near the eastern boundary of Jasper Park, its biggest asset may be the starting point at Miette Hot Springs. What could be a better way to end a scramble than a well-earned soak in the steaming sulphur pools? The view from the summit includes prairies, gentle ridge walks and smaller peaks nearby, plus distant giants like Mounts Robson and Edith Cavell. As part of the approach follows a streambed, the trip is better when the creek level is not too high. Although the mountain would certainly be feasible earlier, because of spring run-off I would suggest trying from about mid-July on.

Follow the Yellowhead Highway (Highway 16) northeast from the Jasper townsite toward Edmonton for 44 km to Pocahontas, then turn right and go southeast 18 km to road's end at Miette Hot Springs. Park in the lot near the picnic area at the far (south) end. Note: Utopia Mountain can be seen from the road about 1 km before reaching the hot springs. The peak sports a wide band of brown shale partway up north-facing slopes. The skyline ridge is the ascent route.

Find a trailhead and map at the south end of the parking lot. A paved pathway descends to Sulphur Creek, passing the old aquacourt and interpretive signs including a small natural hot spring. Continue on the trail to where the stream forks, about 20 minutes away. Leave the trail and follow the right-hand branch of the stream that drains the northwest slopes of Utopia Mountain. Smatterings of a trail are found on the left (east) side of the creek. After about 20 to 30 minutes, watch for a steep animal trail heading left up the hillside. This trail is well trodden by sheep and starts right before a large washout of the hillside. Head up this steep path to tree line, perhaps noting where it emerges to simplify finding it on the return.

Continue up the open, meadowy slope and look for low-angled terrain on the rocky ridge to the right. Scramble up and gain the crest. Follow this ridge up alongside a gully of brown shale, crossing it near the top and continuing up rubble to another ridge above. This second ridge is separated from the mountain by a wide gully of grey scree descending right to tree line. The ridge provides interesting scrambling, particularly where it steepens for a short distance higher up. A couple of spots present brief exposure. Near the top of this ridge, work around right to avoid overhanging rock and gain the top of the wide scree gully adjacent. The flat plateau at the top makes a fine place for a timely rest, a snack and a chance to enjoy the much improved view.

Again the route ascends a slope of rubble on the right, this time to the summit ridge. The snowy cone-shaped summit of Mount Robson is visible to the west on a clear day. Continue along this ridge to the false summit, marked by two

Photo: Don Beers.   *The ascent route, seen from Sulphur Skyline, looking simpler than it actually is.*

survey markers set in the rock and an old wooden tripod. After much ado, finally the real summit is just minutes away.

From the top, the landscape presents many contrasts. Far to the west rise high peaks like Mount Edith Cavell and Tonquin Valley Ramparts while to the east are gentle, eroded ridges along the park boundary whose tops would afford fine, long rambles. The prairie spreads out beyond. To the north, Ashlar Ridge displays its clean-cut slabby face of Palliser limestone. Mighty Athabasca River meanders off in the distance.

The register shows that several parties have reached the summit via Utopia Lake to the south. This would not be a likely direction to descend because of the extra return mileage in- curred. We **returned** the same way, with one small diversion. Rather than downclimb the steepest parts of the upper ridge, it is possible to descend the wide grey scree gully until feasible to traverse to the right and regain the ridge. Then retrace your ascent route. Continuing all the way down the wide scree gully also is an option. Move left at slabs near tree line and descend to the upper valley. This would add more travel alongside the creek, probably boulder-hopping and without benefit of a trail. Holmgren & Holmgren's *Over 2000 Place Names of Alberta* reveals that for the surveyors, Utopia was an escape from the flies. Utopia is also slipping into the relaxing hot pool at the end of a successful day.

ROCHE à PERDRIX 2135 m

Difficulty Moderate scrambling, some exposure near top
Round trip time 4-7 hours
Height gain 1020 m
Map 83 F/4 Miette

Although often climbed by technical climbing routes on the west and north aspects, the normal descent route on this small peak makes for a quick way up. Close to the road and right on Jasper Park's eastern boundary, like nearby Roche Miette, it grants a respectable view and is quite straightforward. Try from mid-June on.

Jasper Park east gate is approximately 50 km east of Jasper on the Yellowhead Highway (Highway 16). Turn south off the highway 0.8 km east of the park gate onto an unmarked road that leads to a rock cut at the end of the north ridge about 50 m from the road. Park here.

At the right edge of the rock cut are many sheep trails heading onto the open north ridge of the mountain. This ridge lies exactly on the Jasper Park boundary. In an hour you pass two brief rock outcrops in close succession. Stop just past these. Do NOT continue to a third and higher rock bluff or it will be necessary to backtrack. Instead, contour left through trees

From the east, N north face, R northeast ridge, G gullies, P damn pole!

From the top, an option to explore further.

until a faint trail appears along the base of slabs on the east side of the ridge. Now the route begins to work around to the east side of the mountain.

Follow this path toward the north face as it hugs the base of vertical limestone walls. It then angles left and rises up a steep shale slope by a small drainage. Still rising rapidly below the northeast face, you soon reach a major watercourse. It is deeply eroded and recognizable by U-shaped folds of rock. A cairn reminds you to cross the drainage and gain the rib separating this major drainage from the next one over. Hike up this steep dividing rib on a good trail through the trees, then turn left across a second gully when the trees end. The way is obvious. If you have not brought ski poles or an ice axe, you might wish you had now. This shale slope is loose and tedious. Continue straight up the hillside until it levels off on a minor northeast trending ridge (467963), a good place to reap the scenic rewards of your toil thus far.

It is but a short, direct scramble to the top from here, whether on the crest or along either side. A stroll west soon leads to the summit cairn and from here you can enjoy a panorama of peaks, boreal forest and the broad Athabasca River. This river served as a vital transportation link during the fur trading era. Bighorn sheep apparently favour this vista too: Be careful not to sit in something.

If you haven't yet had enough, it is also feasible to scramble south along the ridge. Attaining the first high point is no problem; the second point requires a few metres of steep scrambling on the ridge crest. Either side of this steep step is much more exposed and loose. From there you'll no doubt notice that it looks straightforward to continue toward Fiddle Peak, too. The question is, how much is enough? Once you've discovered your limit, **return** via the same route.

The Holmgrens, in *Over 2000 Place Names of Alberta*, relate an apparent resemblance of rock foliations (seen from the highway east) to feathers of a partridge tail. "Perdrix" is French for partridge.

Glossary of Terms

Anticline: Inverted trough-shaped fold in mountain strata. Opposite shape to a syncline.

Arête: Narrow connecting ridge, either snow or rock.

Bergschrund: The crevasse formed between the edge of a body of snow and a rock mass.

Bivouac: A temporary, sometimes unplanned encampment.

Bushwhack: Thrash through bush without benefit of a trail.

Buttress: A column-like feature of rock on a mountain.

Cairn: Pile of rocks usually indicating route or top of a peak.

Castellated: Castle-shaped.

Chimney: A chimney-like feature on a rock face, often climbed using a technique of counter-pressure called stemming.

Cirque: Glacially-carved basin enclosed in steep, high walls.

Col: The crest of a mountain pass between two peaks.

Cornice: An overhanging edge of snow at the crest of a mountain peak or ridge caused by drifting.

Couloir: A steeply ascending gully or gorge in a mountainside that may be filled with snow or ice.

Crampons: A steel framework of spikes strapped to boots to provide traction on snow and ice.

Crevasse: A fissure or crack in a snowfield or glacier, often deep.

Crux: Main difficulty.

Exfoliating: Peeling owing to weathering.

Exposure: Airiness, state of being exposed or open, as in unimpeded distance of a fall.

Gendarme: An isolated rock tower or pinnacle; often along a ridge.

Glen: A small secluded valley.

Glissade: The act of sliding down a steep snow-slope, either standing or seated; normally a voluntary manoeuvre.

Ice axe: Wooden or metal shaft usually 2-3 feet long with an adze-shaped steel head at one end and a sharp spike at the other. Opposite the adze, the head is drawn to a point set with teeth. Used to stop a glissade, to facilitate travel on snow and ice and chop steps.

Massif: A central mountain mass. The dominating part of a mountain range.

Moraine: Rock debris transported and deposited by a glacier at its sides and front.

Rappel: Descending by sliding down a rope while controlling speed with friction.

Scree: Loose, broken rock at the foot of a cliff; slopes of debris caused by disintegration.

Self-arrest: Technique whereby one's ice axe is used to stop a glissade.

Summit: Highest point of a mountain peak.

Syncline: Trough-shaped fold in mountain strata.

Talus: Same as scree. In mythology, Talus was a fearsome brute who did battle with rocks from his home in Crete.

Tarn: A small, high mountain lake typically occupying a glacially-scoured basin.

Thrust: A geological movement where continued folding of layers results in eventual shearing, thereby allowing the upper layer to slide onto and overlay the original rock. The break is known as a thrust fault; the overlying strata are a thrust sheet.

Traverse: To travel laterally without gaining elevation.

Useful Phone Numbers

Park Administrative Offices

Kananaskis Country Office, Canmore	(403) 678-5508
Parks Canada Regional Office	(403) 292-4401

Information Centres

Waterton (mid May to Oct. 31)	(403) 859-5133
Elbow Valley	(403) 949-4261
Bow Valley Prov. Park	(403) 673-3663
Barrier Lake Information Centre	(403) 673-3985
Kananaskis Lakes Visitor Centre	(403) 591-6322
Banff (English and French)	(403) 762-1550
Kootenay	(250) 347-9615
Lake Louise	(403) 522-3833
Yoho	(250) 343-6783
Columbia Icefield	(780) 852-6288
Jasper	(780) 852-6176

Travel Alberta	1-800 661-8888
Tourism British Columbia	1-800 663-6000

Reservations

Alpine Club of Canada Huts	(403) 678-3200
Lake O'Hara Bus & Campground	(250) 343-6433
Canadian Alpine Centre Lake Louise	(403) 522-2200

Peaks by Degree of Difficulty

Easy Peaks

Moderately Difficult Peaks

Alphabetical Index of Peaks

In an Emergency

In an emergency, contact
the Royal Canadian Mounted Police (RCMP) or
the nearest Ranger or Warden Office.

RCMP Offices

Crowsnest	(403) 562-2866
Waterton (May - Oct.)	(403) 859-2244
Waterton (Nov. - Apr.)	(403) 627-4424
Kananaskis	(403) 591-7707
Canmore	(403) 678-5516
Banff	(403) 762-2226
Lake Louise	(403) 522-3811
Field	(250) 489-3471
Jasper	(780) 852-4848

Park Ranger or Warden Emergency Numbers

Waterton	(403) 859-2636
Kananaskis Country	(403) 591-7767
Banff, Yoho and Kootenay National Parks	(403) 762-4506
Jasper National Park	(780) 852-3100

Visit our web site at
www.rmbooks.com